ANDREW BROWN

A New Companion to GREEK TRAGEDY

With a Foreword by P.E. Easterling,
Newnham College, Cambridge

CROOM HELM
London and Canberra

BARNES AND NOBLE BOOKS
Totowa, New Jersey

© 1983 Andrew Brown
Croom Helm Ltd, Provident House, Burrell Row,
Beckenham, Kent BR3 1AT

British Library Cataloguing in Publication Data

Brown, Andrew
    A new companion to Greek tragedy.
    1. Greek drama — Dictionaries
    I. Title
    882'.01'0321   PA 3131
    ISBN 0-7099-0660-9
    ISBN 0-7099-0675-7 Pbk

First published in the United States of America 1983 by
Barnes and Noble Books,
81 Adams Drive,
Totowa, New Jersey 07512

Library of Congress Cataloging in Publication Data

Brown, Andrew, 1950-
    A new companion to Greek tragedy.

    1. Greek drama (Tragedy) — Dictionaries. I. Title.
PA31.B76   1983   882'.01'09   83-3842
ISBN 0-389-20389-0
ISBN 0-389-20396-3 Pbk

Printed and bound in Great Britain
by Billing & Sons Limited, Worcester.

CONTENTS

LIST OF PLATES AND FIGURES

PLATES

FIGURES

Map of Ancient Greece

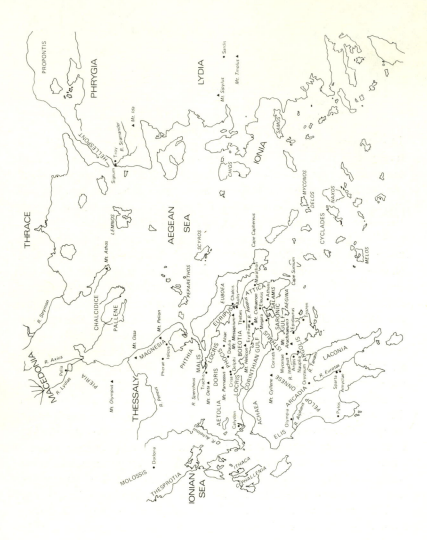

Scale

Miles

0   50   100

PREFACE

This book is intended primarily for those who are reading Greek tragedies in translation, though students of Greek may also find it of some use. Its purpose is simply to provide factual information that will remove some of the barriers separating the modern reader from the plays. The book does *not* contain literary criticism; readers must look elsewhere for accounts of the plays' significance and value.

Although the whole corpus of surviving Greek tragedy has been taken into account throughout the book, 15 of the most widely-read plays have been selected for detailed coverage. These are the *Agamemnon, Choephori* (*Libation-Bearers*), *Eumenides* and *Seven against Thebes* of Aeschylus; the *Prometheus Bound* attributed to Aeschylus; the *Oedipus Tyrannus, Oedipus Coloneus, Antigone, Electra* and *Philoctetes* of Sophocles; and the *Medea, Hippolytus, Electra, Trojan Women* and *Bacchae* of Euripides. The entries, alphabetically arranged, are intended to cover all mythical and geographical names occurring in these 15 plays; all names and technical terms which commonly occur in modern criticism of Greek tragedy; and various features of Greek life, religion and dramatic convention which are likely to seem foreign to the modern reader. The Introduction includes an essay by Mrs P. E. Easterling, setting the plays in the context of Greek literary tradition, and a very brief account of the careers of the three great tragedians. The Bibliography includes a guide to English translations of tragedy, as well as references to a wide range of modern studies.

The word 'New' in the title of the book is included to distinguish it from J. Ferguson, *A Companion to Greek Tragedy* (Austin, 1972), with which it has no connection.

I am most grateful to Dr Audrey Griffin for her work on the map; to Miss A. E. Healey and her colleagues at the Library of the Hellenic and Roman Societies for their helpfulness and efficiency; and to Richard Stoneman of Croom Helm for his advice and encouragement. To Pat Easterling I owe a much greater debt than the habitual clichés of prefaces can possibly convey. She taught me much of what I know about Greek tragedy; the idea for this book was entirely hers; and, besides contributing Part I of the Introduction, she has given unstinting and invaluable advice at every stage in the book's production. In a sense this is as much her book as mine, and my best excuse for not saying so on the title page is my acute awareness of the many defects which would have been avoided if she had done the writing of it her-self.

Finally, since there is a tendency for those catering for 'the Greek-less reader' to write as though Greeklessness were an incurable condi-tion, let me emphasise that it is not, and suggest that anyone in the UK who wishes to know of remedies for it should send a stamped addressed envelope to Dr P. V. Jones, Department of Classics, The University, Newcastle upon Tyne NE1 7RU.

Andrew Brown

INTRODUCTION

Greek Tragedy and Literary Tradition *P. E. Easterling*

From the vantage point of the modern reader Greek tragedy marks a beginning. As one of the most remarkable products of Athenian culture in the fifth century BC it stands at the head of the great tradition of European drama, a norm or a model for later ages to emulate, reinterpret or reject. But seen in the context of Greek literary history this novel creation of the fifth century is itself a deeply traditional phenomenon, which draws much of its peculiar richness and strength from the poetry of the past.

One of the most striking features of Greek tragedy is the fact that nearly all its plots were based on the stories of the Heroic Age, the time of the Trojan War and the generations that came before and after it. These stories were well known all over the Greek-speaking world from the vast corpus of heroic poetry which had been handed down during the archaic period and exercised a profound influence on Greek education, Greek self-consciousness and all subsequent Greek literature and art. In many ways it was the most natural thing in the world for a playwright of the fifth century to choose the doings of **Agamemnon**, **Heracles** or **Odysseus** as the subject matter of tragedy; this is what earlier poets − composers of lyric or elegy − had done when they wanted examples to illustrate their themes, and for the playwright there was the added attraction that many of the stories were already well adapted to dramatic treatment. The epic poets, or some of them at least, had shaped their narratives in ways that brought out their tragic significance: **Plato** was paradoxically right when he called **Homer** 'first of the tragic poets'. The *Iliad* after all gives us a tragic view of human existence: there are many passages which emphasise man's ultimate helplessness in the face of time and change, his blindness and self-destructiveness, his capacity for pity and endurance. Scenes like the meeting of **Priam** and **Achilles** in Book 24 or **Hector**'s farewell to **Andromache** in Book 6 must have given many suggestive hints to dramatists in search of the stuff of tragedy.

But it would be wrong to think of the tragedians as antiquarian writers harking back to a vanished past, as if their aim were actually to recapture Homer's world in dramatic form. There is every reason for thinking that despite the heroic plots and characters the situations enacted in the plays were related to the contemporary issues of **Athens** in the fifth century. When **Phaedra** and **Medea** talk about the experiences of women, or when Athena in *Eumenides* and **Creon** (i) and **Haemon** in *Antigone* discuss political institutions, or when innumerable characters in Euripides stress the importance of speaking well and winning their case, they are all giving expression to a consciousness which recognisably belongs to the fifth century. Even the figure of the king in tragedy, seemingly remote from the concerns of democratic Athens, could be made to serve more relevant purposes, now as the model of all that was un-Greek, the oriental absolute ruler like Xerxes in the *Persae* (while Darius in the same play represented the most solemn moral authority), now as the ideal first citizen who typified all that the Athenians most valued about themselves and their traditions, like **Theseus** in *Oedipus Coloneus*.

We can find a similar combination of traditional and contemporary in the form and language of Greek tragedy. The lyrics that the **choruses** performed in dance and song echoed in their rhythms and language the different kinds of lyric compositions that were traditionally performed by choirs at festivals: hymns of praise or entreaty to the gods, dirges, victory odes and so on. So when the Chorus of *Oedipus Tyrannus* appeal to **Apollo** and other gods for deliverance from the plague they are echoing the form and spirit of a **paean**, and in the *Bacchae* the rhythms and ritual cries of some of the lyrics are thought to recall the cult songs of Dionysiac worshippers in real life. But each lyric is intimately connected in the detail of its language and themes with the other parts of the play: no ode in our extant plays stands alone as a quite separate and independent interlude (though we hear that this was a tendency which began to develop late in the fifth century). This interplay between the choral songs and the spoken dialogue, which gives tragedy its characteristic form, must be seen as a 'modern' innovation not paralleled by anything we know in earlier literature. Similarly the duality of tragedy is reflected in the formal division between individual characters of heroic standing and a chorus of 'ordinary people' — citizens, household slaves, friends and neighbours, sailors — who make the action seem more familiar and accessible while the grandeur of the heroes brings out its distance from the humdrum present. The language, too, is a mixture of the traditionally poetic and elevated and the contemporary: echoes of Homer and the lyric poets are juxtaposed with words for concepts unknown in the heroic age, the language of medicine, for instance, or of the law courts and the democratic assembly.

Not surprisingly the tragedians found ways of exploiting this complexity inherent in the very nature of tragedy. One of the most interesting possibilities open to them was the ironic use of allusion. It is true that they were composing for large popular audiences, not for a sophisticated élite, but they could still be sure that a large proportion of the spectators would be familiar with the most famous, at least, of the epic stories, just as Biblical stories used to be widely known in our own culture. Even a person with the most rudimentary sort of education would have heard passages of Homer recited or himself learned some by heart, so that an echo of a Homeric passage need not be an esoteric device even if its effects are highly sophisticated. Tragedy is full of such allusions: sometimes a famous scene is recalled, as when in *Choephori* **Clytemnestra** bares her breast to **Orestes** and implores him not to kill her and we are grimly reminded of the true appeal of mother to son in *Iliad* 22, when **Hecabe** makes the same gesture to Hector, pleading with him not to fight Achilles. In Sophocles' *Electra* the lying tale of the old tutor about the death of Orestes in a racing accident is made all the more exquisitely ironic because it is a rewording of the story of **Antilochus** and the chariot race in *Iliad* 23. Or to take a finer point of detail: in the prologue of *Agamemnon* when the watchman tells us that he has been watching for a year on Clytemnestra's instructions for a message from **Troy**, the spectator who remembers *Odyssey* 4. 524-7 will find this a disturbing detail. In Homer Clytemnestra's lover **Aegisthus** posted a watchman who kept look-out for a year for Agamemnon's return and thus made possible the treacherous ambush in which Agamemnon was killed. What of the watching in this play: is it sinister or innocent? In *Trojan Women* the contest between **Helen** and Hecabe is used in an interesting way: Hecabe wins, and Menelaus, who has been the judge, promises that he will have Helen executed when they get back to Greece. But Hecabe suspects that in fact he will succumb to Helen's beauty; and the audience, remembering the *Odyssey*, must surely suspect that she is right. Euripides could afford to leave the scene open-ended without making it simply perplexing, because the happy domestic scenes of Menelaus and Helen at **Sparta** after their return from Troy were so well known from the *Odyssey*.

One of the most obvious advantages which tragedy gained from its use of heroic settings and its echoes of past poetry was dignity. A genre that confined itself strictly to the contemporary world could not easily have created the same degree of glamour and grandeur as we find in the **Argos** of *Agamemnon* or the **Thebes** of *Oedipus Tyrannus*. But at the same time the tragedians seem often to have felt the need to remind their audiences, sometimes rather pointedly, of the ironic contrasts between past and present. So Sophocles in *Philoctetes* presents an Odysseus who talks in the tones of voice of a contemporary **sophist** and sets traditional morality in a new and problematic perspective. Euripides goes much further, and often seems almost to be subverting the heroic world from within. When he makes his **Electra** the wife of a humble farmer living in a squalid hut in the country and elaborates such homely details as fetching water from the spring and finding supper for unexpected guests, we are reminded more of comedy than of tragedy. And when divine authority in the shape of **Castor** at the end of the play questions the rightness of Apollo's command to Orestes to avenge his mother we are made to feel that the very basis of the heroic story is put in question. On the other hand, the overall effect of the play is tragic and disturbing. The unheroic and subversive details do not detract from the seriousness of the situation, although they compel us to look at it in a new light. It is worth noting that Euripides did not abandon the old stories, as he could well have chosen to do. By keeping to the traditional themes, but giving them a fresh and often ironic interpretation, he was able to achieve an arresting mixture of modes which made a challenge to established ways of thinking and feeling. Of course there was an ever-present danger that tragedy would lapse into convention and cliché; this is what seems to have happened in the fourth century and after, but during the fifth century the precarious balance between tradition and innovation was maintained with extraordinary brilliance.

It is difficult for translations to convey the peculiar effects of language that reflect tragedy's simultaneous links with past and present. But no careful reader of a Greek play in translation can fail to notice the richness of the medium, with its references to people, places and times beyond the relatively small world of Athens.

P.E.E.

Purpose and Scheme of This Book

The 15 plays listed in the Preface have been selected for detailed coverage in this book in order to save space and cost, and not from any wish to suggest that only these 15 are worth reading. Even if one reads all the 32 tragedies and one **satyr** play that survive, these are a minute fraction of the number that were written, and may well be too few to give a balanced picture of the genre. The *Persians* of Aeschylus is of great interest as the earliest surviving play and the only one on a historical theme, and it makes an excellent introduction to Aeschylus's work; the reason why it is not in my selection is simply that it contains a great number of oriental names which do not occur in other plays. The five plays of Sophocles which I have selected are all masterpieces, but then so are the two which I have not, and each of the seven sheds light on all the others. The five selected plays of Euripides are among the most widely read, but they are less than a third of his surviving work, and cannot even be called a representative sample, since they include no example of his lighter plays, such as *Iphigenia in Tauris*, or of his more melodramatic ones, such as *Orestes*. Many of the entries, however, apply equally to all surviving tragedies, and I trust that the usefulness of this book will not prove limited to the selection of 15.

The aim of providing factual information is easier to state than to fulfil, since one cannot proceed far in the study of Greek tragedy without coming to issues where the facts are highly controversial. I have done my best, however, not to impose any personal views of my own; and indeed I claim no originality for any of the discussions in this book. I have unavoidably ignored certain minority opinions which seem to me clearly wrong, but I hope that, wherever genuine uncertainty exists, I have honestly acknowledged it; and there are only a few entries in which I have had to admit that an opinion held by most reputable scholars today is not one that I share. The reader may well find that I contradict existing handbooks in places, but no apology is needed for that; the study of Greek literature, life and religion does make progress, and many matters are better understood now than they were only a few years ago. On some issues I have been consciously influenced by particular modern discussions, several of which are listed on pages 207-9.

Some of the entries on technical terms include explicit or implicit protests against their misuse. Such misuse is not characteristic of reputable scholars today, but I have thought the protests worth including because popular notions about Greek tragedy seem capable of being influenced, in some inexplicable way, by books that no one can actually have read for a good half century. And the idea persists, at least among those who encounter Greek tragedies in educational establishments, that the best way of dealing with them is to stand at a safe distance and to fling in their general direction a few imposing Greek words taken from **Aristotle** and elsewhere, without making much effort to discover what these words might mean. It may, then, be worth emphasising at the outset that jargon has never provided a means of understanding any subject; the only valid use of jargon is to provide a compendious way of conveying a precise and agreed meaning to those to whom the subject is already familiar. As can be seen from this book, a precise and agreed meaning can hardly be said to exist even for such basic structural terms as **prologue** and *exodos*; and anyone who talks of **catharsis**, *hamartiā* or *hybris* without explaining exactly what he means by the word will merely be revealing his own ignorance and plunging his readers into needless confusion.

In entries on mythical figures I have usually given only a single version of the myths in question. That should not, however, be taken to mean that these myths necessarily had a fixed and canonical form (see the entry on **myth**, where I attempt to guard against possible misconceptions of the relation between the myths and the plays). The version of a myth that is given here is the one that occurs in, or that seems to be presupposed by, Greek tragedy, especially (though not exclusively) the set of 15 plays named in the Preface; and this version will not necessarily be the best known, the most developed, the earliest or the most interesting. Moreover, I have not as a rule attempted to distinguish between features taken over by the tragedians from existing accounts and ones which they themselves invented, since in most cases the evidence does not enable us to make such a distinction with any confidence (see **originality**). Where there are conflicts between different tragedies, however, I have drawn attention to them; and I have given some account of the historical development of the myths where this happens to be known and to seem relevant — where, for instance, a tragedian is clearly referring to, or deliberately departing from, a version found in **Homer** or **Hesiod**. There are also places where a tragedian alludes to a myth in vague terms which do not allow us to be sure what version he has in mind (of some myths our only connected accounts are found in sources much later than the fifth century), and here I have mentioned alternative possibilities. I have avoided, however, all discussion of the 'origin' or 'true meaning' of the myths; any readers who enjoy being told that almost every mythical character they meet was 'really' or 'originally' a fertility god or goddess will easily find other handbooks whose authors are eager to oblige them.

I have not worked from any existing translation, but have sought to include all names that would be likely to occur in the most literal rendering of the Greek text of the 15 selected plays. When the translation is less literal, the names will tend to be fewer; for instance, a translator may call a god by his most familiar title where the Greek text uses a more abstruse one. On occasion, however, a dramatist alludes to a mythical character without naming him, and here the name may reasonably be inserted by the translator (e.g. at Eur. *Hipp*. 339, where **Phaedra** says 'And you, unhappy sister, bride of Dionysus', a translator might insert the name **Ariadne**). The subjects of such implicit allusions have therefore been given entries or cross-references in their alphabetic place, though I have also tried to ensure that they can always be identified from cross-references elsewhere (the reader can find his way to Ariadne by looking up **Phaedra**, **Dionysus** or Fig. 4). I have not, however, attempted to take account of wilful and arbitrary alterations by translators; the only way of guarding against these is for the reader to use more than one translation, or to look up the Greek text. In all quotations in this book the translation is my own, and is without literary pretentions.

Since there are already several introductory books on the Greek theatre (see p. 203), I have said little about the physical conditions of performance (though there are entries on **actors**, **masks**, etc., and such technical terms as *orchēstrā* and *skēnē* are briefly explained). And, since I am concerned with the surviving plays rather than with literary history, I have said little about the origins of tragedy (see **tragedy**); the minor tragedians are confined to three brief entries (**Agathon**, **Phrynichus**, **Thespis**); and the accounts of the careers of Aeschylus, Sophocles and Euripides on pages 21-4 include few biographical details.

Since the book is not intended as an *index* to Greek tragedy, I have not specified where each name occurs, except when there is some special point in doing so. References to Greek works other than tragedy are limited to ones likely to be available to the general reader (in practice mainly **Homer**, **Hesiod**, **Herodotus** and **Aristotle**'s *Poetics*). References to the plays and to other works in verse are by line numbers of the Greek text, which are printed in most translations (but translators are often careless in this matter, and in any case Greek word-order makes it impossible for the lines of any translation to correspond exactly with those of the text, so some searching may be needed). References to Aristotle are by chapter numbers (there is an alternative system, which many books use). References to modern works are confined to the Bibliography.

For the abbreviated play-titles used throughout this book see pages 22-4. The *Prometheus Bound* and the *Rhesus* are referred to for convenience as Aesch. *PV* and Eur. *Rhes.*, despite their uncertain authorship (see **Prometheus**, **Rhesus**).

Titles of gods, with their pronunciation, are given in their alphabetic place (except for those which I would expect any translator to turn into English), but their meaning is explained in the main entries on the gods in question.

The use of bold type within an entry indicates that the word so printed has an entry of its own (consisting of something more than a note on its pronunciation and a cross-reference) in its alphabetic place. But, unless there is some particular reason for drawing attention to the reference, bold type is *not* used for words other than names and technical terms, nor for any word that has occurred earlier in the same entry.

Spelling and Pronunciation

Names

There exists in English an old convention whereby most Greek personal names, and many place names, are written as though they were Latin, and all are pronounced as though they were English. Not everyone now follows this convention, and it may seem perverse to do so; but, besides perpetuating the pleasant illusion that Greek names form part of the daily vocabulary of every English gentleman, it at least avoids the barbarisms that result from attempts to compromise. An actor, for instance, who feels, reasonably enough, that Krĕŏn (which is Greek) sounds mannered in an English sentence had better say Crĕŏn (which is English) and not Crayon.

Unfortunately, it is impossible in practice to follow this system with complete consistency, unless one is prepared to unleash such monsters as Delus and Posido. My practice, then, is simply to give Latinised spelling and Anglicised pronunciation wherever established usage permits. It should be noted that 'Latinised spelling' sometimes involves writing names in a form that was not used by the Romans themselves; they talked, for instance, not of **Hecabe**, **Heracles** and **Hephaestus** but of Hecuba, Hercules and Volcanus. One Greek diphthong causes particular problems and has had to be rendered quite inconsistently, appearing sometimes as ei (e.g. **Poseidon**), sometimes as i (e.g. **Polynices**) and sometimes as e (e.g. **Areopagus**).

For practical purposes the user of this book must bear the following points in mind.

1. The spelling of names here will differ from that found in some translations and other books (as is inevitable, whatever system is adopted). In particular most names beginning with K must be sought here under **C**, and most beginning with Ai must be sought under **Ae**.

2. The guides to pronunciation (in square brackets) have hardly anything to do with the way in which the names were pronounced by the Greeks themselves. In particular, English stresses one syllable in each word, and often lengthens the vowel of a stressed syllable and shortens that of an unstressed one, irrespective of their original length (in **Eros** and **Trozen**, for instance, as in **Creon**, the first vowel was actually short, the second long). And all soft Cs (shown as [s] in the guides to pronunciation) and Gs (shown as [j]) were originally hard.

3. These guides to pronunciation employ the sort of unscientific system which is found in many non-specialist English dictionaries, and which more or less adapts itself to different accents of English (as a strictly phonetic system would not). The reader should inter-pret them as though the words in question were English, forgetting any-thing he may know about foreign languages and phonetic principles.

Thus [ā] is the sound heard in mate;
    [ē] „ „ „ „ „ meet;
    [ī] „ „ „ „ „ mite;
    [ō] „ „ „ „ „ moat;
    [ū] „ „ „ „ „ mute (strictly two sounds, yo͞o, as opposed to the pure o͞o of moot).

All vowels not marked long are short, as in gnat net knit not nut.
[g] is always hard, as in gun.

If there is more than one syllable, an accent is placed after the vowel sound of the accented syllable: [agame′mnon] , [ar′gos] (with apologies to the Scots, who would expect [a′rgos]).

Syllables are separated by a hyphen where there might otherwise be ambiguity, but not elsewhere.

The reader should reduce the vowel of an unstressed syllable to a neutral 'er' (e.g. agerme′mnon) where he finds it natural to do so.

Other Greek Words

Unless they have become naturalised in English, Greek words other than names are printed in italics and more directly transliterated. A vowel that is marked long in these words is one that is long in the original Greek (but the long vowels in the Latin phrases *deus ex māch-inā* and *drāmatis persōna* are not marked). Since an authentically Greek pronunciation would hardly be attainable (or worth attaining), no guides to pronunciation are given for these words.

Those who wish to know how the Greeks pronounced Greek will find an accessible account in K. J. Dover, *Aristophanic Comedy* (London, 1972), pp. xii-xiv.

Classified List of Entries (other than names occurring in the text of Greek tragedy)

Technical Terms

agōn	dithyramb	*koros*	prologue
amoibaion	*ekkyklēma*	*mimēsis*	scholia
anagnōrisis	episode	monody	*skēnē*
antilabē	*exodos*	nemesis	*stasimon*
ātē	*hamartiā*	ode	stichomythia
aulos	hero	*orchēstrā*	tetralogy
catastrophe	*hybris*	*paidagōgos*	thyrsus
catharsis	hyporcheme	*parodos*	*tychē*
choregus	hypothesis	*peripeteia*	tympanum
deus ex machina	*kommos*	phratry	*tyrannos*
dianoia			

Authors

Agathon	Herodotus	Phrynichus	Solon
Aristophanes	Hesiod	Pindar	Stesichorus
Aristotle	Homer	Plato	Thespis
Freud	Nietzsche	Seneca	

Greek Life and Religion

city	hymns	persuasion	satyrs
curses	justice	politics	seers
death and burial	lamentation	pollution	sophists
democracy	libation	priests	supplication
dreams	myth	rhetoric	temples
fate	nymphs	ritual	Underworld
gods	omens	sacrifice	women
house	oracles		

Greek Theatre and Drama

actors	Great Dionysia	stage directions
attendants	imagery	text
character	irony	tragedy
chorus	masks	unities
extras	messengers	verse
fragments	originality	

Miscellaneous Topics

adamant	eagle	nightingale
amphisbaena	Glauce	olive
barbarians	Io's wanderings	Peloponnesian War
Beacon Speech	lotus	Seven against Thebes
Choephori	lyre	swan

Careers of the Tragedians

Note: Since the Greek year began at midsummer, some dates are given in the form 525/4, meaning the Greek year which ran from midsummer 525 BC to midsummer 524 BC.

In the lists of extant plays the four columns show respectively: the usual Greek or Latin title of each play (the Greek title being given separately in parentheses where it differs substantially from the Latin); its usual English title; the abbreviated title used in this book (and in others); and the date of first production, if this is known, with sometimes some other details.

Aeschylus, 525/4 to 456/5

Aeschylus was born at **Eleusis**. He had begun his career as a dramatist by the 490s. For his participation in the Persian Wars see **Persia**. He became the most popular tragedian of his day, winning 13 victories at the **Great Dionysia** at **Athens** (so that he was victorious with 52 plays), and also visiting **Sicily** to produce plays for the tyrant (*tyrannos*) Hieron of Syracuse. According to tradition he was prosecuted, but acquitted, on a charge of revealing the Eleusinian Mysteries (see **Eleusis**) in a play. He died at Gela in Sicily, and the only distinction recorded in the grave-epigram which he is said to have written for himself was his courage in the Battle of Marathon.

He is said to have been responsible for reducing the role of the

chorus in tragedy and for introducing the second **actor** (and later, perhaps, the third). Many, perhaps most, of his plays belonged to connected **tetralogies**.

He is said to have written 90 plays, and we know the titles of over 70. The following seven survive under his name.

Latin/Greek title	English title	Abbreviation	Date etc.
Persae	Persians	Pers.	472
Septem contra Thebas (Hepta epi Thēbās)	Seven against Thebes	Sept.	467, 3rd play of a connected tetralogy
Supplices (Hiketides)	Suppliant Women	Supp.	466-459, 1st play of a connected tetralogy
Agamemnon	Agamemnon	Ag.	458, forming a connected trilogy, the Oresteia
Choephori	Libation-Bearers	Cho.	
Eumenides	Eumenides	Eum.	
Prometheus Vinctus (Promētheus Desmōtēs)	Prometheus Bound	PV	date unknown, probably not by Aesch.

Sophocles, c. 496 to 406/5

Sophocles was born at **Colonus**. It is said that as a boy he led a choir celebrating the Greek victory at **Salamis** (480), but that he later had to give up acting in his own plays because of a weak voice. His first production was in 468, when he won first prize although he was competing against Aeschylus. He took an active part in public life; his offices included a generalship (an elective post held for one year) as a colleague of the statesman Pericles in 440/1. Stories are told of his piety: he was the **priest** of a certain **hero**, and when the Athenians were establishing a cult of **Asclepius**, the god was accommodated in Sophocles' house until a temple could be built.

He is said to have written 123 plays (we know the titles of over 110) and never to have been placed third in the competitions. He probably won 18 victories at the **Great Dionysia** (making 72 successful plays) and others at a lesser festival, the Lenaea. The introduction of the third **actor** is attributed to him by some authorities and to Aeschylus by others, and evidently occurred in the period when both poets were competing. He is also said to have increased the number

of the **chorus** from twelve to fifteen. It is doubtful whether he ever
wrote connected **tetralogies**.

The following seven plays survive. The dates of at least four of them
are quite uncertain.

Latin/Greek title	English title	Abbreviation	Date etc.
Ajax (*Aias*)	*Ajax*	*Aj.*	before 440?
Antigone	*Antigone*	*Ant.*	c. 442?
Trachiniae	*Women of Trachis*	*Trach.*	before 430?
Oedipus Tyrannus or *Rex*	*King Oedipus*	*OT*	the 420s?
Electra	*Electra*	*El.*	the 410s?
Philoctetes	*Philoctetes*	*Phil.*	409
Oedipus Coloneus	*Oedipus at Colonus*	*OC*	produced post-humously in 401

Euripides, 485/4? to 407/6

Euripides' family came from Phlya, a village in **Attica**. His first plays
were performed in 455. He seems to have taken little part in public life,
but he became a favourite target for the mockery of **Aristophanes** and
other comic poets. In 408 or 407 he left Athens for the court of
Archelaus, King of Macedon (see **Bacchae**), and it was there that he
died.

He is said to have competed 22 times at the Great Dionysia and
to have written 92 plays; we know the titles of about 80. He won
first prize only four times during his life, though he became by far the
most popular of the tragedians after his death. A few of his plays
belonged to loosely connected **tetralogies**, but most did not.

Nineteen plays survive under his name. Progressive changes in his
metrical practice mean that even those which cannot be dated on
external evidence can be fitted into a fairly reliable chronological
sequence (except for *Cycl.* and *Rhes.*).

Latin/Greek title	English title	Abbreviation	Date etc.
Alcestis	*Alcestis*	*Alc.*	438 (a tragedy performed in place of a satyr play)
Medea	*Medea*	*Med.*	431
Heraclidae	*Children of Heracles*	*Heracl.*	430-428
Hippolytus	*Hippolytus*	*Hipp.*	428

Andromache	*Andromache*	*Andr.*	*c.* 425, possibly not produced at Athens
Hecuba (Hekabē)	*Hecabe*	*Hec.*	*c.* 424
Supplices (Hiketides)	*Suppliant Women*	*Supp.*	*c.* 423
Electra	*Electra*	*El.*	*c.* 420-416
Hercules (Furens) (Hēraklēs (Mainomenos))	*Heracles (Mad)*	*HF*	close to 415
Troades	*Trojan Women*	*Tro.*	415, 3rd play of a connected tetralogy
Iphigenia in Tauris	*Iphigenia among the Taurians*	*IT*	*c.* 414
Ion	*Ion*		*c.* 413
Helena	*Helen*	*Hel.*	412
Phoenissae	*Phoenician Women*	*Phoen.*	*c.* 409
Orestes	*Orestes*	*Or.*	408
Bacchae	*Bacchants*	*Bacch.* ⎫	posthumously
Iphigenia Aulidensis	*Iphigenia at Aulis*	*IA* ⎬	produced
Cyclops	*Cyclops*	*Cycl.* ⎭	a satyr play, probably late
Rhesus	*Rhesus*	*Rhes.*	probably fourth-century and not by Eur.

A

Abae [a'bē]   A city in **Phocis**; site of a famous **oracle** of **Apollo**. The place mentioned before Abae at Soph. *OT* 898-9 is **Delphi**.

Acastus [aka'stus]   Son of **Pelias** of **Iolcus**. When **Peleus** of **Phthia** was Acastus's guest, Acastus's wife fell in love with him, and, since he resisted her advances, falsely accused him of trying to seduce her. Thus there arose a feud between Acastus and Peleus, of which various accounts are given.

Achaea [akē'a]   A region of the northern **Peloponnese** (also a region of **Thessaly**, mentioned only at Aesch. *Pers.* 488). **Homer**, however, uses 'Achaean' as his commonest word for 'Greek' (see **Hellas**). In tragedy 'Achaean' bears its strict sense at Soph. *El.* 701, but normally means 'Greek' or sometimes 'Peloponnesian'; the 'Achaean land' of Eur. *El.* 1285 is apparently the Peloponnese.

Achelous [akelō'us]   A large river of western Greece, thought of, when personified, as the father of all other streams and rivers. At Eur. *Bacch.* 625 the name is used to mean simply 'water'.

Acheron [a'keron]   One of the rivers of the **Underworld**. The name suggests *achos*, 'pain, distress'. Those newly dead might be thought of as crossing Acheron on a ship, and at Aesch. *Sept.* 854-60 that ship is pictured as a *theôris* rowed by the arm-beats of mourners and carried down-wind by their sighs (see **lamentation**). Acheron can also be personified as a god of death.

Achilles [aki'lēz]   The greatest of the Greek warriors at **Troy**. He was the son of **Peleus**, King of **Phthia**, and of the sea-**nymph Thetis**. As a boy he was brought up on Mount **Pelion** (or **Ossa**) by the wise **Centaur** Chiron (the 'horse-father' of Eur. *El.* 448-9; but the 'tutor' or 'foster-father' of Soph. *Phil.* 344 is **Phoenix**). Later, fearing that he would be killed if he joined the expedition to Troy, his mother took him to **Scyros**, where she left him, disguised as a girl, in the

care of the King, **Lycomedes**. There he fell in love with the King's
daughter, Deidamia, and by her became the father of **Neoptolemus**.
His identity was discovered, and he was forced to go to Troy.

The *Iliad* of **Homer** is the story of the Wrath of Achilles in the
tenth year of the war. Thinking himself slighted by the Greek
commander-in-chief, **Agamemnon**, he refuses to fight for most of the
poem, and the Trojans, led by **Priam**'s son **Hector**, come near to victory. Achilles' close friend **Patroclus**, however, borrows his armour,
goes out to fight, and is killed by Hector. Achilles' wrath is now turned
against Hector, so he makes peace with Agamemnon and re-enters the
battle. He succeeds in killing Hector, but finally allows Priam to ransom
his son's body.

Homer's Achilles embodies the Homeric ideal of personal honour
and martial prowess at its most fierce, proud and uncompromising.
Some famous lines at *Iliad* 9. 312-13, in which he proclaims to **Odysseus** his hatred of duplicity, were evidently much in Sophocles' mind
when he wrote *Philoctetes*.

At *Iliad* 18. 369-19. 39 Thetis procures fresh arms for Achilles
from **Hephaestus**, to replace those worn by Patroclus. At Eur. *El.*
442-51, however, the arms of Hephaestus are brought to Achilles by
Nereids when he is still a boy in **Thessaly**. Homer (*Il.* 18. 478-608)
and Euripides (*El.* 452-75) both give elaborate, but different, descriptions of the decoration on his shield.

Achilles was killed before the end of the war by **Paris** with the help
of **Apollo**; or by Apollo alone (the 'Achilles heel' is a much later addition to the story). His arms were then allotted by the other Greek
leaders to Odysseus (see also **Ajax (i)**). He was buried at **Sigeum**, and
Polyxena was sacrificed at his tomb.

Aeschylus wrote more than one play concerning Achilles, probably
belonging to a connected **tetralogy**; and he is a character in Eur. *IA*.

Acraea [akrē'a]   A title of **Hera**.

Acropolis [akro'polis]   The word, meaning 'upper city', can be
applied to any raised citadel, but is used chiefly of the citadel of
Athens, on which the Parthenon and other **temples** were built.

Actaeon [aktē'on]   A Theban prince and huntsman, son of **Aristaeus** and **Autonoe** (Fig. 3). He offended **Artemis** by boasting that he
was better at hunting than she (this is according to Eur. *Bacch.* 337-40;
the familiar story that he saw her bathing is not found until later). She

therefore turned him into a stag, and he was torn apart on Mount **Cithaeron** by his own hounds. He is mentioned several times in Eur. *Bacch.*, evidently because of the resemblance between his fate and that of his cousin **Pentheus**.

Actor [a'ktor] One of the seven defenders of **Thebes**; brother of **Hyperbius**.

actors The Greek for 'actor' is *hypokritēs*, of which the basic meaning is either 'answerer' (of the **chorus**?) or perhaps 'interpreter, expounder'.

The speaking parts in any tragedy were shared between a very small number of actors (but see also **extras**), who were always male. The use of **masks** clearly made doubling easier, but great versatility must still have been required. We are told that the first actor (or protagonist) was introduced by **Thespis**; the second (or deuteragonist) by Aeschylus; and the third (or tritagonist) by Aeschylus according to some authorities, and by Sophocles according to others. This doubtless means that the tritagonist was first used in the period in which both Aeschylus and Sophocles were competing, i.e. 468-456; and that is borne out by the evidence of the plays, since the *Oresteia* (458) requires three actors, while the earlier plays of Aeschylus require only two (assuming that **Antigone** and **Ismene** do not belong in Aesch. *Sept.*). Of later plays, Eur. *Alc.* can be performed by two actors (but this need not mean that it was), while Soph. *OC* and Eur. *Rhes.* seem to require four (unless a single part could be divided between two). The indications are that, as far as possible, the protagonist always took the most important parts and the tritagonist the least important, with little or no type-casting.

At the earliest period the protagonist was the poet himself. Late sources tell us that this practice was first abandoned by Sophocles, but also claim to know the names of actors employed by Aeschylus, apparently as protagonists; thus it is uncertain whether Aeschylus performed in all his own plays. Euripides evidently did not act.

It is also uncertain how actors were selected at different periods; we hear of particular protagonists being selected by particular poets, but also of protagonists being chosen by the state and then assigned to the three competing poets by lot. It is clear in any case that each poet in any one year acquired his own set of three actors whom he used in all the four plays which he produced at the **Great Dionysia**. From 449 there was a prize for the best protagonist in each year as well as one for the best poet. From at least the late fifth century actors seem to have been more or less professionals, trained at the expense of the state.

For styles of acting we have little evidence. The thick-soled boot and high, narrow stage, which in their day must have severely restricted movement, were introduced later than the fifth century (see also **masks**), but the scale of gestures must always have conformed to that of the theatre, and the lines, even if not delivered at great volume, must have been very clearly articulated. The texts of the plays, while avoiding violence on stage, often suggest quite vigorous actions. Various anecdotes imply that naturalism was prized, but many acting conventions that would seem highly stylised to us have been regarded as naturalistic in their day; the conditional 'naturalism' which can be attained by opera singers may well be a good analogy (see also **character**).

adamant [a'damant]   A legendary material of extreme hardness.

Adrasteia [adrastī'a]   'The Inescapable', a divinity who punishes rash speech; identified with **Nemesis**.

Adrastus [adra'stus]   King of **Argos**; father-in-law of **Polynices**, with whom he led the expedition of the **Seven against Thebes**. In Eur. *Phoen.* he is reckoned as one of the Seven, but in other plays he is not. He survived the defeat of the expedition, and is a character in Eur. *Supp.*, where with the help of **Theseus** he obtains burial for his fallen comrades.

Adria [ā'dria]   A region of north **Italy**. At Eur. *Hipp.* 735-6 the sea called after it is probably the Gulf of Venice, at the head of the Adriatic, rather than the Adriatic as a whole (see also **Eridanus**).

Aegean [ējē'an]   The sea between the Greek mainland and Asia Minor, supposedly called after **Aegeus**.

Aegeus [ē'jūs]   King of **Athens**: son of **Pandion**; father of **Theseus** (Fig. 4).

According to one story he was childless, and went to **Delphi** to ask the reason for this. The **oracle** told him, in riddling language, to touch no woman until he returned to Athens. On his way back, however, he visited **Pittheus**, King of **Trozen**, to consult him about the oracle, and Pittheus contrived that his daughter Aethra should seduce

Aegeus. This was how Aegeus's son Theseus came to be born and brought up at Trozen instead of Athens.

In Eur. *Med.*, however, Aegeus visits **Medea** at **Corinth** on his way from Delphi to Trozen. He promises her sanctuary at Athens, and she promises in return to cure his childlessness by her spells when she arrives there. Although Pittheus is mentioned (683), it is difficult to fit the birth of Theseus at Trozen into this version.

For the death of Aegeus see **Theseus**. The sea into which, by one account, he had flung himself was then called the **Aegean** after him.

Aegiplanctus [ējipla′nktus]   See **Beacon Speech**.

Aegis [ē′jis]   The word should mean simply 'goat-skin', but is used to mean a miraculous cloak, worn by **Athena**, which strikes terror into her enemies. At Aesch. *Eum.* 404 it apparently helps her to fly. At Eur. *El.* 1257 it is pictured as a round shield.

Aegisthus [ēji′sthus]   Son of **Thyestes**; lover of **Clytemnestra** (Fig. 2). For the murder of his brothers and sisters see **Atreus**. At Aesch. *Ag.* 1605 he apparently calls himself the thirteenth child, though some think that the **text** should read 'third'. He grew up determined to take vengeance for Atreus's crime, but his part in the murder of **Agamemnon** varies in different sources; see **Clytemnestra**. For his own death see **Clytemnestra**, **Orestes**, Plate IIb.

Aenianes [ēniā′nēz]   A tribe living round the upper **Spercheus** river.

Aethiops [ē′thiops]   See **Io's wanderings**.

Aetna   See **Etna**.

Aetolia [ētō′lia]   A region of western Greece, north of the Corinthian Gulf.

Agamemnon [agame′mnon]   Son of **Atreus**; brother of **Menelaus** (Fig. 2); commander-in-chief of the Greek army at **Troy**. For the name of his city (Argos or **Mycenae**) see **Argos**.

When **Helen** had been abducted by **Paris**, Agamemnon raised an army from all the cities of Greece to punish Troy. The kings of the other cities were thought of as bound to him by rather loose ties of loyalty; he had a right to expect their allegiance, at least as long as

Figure 2: The Family of Agamemnon

(a)

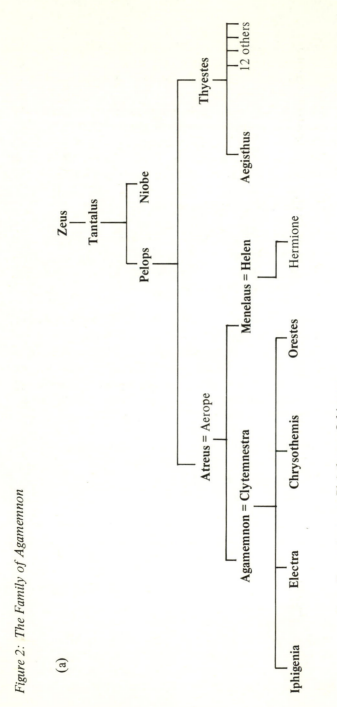

Note For variants see **Pleisthenes, Iphianassa**.

(b)

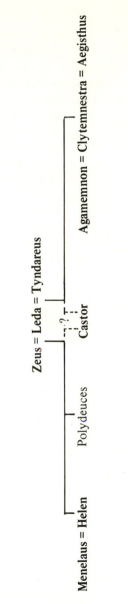

Zeus = Leda = Tyndareus

Menelaus = Helen   Polydeuces   Castor   Agamemnon = Clytemnestra = Aegisthus

he commanded well, but could not compel it.

The army and its fleet assembled at **Aulis**. But the goddess **Artemis** was for some reason angry with Agamemnon. According to one version he had killed a stag belonging to her and had boasted of the deed (Soph. *El.* 566-9); according to another he had once promised to **sacrifice** to her the fairest thing born in his house in a certain year, and, when his daughter **Iphigenia** was born in that year, had broken his vow (Eur. *IT* 20-4); Aesch. *Ag.* 133-8 does not mention any offence on Agamemnon's part at all, and there has been much debate as to Aeschylus's intention here. In any case, the goddess sent contrary winds at Aulis, and would not permit the fleet to set sail until Agamemnon had sacrificed Iphigenia.

For the quarrel between Agamemnon and Achilles, the subject of **Homer**'s *Iliad*, see **Achilles**. In some passages, as at the beginning of this quarrel in *Iliad* 1, Homer makes Agamemnon appear vain and weak-willed, but in others he is a great king and warrior. The tragedians were thus able to make use of either conception; Aesch. *Ag.* perhaps combines elements of both.

When Troy was finally sacked, Agamemnon took **Cassandra** as his concubine and returned to Greece. Meanwhile, however, his cousin **Aegisthus** had become the lover of his queen, **Clytemnestra**. Both wanted revenge on him, Clytemnestra for the killing of Iphigenia, Aegisthus for the death of his brothers and sisters at the hands of Atreus. On their arrival at Mycenae/Argos, therefore, Agamemnon and Cassandra were murdered by Clytemnestra and/or Aegisthus; for the different accounts of this see **Clytemnestra**, Plate IIa.

Agamemnon's return and death are the subject of Aesch. *Ag.*, the first play in the **tetralogy** the *Oresteia*. He is also a character in Soph. *Aj.*, Eur. *Hec.*, *IA*.

Agathon [a'gathon]   A tragedian, active in the late fifth century; portrayed as the host in **Plato**'s *Symposium*. Like Euripides, he left **Athens** in about 407 and died at the court of Archelaus of Macedon. From **Aristotle** we learn that he wrote at least one tragedy (*Antheus*) with purely invented characters instead of mythical ones, and another containing enough material for an epic; also that he was the first to write choral songs which were mere interludes, unrelated to the rest of the play (see **chorus**). In all these respects he was taking to their logical conclusion tendencies which are detectable in the later work of Euripides.

Agave [agā'vē]   Daughter of **Cadmus**; mother of **Pentheus** (Fig. 3), whom she and her sisters tore apart when driven mad by **Dionysus**, as Eur. *Bacch.* tells. We know that in a passage which has dropped out of the play (after *Bacch.* 1300 or 1329; see **text**) she lamented over the dismembered body of her son, picking up his limbs in turn and mourning for each of them. One of the missing decrees of Dionysus before *Bacch.* 1330 was that she and her sisters should live in perpetual exile from **Thebes** because of the **pollution** that they had incurred.

Agenor [ajē'nor]   King of Tyre or **Sidon** in **Phoenicia**; father of **Cadmus**, Europa (Fig. 3) and others.

agōn (plural *agōnes*)   The word means 'contest', and is used by modern critics to denote a set-piece legalistic debate between two or more characters. In Greek tragedy the structure of such debates varies considerably, and it is often a matter of opinion whether a scene should be classed as an *agōn* or not. Typically, however, a debate will start with a long speech for the prosecution and a corresponding speech for the defence, each followed by a comment (often of two lines) from the Chorus-Leader, and will end with more rapid dialogue, generally including **stichomythia**. Every surviving tragedy of Euripides has at least one scene close enough to this pattern for the *agōn* form to be recognisable. In Sophocles the form is less clearly defined, but there is something of the sort in every play except *Trach.* In Aeschylus there seems to be no genuine example (but note *PV* 307-96, 944-1079); there are conflicts, often rhetorically expressed, between characters, but even the trial of **Orestes** in *Eum.* has nothing like the structure or flavour of a Euripidean *agōn*.
    Sometimes the debate is conducted before a third party who acts as judge (as **Menelaus** judges the issue between **Hecabe** and **Helen** at Eur. *Tro.* 914-1059, and **Theseus** judges that between **Creon (i)** and **Oedipus** at Soph. *OC* 939-1015); sometimes one party seeks to persuade the other (as **Haemon** seeks to persuade Creon (i) at Soph. *Ant.* 631-780, and **Hippolytus** seeks to persuade Theseus at Eur. *Hipp.* 936-1101); sometimes the debate is on a matter of principle, and hardly designed to achieve a positive result (as are those between **Electra** and **Clytemnestra** at Soph. *El.* 516-633, Eur. *El.* 1011-123). Generally the *agōn* throws into sharp relief a conflict that is central to the play, but in many cases it seems that some, at least, of the arguments employed are there simply for their ingenuity and rhetorical effectiveness. Certainly the form reflects the rise of interest in techniques of **rhetoric** which is associated with the **Sophists**.

Ai- See also **Ae-**.

Aias See **Ajax**.

Aidoneus [ă-idŏ'nŭs]   A name of **Hades**.

aisa See **fate**.

Ajax [ă'jaks]   The Latin form of *Aiās*, the name of two Greeks who fought at **Troy**.

(i) The greater Ajax, son of **Telamon** of **Salamis**, is portrayed by **Homer** as the finest of the Greek warriors after **Achilles**, but as a defender rather than an attacker. After the death of Achilles, both Ajax and **Odysseus** laid claim to his armour, and the Atridae (see **Atreus**) decided the issue in favour of Odysseus. Ajax then sought to kill Odysseus and the Atridae, but **Athena** drove him mad so that he killed their cattle and sheep instead. Soph. *Aj.* tells how he then recovered his senses and killed himself in shame, and how his brother **Teucer** obtained honourable burial for him with the unexpected help of Odysseus.

(ii) The lesser Ajax, son of Oeleus of Locris, was a much inferior character. During the sack of Troy **Cassandra** took refuge at an image of **Athena** (see **supplication**), but Ajax dragged her away and perhaps raped her, thus earning Athena's wrath. On his way home he was shipwrecked by **Poseidon**, but emerged from the sea boasting that he had escaped in spite of the gods; he was at once blasted with a thunderbolt.

Alastor [ala'stor]   A spirit of vengeance similar to an **Erinys**. At Aesch. *Ag.* 1505-8 the Chorus deny that the Alastor of the **House** of **Atreus** can have taken the form of **Clytemnestra**, but admit that it may have helped her.

Alcestis [alse'stis]   Daughter of **Pelias**; wife of Admetus, King of Pherae in **Thessaly**; daughter-in-law of **Pheres**. **Apollo** worked for a year as a serf to Admetus in order to expiate a crime, and was so well treated that he tricked the **Fates** (by making them drunk, according to Aesch. *Eum.* 728) into allowing Admetus not to die when his time came, provided that he could find a substitute to die in his place. The only person willing to do so was Alcestis. In Eur. *Alc.* Alcestis dies, but on the same day **Heracles**, on his way to one of his Labours, calls at Admetus's house, and manages to bring Alcestis back from the grave by wrestling with Death himself (see also **satyrs**).

Alcmene [alkmē'nē]   Mother of **Heracles**.

Alexander [aleksah'nder]   See **Paris**.

Alpheus [alfē'us]   The river that flows past **Olympia**. Its upper reaches are not far from Oresteum (see **Orestes**).

altars   See **sacrifice, supplication**.

Althaea [althē'a]   Daughter of **Thestius**; wife of **Oeneus**; mother of the hero Meleager. When Meleager was born she overheard the **Fates** prophesying that he would live no longer than a brand that was then burning on the fire; so she snatched the brand from the flames and kept it. In manhood, after heroic exploits, Meleager quarrelled with his mother's two brothers, and killed them. In revenge Althaea deliberately burnt the brand, thus killing her son.

Amazons [a'mazonz]   A race of warrior women living somewhere near the Black Sea (by the River Thermodon in Asia Minor by most accounts, but see **Io's wanderings**). During the reign of **Theseus** they attacked Athens and encamped on the **Areopagus**, where they sacrificed to their god **Ares**. Theseus defeated them, however, and married their queen (unnamed in Eur. *Hipp.* but called Antiope or Hippolyta elsewhere), who became the mother of **Hippolytus** (Fig. 4).

Ammon [a'mon]   Site of a famous **oracle** in the Libyan desert.

amoibaion (plural *amoibaia*)   This is probably the best term (compare *kommos*) for any exchange between the **chorus** and one or more **actors** in which one or more of the parties delivers sung lyrics (see **verse**). Sometimes all the parties sing, as in the 'Great *Kommos*' between **Orestes**, **Electra** and the Chorus at Aesch. *Cho.* 306-478; sometimes the lyrics alternate with iambic dialogue, as in the exchange between **Clytemnestra** and the Chorus at Aesch. *Ag.* 1401-47; sometimes they alternate with non-lyric anapaests, as in the continuation of that exchange at 1448-576. *Amoibaia* are more frequent in Aeschylus than in Sophocles or Euripides, by contrast with **monody**.

Amphiaraus [amfiarā'us]   Son of **Oecles**; one of the **Seven against**

Thebes, and the only virtuous man among them according to Aeschylus; a great **seer** as well as a great warrior. He foresaw that he would be killed in the campaign against **Thebes**, but was persuaded to take part by his wife Eriphyle, whom **Polynices** had bribed with a golden necklace. During the battle the earth opened up and swallowed him and his chariot. After his death he was honoured as an **oracle**-giving **hero**, and his son Alcmeon avenged him by killing Eriphyle.

Amphion [amfī′on]   Son of **Zeus**; husband of **Niobe**. He and his brother Zethus ruled **Thebes** for a period, and provided it with walls; thus he is sometimes regarded as its second founder (after **Cadmus**).

amphisbaena [amfisbē′na]   A fabulous kind of snake with a head at each end.

Amphitrite [amfītrī′tē]   Consort of **Poseidon**. At Soph. *OT* 195 the 'great chamber of Amphitrite' is the Atlantic.

Amyclae [ami′klē]   A town just south of **Sparta**, where **Tyndareus** and his family were sometimes said to have lived.

anagnōrisis   'Recognition', defined by **Aristotle** in *Poetics* 11 as 'a change from ignorance to knowledge, tending to the friendship or enmity of people whose state is defined [?] with reference to good or bad fortune; and', he continues, 'the finest recognition is one that occurs together with reversal [see *peripeteia*], as in the *Oedipus* [Soph. *OT*]'. Earlier he says that the presence of *peripeteia* or *anagnōrisis* or both makes a plot complex, not simple; later he makes it clear that the recognition which he has in mind is of a person's identity; and in *Poetics* 16 he lists different types of *anagnōrisis* in order of merit.

It is certainly true that a change from delusion to enlightenment is important in many Greek tragedies (see **irony**); and the 'recognition scene', often elaborately contrived to create as much suspense and pathos as possible, is a fairly common feature of the genre (fine examples at e.g. Soph. *El.* 1174-231, Eur. *Bacch.* 1259-97).

ananke   See **fate**.

anapaests   See **verse**.

Andromache [andro′makē]   Wife of **Hector**. After the sack of **Troy**, as Eur. *Tro.* tells, she was chosen as the concubine of **Neoptolemus**, and her baby son **Astyanax** was hurled from the city wall. The audience of the play were certainly expected to remember **Homer**'s famous and moving scene between Hector, Andromache and Astyanax at *Iliad* 6. 392-502; note also Andromache's lament at *Iliad* 24. 723-46.

Eur. *Andr.* is concerned with later intrigues in **Phthia**, after Neoptolemus has married Hermione (daughter of **Menelaus** and **Helen**), who tries to kill Andromache.

Antigone [anti'gonē]   Daughter of **Oedipus** and **Jocasta** (Fig. 3). In Soph. *OC* she tends her blind father in his wanderings and tries to prevent the war between her brothers **Eteocles** and **Polynices**.

Soph. *Ant.*, though written much earlier, is set on the day after the end of that war, when the **Seven against Thebes** have been defeated, Eteocles and Polynices have killed each other, and **Thebes** is ruled by Jocasta's brother **Creon (i)**. Creon has issued an edict that Polynices, who attacked his own city, must be left unburied; but Antigone is determined to disobey, and disaster follows for all concerned.

According to the manuscript **text** of Aesch. *Sept.*, Antigone and her sister **Ismene** take part in the mourning for their brothers towards the end of the play, and Antigone then insists on burying Polynices, as she does in Sophocles. Most scholars agree, however, that the end of the play was reworked at some time after the performance of Soph. *Ant.*; the sisters have no place in the play as Aeschylus wrote it, all the mourning belongs to the Chorus, and lines 861-74, 996-7 and 1005 to the end (if not others) are spurious. (The present writer has suggested, however, that, although the sisters have indeed no place in the play, lines 1005-25, 1054-63 and 1065-78 should be retained, to make a final scene between the Herald and the Chorus.)

If Antigone does not belong in Aesch. *Sept.*, there is no reference to her in surviving literature earlier than Sophocles, and the plot of *Ant.* may be almost entirely his invention (see **originality**). Her role in Eur. *Phoen.* is certainly dependent on Sophocles' play. Euripides also wrote an *Antigone*, which seems to have had a romantic plot; here Antigone married **Haemon** and bore him a son.

See also **character, women**.

antilabē   Division of line of **verse** between two or more speakers. As a rule this happens only at moments of excitement or for special effect, and it probably does not happen at all in the genuine work of Aeschylus (but note *PV* 980). For hemistichomythia, involving repeated *antilabē*, see **stichomythia**.

Antilochus [anti'lokus]   Son of **Nestor**, killed during the Trojan War.

Aphrodite [afrodi'tē]   Goddess of sexual love and desire, which were naturally ascribed to divine power like any other forces beyond men's conscious control (see **Eros**; **gods**). She was either the daughter of **Zeus** and Dione (according to **Homer**) or born from the severed genitals of **Uranus** when they fell into the sea (according to **Hesiod**); because of the latter story she can be referred to as sea-born. She was worshipped in many parts of Greece (for a cult at **Athens** see **Hippolytus**), and especially at **Paphos** on **Cyprus**, where she was supposed to have risen from the sea; hence she is very often called Cypris or the Cyprian. In literature she can be regarded as a cruel and irresistible power or as a bringer of delight to mankind, according to the different ways in which love can be thought of. Sometimes her concern with beauty and pleasure is made to extend beyond the sexual sphere, as at Eur. *Med.* 835-45.

Being victorious in the Judgement of **Paris**, she rewarded Paris with the gift of **Helen**, and thereafter she continued to favour **Troy**. Her role in Helen's seduction is the subject of a debate at Eur. *Tro.* 914-97, which raises the whole question of divine and human responsibility; at 985-90 **Hecabe** distinguishes between Aphrodite as an all-powerful goddess and as a mere projection of human lust, playing on the name Aphrodite and the word *aphrosynē*, 'folly'.

As the mother of **Harmonia (ii)** she was an ancestress of the Thebans. In referring to a hypothetical mortal favourite of hers at *Hipp.* 1420-2 Euripides may be thinking of her lover Adonis, though he is elsewhere said to have been killed by a boar, not by the arrows of **Artemis**.

Apian [ā'pian] **Land**   Either **Argos** (Aesch. *Ag.* 256) or the whole Peloponnese (Soph. *OC* 1303), supposedly from a King Apis.

Apollo [apo'lō]   Son of **Zeus** and **Leto**; brother of **Artemis**; one of the most important and popular of the gods, worshipped all over Greece but especially at his birthplace on **Delos** and at the oracular shrine of **Delphi**.

His functions and attributes are very varied. He is the archer god (though at Soph. *OT* 470 his weapon is his father's thunderbolt); the god of music and poetry; the god of purification (see **pollution**);

the healer of disease, though he also causes plague and sudden death with his arrows; a protector of flocks and pastures, though also a hunter like his sister; but in tragedy he is above all the god of prophecy. In this capacity he acts as the 'prophet' or spokesman of his father Zeus through his **oracles** at Delphi and elsewhere, and is responsible for the inspiration of **Cassandra**. At times he becomes personally involved with events that his oracle has foretold or ordained; thus he can be held responsible for the misfortunes of the house of **Laius** (e.g. Aesch. *Sept.* 800-2, Soph. *OT* 1329-30), and in Aesch. *Eum.* he actively protects **Orestes** who obeyed his oracle and trusted him.

Even more than other Olympians he tended to shun anything sorrowful, unclean or ill-omened. An altar to him often stood in front of a house, which he was expected to protect. His association with the sun does not often appear as early as the fifth century, but there may be a hint of it at Aesch. *Sept.* 859. The laurel (bay) tree was sacred to him, and was associated with prophetic inspiration.

For his dealings with Admetus see **Alcestis**. For his building of the walls of **Troy** (with **Poseidon**) see **Laomedon**. Thereafter he continued to favour the Trojans, and he directly or indirectly caused the death of **Achilles**. He pursued several mortal women besides Cassandra, generally meeting with greater success; his children included **Asclepius**.

Among his names and titles are Phoebus (the Bright or Pure One), **Paean** (the Healer), Loxias (of doubtful meaning but used in the context of oracles), **Lyceus** (again doubtful, but sometimes connected with **Lycia** and sometimes with *lykos*, 'wolf'; at Soph. *El.* 6 he is a wolf-killer, but at Aesch. *Sept.* 145 the sense is probably that Lyceus should be truly wolf-like to the enemy), Agyieus (God of the Roadside, as represented by roadside images), the Delian, the Pythian (see **Pytho**), the Far-Shooter. He had associations with the number seven, and at Aesch. *Sept.* 800 *hebdomágetãs*, 'leader of seven' (?), is perhaps a genuine cult title, chosen here to suit the context.

The name Apollo (*Apollōn*) itself, though probably of non-Greek origin, is identical (in the nominative case) with a Greek word for 'destroyer'; hence there is word-play when Cassandra calls him 'my Destroyer' at Aesch. *Ag.* 1081.

Apollo is the god addressed at Aesch. *Cho.* 807-8; for this and for *Cho.* 953-4 see **Delphi**. It is uncertain why he is named, along with **Pan** and Zeus, at Aesch. *Ag.* 55. He is a character in Aesch. *Eum.*, Eur. *Alc.*, *Or.*

Arabia [arā′bia]   The peninsula, known to the Greeks for its spices.

Those texts and translations which place the Arabians near the **Caucasus** at Aesch. *PV* 420 are probably wrong; the Arabians and the dwellers near the Caucasus should be two separate groups.

Arachnaeum [araknē'um]   See **Beacon Speech**.

arai   See **curses**.

Arcadia [arkā'dia]   A mountainous region of the central **Peloponnese**.

Arcturus [arktū'rus]   The star, in Bootes. Soph. *OT* 1137 refers, by a common method of date-reckoning, to the time of year at which Arcturus first rose early enough to be visible before dawn, i.e. mid-September.

Areopagus [arēo'pagus]   The word, meaning 'Hill of **Ares**', is primarily the name of a hill within the city of **Athens**, west of the **Acropolis**. According to the usual account (Eur. *El.* 1258-63) this hill acquired its name when Ares was put on trial there for the murder of **Halirrhothius**. Aeschylus, however, wanting the trial of **Orestes** (which was probably his own invention) to be the first that ever took place there, gives a different explanation for the name at *Eum.* 685-90 (see **Amazons**).

The Council of the Areopagus (also called simply 'the Areopagus') was an ancient body that traditionally met on the hill. In the fifth century its members were men who had previously held any of the nine annual magistracies (archonships), and they remained members for life. Although the archons, from the 480s on, were democratically appointed, the Council of the Areopagus apparently continued to be regarded as a conservative body.

One of its ancient functions, which it retained through the fifth century, was to act as a court in cases of deliberate homicide. Like jurors in other Athenian courts, its members cast their votes by dropping pebbles into urns (at Aesch. *Ag.* 813-17 the gods are metaphorically credited with the same voting procedure). There was a tradition that, when the votes were equal, the defendant was acquitted, the goddess **Athena** having notionally cast a vote in his favour; this tradition is explained in mythical terms at Aesch. *Eum.* 734-41, Eur. *El.* 1265-9. The number of jurors was not fixed, however, and there has been much dispute as to whether the number seen in *Eum.* is odd or even; does Athena vote as one of the jury, thus helping to produce the tie that secures Orestes' acquittal, or does her casting vote break a tie produced by human jurors alone? The latter seems to make much better sense.

In addition, before 462/1 the Council retained, or had recently usurped, some political function which is vaguely described as a 'guardianship of the constitution'. In 462/1 this function was abolished on the motion of a certain Ephialtes. Ephialtes died soon afterwards, allegedly murdered, but the political function was not restored.

This reform must have some relevance to Aesch. *Eum.*, which was performed in 458 and is much concerned with the Areopagus. But is Aeschylus applauding the reform, since he treats the Council purely as a murder court? Or is he deprecating it, since Athena praises the Council highly and regards it as important in preserving the stability of Athens (681-710)? Or is he studiously neutral? The question is remarkably difficult to answer. On the one hand we cannot assume that Aeschylus was a staunch democrat on the ground that he favoured alliance with **Argos** (*Eum.* 762-74), since the link between a policy of alliance with Argos and democratic reforms at home may have been less apparent to contemporaries than it is to some modern historians. On the other hand we cannot assume that he was a conservative on the ground that Athena warns against innovations at 693-5, since any Athenian who favoured a reform tended to claim that it represented a return to the true ancestral constitution.

See also **democracy, politics.**

Ares [air'rēz]   God of war; son of **Zeus** and **Hera**; father of **Harmonia (ii)** and of **Phobos**. His name often means little more than 'war', and is not often found in any other context. Although an Olympian, he is a savage and bloodthirsty being, inspiring fear and hatred; the glory of victory belongs not to him but to **Athena**.

Despite his connection with **Thebes** as the father of Harmonia (ii), he is as much feared by Thebans in tragedy as by others; at Aesch. *Sept.* 104-7, 134-7, it is implied that he *ought* to care for the city, but may in fact destroy it. At Soph. *OT* 190-1 he attacks Thebes by means of plague instead of war; this is unusual, and has been connected with the Great Plague of **Athens**, which began in the second year of the **Peloponnesian War** (430 BC), and was far more destructive than the actions of the enemy.

He has associations with **Thrace**, and that is why he is a neighbour of the Thracian city of **Salmydessus** at Soph. *Ant.* 970 (where he 'saw' the blinding of the sons of **Phineus** and **Cleopatra**, the sort of cruel and bloody deed that he presides over). He was also said to be worshipped by the savage archers of **Scythia** (hence he has a Scythian bow at Aesch. *Cho.* 162), and by the similarly warlike and barbarian **Amazons**.

In a justly famous image at Aesch. *Ag.* 437-44 Ares is described as a 'gold-changer'; as a certain type of merchant gives a small amount of gold dust, weighed in a balance, in return for bulky goods, so War, who holds a balance on the battlefield, takes men from their homeland and sends back a little ash, 'conveniently packed' in urns (see **death and burial**).

For the Hill of Ares see **Areopagus**.

Argives [ar'gīvz]   See **Argos**.

Argo [ar'gō]   See **Jason**.

Argos [ar'gos]   An important city in the eastern **Peloponnese**; or the region which the city controlled, and which can also be called Argolis or the Argolid. A number of myths traditionally belong here: Argos is the home of **Io** and of **Danae**; the city of **Pelasgus** to which the **Danaids (i)** fled; the city of **Adrastus** where **Polynices** raised the army of the **Seven against Thebes**; and the city of **Diomedes**.

In the fifth century, however, a further set of myths was transferred to Argos. In **Homer** the city of **Agamemnon** is **Mycenae** (though he is sometimes called king of 'all Argos', meaning the region), and that of **Menelaus** is **Sparta**. **Stesichorus**, however, placed both brothers in Sparta, and Aeschylus places them both in Argos, about six miles from Mycenae. Since the *Oresteia* was performed in 458, this innovation must be connected with the alliance which **Athens** had concluded with Argos (breaking off an earlier alliance with Sparta) in about 462/1, and which is explicitly foreshadowed at *Eum.* 289-91, 670-3, 762-74. It is also worth noting that Argos had recently (and perhaps very recently, after the treaty with Athens) attacked and destroyed Mycenae. Argos was a **democracy**, and there is some reason to think that the policy of alliance with her was supported by strongly democratic politicians at Athens; but it need not follow that Aeschylus, because he supported the alliance, was strongly democratic in all respects (see **Areopagus**).

Faced with conflicting traditions, Sophocles and Euripides tend, when dealing with Agamemnon and his family, to write as though Argos and Mycenae were alternative names for the same place (e.g. Soph. *El.* 4-10), though sometimes Argos is the district and Mycenae the city, and at Eur. *El.* 35 the Mycenaeans are the Argive nobility.

Alliance between Athens and Argos is again advocated at Eur. *Supp.* 1183-212, written when no such alliance was in force.

Argos is also an adjective meaning 'white', and the army of Argos therefore carried white shields (at Soph. *Ant.* 106-7 the 'man of the white shield' refers collectively to the whole army). The adjective corresponding to the noun Argos is 'Argive', but the tragedians (following Homer) also use 'Argive' to mean either Greek (see **Hellas**) or Peloponnesian; e.g. Argives are Greeks at Eur. *Tro.* 179, Peloponnesians at *Tro.* 187. See also **Argus**.

Argus [ar'gus]   An earth-born monster with many eyes (the number is variously given), sent as a herdsman to watch over **Io** after her transformation into a cow and before she was set wandering by the gadfly. From Aesch. *Supp.* 302-5 and other sources it appears that it was **Hera** who sent him, in order to keep **Zeus** away from Io, and that he was then killed by **Hermes** at Zeus's behest, but at Aesch. *PV* 566-75, 677-81, where the story is seen from Io's viewpoint, his role and death are made more mysterious. In the former passage he is pictured (whether in reality or in Io's maddened imagination) as continuing, after his death, to haunt her in the form of the gadfly, whose buzzing replaces that of the herdsman's reed pipe.

In Greek the name is *Argos*, fortuitously identical, in the nominative case, with the place-name **Argos**, but it is convenient to make a distinction in English.

Ariadne [aria'dnē]   Daughter of **Minos** and **Pasiphae**; sister of **Phaedra**; bride of **Dionysus** (Fig. 4). According to the version of her legend which Euripides has in mind at *Hipp.* 339 (not the version most familiar today), it was in **Crete** that she married the god Dionysus, and it was after this that she fell in love with **Theseus** and helped him to escape from the Labyrinth. She then fled from Crete with Theseus, but when the lovers reached the island of Dia (Naxos), she was killed by **Artemis** in punishment for her infidelity to Dionysus. She was thus the victim of an illicit passion, like Pasiphae and Phaedra.

Arians [a'rianz]   An old name for the **Medes**. At Aesch. *Cho.* 423 both 'Arian' and 'Cissian' are in effect simply exotic terms for 'Persian' or 'oriental', extravagant **lamentation** being associated with such people (see **Persia**). The Chorus themselves are presumably of oriental origin, like the Nurse **Cilissa** (though they can hardly be Trojans, as is often claimed, in view of their devotion to the memory of **Agamemnon**).

Arimaspians [arima′spianz]   See **Io's wanderings**.

Aristaeus [aristē′us]   Father of **Actaeon** (Fig. 3).

Aristophanes [aristo′fanēz]   A younger contemporary of Sophocles and Euripides (active from 427 to after 388); the leading writer of early Greek comedy ('Old Comedy'), and the only such writer whose works survive (we have eleven plays).

One of his favourite themes is parody of tragedy, and this can take various forms. Often it is mere buffoonery, as where a character uses high-flown tragic language in an incongruous context; but there is also ingenious mockery of the work of particular tragedians, implying a considerable knowledge of tragedy among the audience. Aristophanes' favourite target is Euripides, who appears in person in *Acharnians*, *Thesmophoriazusae* and *Frogs* and is frequently mentioned elsewhere; he is attacked as a **sophist**, an atheist, a misogynist, and one who prostitutes the tragic **Muse** by his use of immoral themes, deliberate squalor, and trivial realism. Other targets are Aeschylus (a character in *Frogs*) and **Agathon** (a character in *Thesmophoriazusae*). When due allowance has been made for comic exaggeration and distortion (often gross), Aristophanes' plays provide very valuable indications of the way in which ordinary members of the audience reacted to tragedy and the conventions which tragedians were expected to observe.

Aristotle [a′ristotl] (384-322 BC)   Philosopher; pupil of **Plato**; author of numerous works concerning logic, the natural world, and human activities.

From his *Poetics*, probably written in the 330s or 320s, we possess only one book out of two, and that in such a compressed, disordered and corrupt form (see **text**) that its meaning is often uncertain and at times irrecoverable. Aristotle approaches poetry not as a literary critic but as an analytical philosopher, and thus treats it as a phenomenon among other phenomena, requiring definition, explanation of its existence, and classification into its varieties, each of which must then be analysed into its constituent parts. Any phenomenon, however, is best exemplified by its highest forms, and Aristotle must therefore establish what is the highest form of poetry — in his opinion tragedy — and what is the best kind of tragedy. It is in this way that literary evaluation enters in; although, when Aristotle is defending poetry in general and tragedy in particular (*Poetics* 4, 9, 26, etc.), it is often possible to detect the ulterior motive of replying to Plato's charges against them.

The factual information which Aristotle gives, especially on the origins of tragedy (see **dithyramb, satyrs, tragedy**), can seem contradictory and implausible, and there has been much dispute as to how far it is based on evidence and how far on mere theorising. His definitions, such as that of tragedy in *Poetics* 6, tend to reflect his philosophical preoccupations rather than ordinary usage (and the very unsatisfactory ones in *Poetics* 12 may not be Aristotle's work at all; see **episode,** *exodos, kommos, parodos* (**i**), **prologue,** *stasimon*). His literary judgements are often based more on *a priori* reasoning than on a direct response to literature, though at times we may feel that he is attempting to rationalise the latter. His unargued assumptions are sometimes of greater interest than his conclusions.

The *Poetics* has been constantly misunderstood and misused from the Renaissance to the present, and is quite capable of doing more harm than good. There *are* valuable insights to be gained from it, for those who are prepared to take some time and trouble determining what Aristotle actually meant. Those who are not would probably be well advised to ignore it altogether and to confine their attention to the plays.

See also *anagnōrisis*, **catastrophe, catharsis, character,** *hamartiā, mīmēsis, peripeteia*, **rhetoric**.

Artemis [ar′temis]   A goddess; daughter of **Zeus** and **Leto**; sister of **Apollo**. Like her brother she is usually benevolent but has her darker side. She is a virgin huntress, roaming the mountains with bow and arrows, but also a protectress of wild animals, especially young ones, and a spirit of untamed nature in general. Her arrows are responsible for sudden death in women, but she can also help them in childbirth, and women commonly invoke her in oaths. She is associated with marshes and lagoons, including a lagoon at **Trozen**, beside which she had a temple.

In certain places she was called the Goddess of Fair Fame and of the Market Place, both titles being probably alluded to at Soph. *OT* 161. Elsewhere in tragedy she is the Fair or Fairest. As a goddess of the wild she can be identified with **Dictynna**.

Although chaste herself, she is not usually thought of as demanding constant chastity from her votaries or as a positive enemy to **Aphrodite**. This side of her nature is exaggerated by Euripides for the sake of the schematic pattern of his *Hippolytus*.

She took the side of **Troy** in the Trojan War. For her motive in demanding the **sacrifice** of **Iphigenia** see **Agamemnon**. It is unclear why she is singled out at Aesch. *Sept.* 450.

Asclepius [asklē′pius]   Son of **Apollo**; a miraculous healer. He transgressed the natural order by bringing to life a dead man (sometimes named as **Hippolytus**, but there is no hint of this in tragedy), and **Zeus** therefore killed him with a thunderbolt (this is the myth alluded to at Aesch. *Ag.* 1022-4). He was then worshipped as a **hero** or god, especially at **Epidaurus**, where the rock of Asclepius (Eur. *Hipp.* 1209) was doubtless situated.

His sons Machaon and Podalirius served as physician and surgeon to the Greek army at **Troy**. At Soph. *Phil.* 1333-4 we are told that they will cure the wound of **Philoctetes**, but at 1437-8 Asclepius himself will do so; perhaps the deified father will miraculously inspire the sons in their work.

Asia   Usually the continent (or as much of it as the Greeks knew), as opposed to Europe (see **Bosporus**) and Africa. At Eur. *Bacch.* 17, however, where 'all Asia' is inhabited by a mixture of Greeks and **barbarians**, the meaning must merely be western Asia Minor; and it is evidently restricted in a similar way at Eur. *Tro.* 748.

Asopus [asō′pus]   A river that flows south of **Thebes** and north of Mount **Cithaeron** (see also **Beacon Speech**).

Astacus [a′stakus]   Father of **Melanippus**.

Astyanax [astï′anaks]   Baby son of **Hector** and **Andromache**, thrown to his death from the walls of **Troy** after the sack of the city.

Atalanta [atala′nta]   A maiden of **Arcadia**, who could run faster than any man, and who vowed not to marry until she encountered a man who could defeat her in a foot-race. Eventually Melanion did so by trickery, and she became the mother of **Parthenopaeus**.

ātē   A poetic word, used by the tragedians in two different but related senses. The commoner of these is 'ruin, destruction', generally visited on men by the gods. Where the gods' motive can be discerned, *ātē* is found to be a punishment for crime, sometimes for *hybris*, though there is no necessary connection between the two words.

Such destruction may (but need not) be brought about by some fatal infatuation or mental blindness; and 'infatuation, mental blindness' is the second sense of *ātē*. This sense is unusual in tragedy (though some instances of the word are difficult to classify), but has received much attention from critics; two clear examples are Aesch. *Sept.* 687 (**Eteocles** is warned against *ātē* in wishing to fight his own brother) and Eur. *Hipp.* 276 (*ātē* may be the cause of **Phaedra**'s refusal to eat). In this sense too *ātē* is explained by the agency of the gods (e.g. *Hipp.* 241), like anything else which 'comes over' a man from outside his conscious personality. This does not mean, however, that a man is not accountable for reckless or criminal acts committed under the influence of such infatuation; in a famous passage of **Homer** (*Iliad* 19. 78-144) **Agamemnon** accepts blame for the quarrel with **Achilles** precisely *because* **Zeus** sent *ātē* to take away his wits.

When the gods wish to punish a person for a crime that he or an ancestor has committed in the past, they may visit him with infatuation so that he brings his destruction on himself; a famous **fragment** of Aeschylus's *Niobe* says that 'a god plants a fault in men when he wishes utterly to destroy a house'. Something like this happens to Xerxes and the Persians in Aesch. *Pers.* (where the operation of *ātē* is described in general terms at 93-100) and to **Ajax (i)** in Soph. *Aj.* (whose madness is called *ātē* at 363). At Aesch. *Ag.* 223, in a very difficult and much discussed passage, a word close to this sense of *ātē* is used in the context of Agamemnon's **sacrifice** of **Iphigenia**; and at 1192 the troubles of the **house** are traced back to an 'original *ātē*' (here not much more than 'crime', for the Greeks tended to attribute *any* crime to some mental failing), namely the adultery of **Thyestes**. See also **curses**, *hamartiā*.

A classic account of *ātē* is the Second **Stasimon** of Soph. *Ant.*, describing the destruction of an accursed house. Here the word means 'destruction' at 584, 614, 625, but seems poised between 'destruction' and 'infatuation' at 624 ('evil at last seems good to a man when a god wishes to bring his mind to *ātē*'); in any case the *idea* of an infatuation sent by the gods is vividly described here.

As every solver of crossword puzzles knows, *ātē* can be personified as a goddess. She then embodies the abstract noun in either of its senses; at Aesch. *Ag.* 385-6 **Persuasion** is the child of Infatuation.

Athena [athē′na] or Athene [athē′nē] Daughter of **Zeus**; an important goddess. She sprang in full armour from her father's head after **Hephaestus** had split it with an axe in order to release her. She can thus be said to have had no mother (though **Hesiod** says at *Theogony* 886-900 that her mother was Metis, Wisdom, who was swallowed by Zeus when she was about to give birth to Athena). For her birth see also **Triton**.

She is a virgin warrior who terrifies her enemies by shaking her **Aegis** before them, and who brings victory to those mortals whom she favours. She was prominent in the battle against the **Giants**, and it is usually said that as her father's favourite she alone may borrow his thunderbolt (but see **Apollo**).

She is also, however, a goddess of arts, crafts and wisdom in general; and of cities and citadels, especially **Athens**, her principal home, where she was naturally very popular. She became its patroness after a competition with **Poseidon**, when she gave it the gift of the **olive** and he could only produce a salt spring (though at **Colonus** she was worshipped beside Poseidon as a goddess of horses). Her most sacred image, an ancient olive-wood statue, was housed in a **temple** (replaced in the late fifth century by the Erechtheum) on the **Acropolis**, the site of the competition; **Orestes** is seen grasping this image in **supplication** at Aesch. *Eum.* 276 (compare *Eum.* 80).

In the Trojan War she took the side of the Greeks, having been rejected in the Judgement of **Paris**. In particular she was the patroness of **Odysseus**. She advised on the building of the Wooden Horse (see **Troy**), which was supposedly dedicated to her, and which the Trojans intended to place in her temple when they hauled it into the city. In the sack of Troy, however, she was angered by the impiety of **Ajax (ii)** in dragging **Cassandra** away from her image.

She is very often called Pallas, a name of unknown origin. Hence the City of Pallas is Athens, the Shores of Pallas are those of **Attica**, and the Rock of Pallas is the Athenian Acropolis. At **Delphi** there was a shrine of Athena Pronaia, 'Athena Before the Temple' (of Apollo). She is also identified with **Nike** (Victory), and with **Onca** of **Thebes**, and she is called Polias as protectress of cities and citadels. At Eur. *Tro.* 536 she is the 'maiden of immortal steeds'; and at *Tro.* 1113 she is the 'goddess of the Bronze Gates', with reference to a bronze-covered temple at **Sparta**. She is a character in Aesch. *Eum.*, Soph. *Aj.*, Eur. *Supp.*, *Tro.*, *IT*, *Ion*, *Rhes.*

Athens Although Athens was an important site from the Bronze Age on, there are for some reason relatively few **myths** that properly belong there (even **Theseus** is not exclusively Athenian), and Athenians played only a small part in the Trojan War according to **Homer**. By the time of the tragedians, however, many myths had been given an Athenian connection, and the tragedians themselves made further contributions to this process (see **Heracles, Medea, Oedipus, Orestes, Seven against Thebes**).

By the sixth century Athens controlled the whole of **Attica** and was one of the most prosperous of Greek states. In that century the foundations of Athenian **democracy** were laid, and **tragedy** (or certainly tragedy as we know it) was invented there (see **Thespis**). For the Persian Wars of the early fifth century, in which Athens won great prestige, see **Persia**. When the Persians had been driven from Greece in 479, the most powerful Greek states were **Sparta** by land and Athens by sea; and Athens acquired control of a maritime alliance or empire that soon included almost all the islands of the **Aegean** and the cities on its northern and eastern coasts. For much of the fifth century, however, Athens was at war with Sparta and other mainland states (see **Peloponnesian War**), until a crushing defeat in 404 caused the 'Athenian Empire' to be dissolved.

In the intervening period (479 to 404) Athens was the unquestioned centre of Greek culture. All surviving tragedies were written in that period (with the probable exception of Eur. *Rhes.*) for performance at Athens (with the possible exceptions of Eur. *Andr.*, *Bacch.*, *IA*).

In the fourth century Athens was the home of **Plato** and **Aristotle**, and, although less powerful than before, retained its democracy and its independence until conquered by Philip of Macedon in 338.

Athos [ā′thos]   See **Beacon Speech**.

Atlas [a′tlas] (adjective Atlantic)   A **Titan**, who, when the Titans had been defeated by **Zeus**, was condemned to stand for ever in North Africa, near the western end of the Mediterranean, supporting the sky on his shoulders.

When **Heracles** came to the far West to fetch the Golden Apples of the **Hesperides**, he tricked Atlas into picking them for him while he (Heracles) held up the sky; this story may have been narrated in the course of the *Prometheus Unbound* (see **Prometheus**).

The 'Bounds of Atlas', 'Atlantic Regions', etc. are the westernmost limits of the world, near the Pillars of Heracles (Straits of Gibraltar).

Atreus [ā′trūs]   Son of **Pelops**; father of **Agamemnon** and **Menelaus** (Fig. 2), who are often referred to as the Atridae [atrī′dē], i.e. Sons of Atreus. For his crime see **Thyestes**.

attendants   Royal or noble characters in Greek tragedy are accompanied, where appropriate, by a few mute servants, of whom no notice is taken in the text until they are needed for some purpose, when a command is addressed to them. See also **extras**.

Attica [a'tika]   The region surrounding, and controlled by, **Athens**, stretching from Cape Sunium to Mount **Cithaeron** and including **Eleusis**, Marathon, etc. Since all free natives of Attica were citizens of Athens, 'Attic' often means the same as 'Athenian'.

Aulis [aw'lis]   A port on the coast of **Boeotia** (opposite **Chalcis**), where **Iphigenia** was sacrificed and from which the Greek fleet set sail for **Troy**.

aulos   Commonly translated 'flute', but in fact a reed instrument with a penetrating tone. It accompanied dirges (see **lamentation**), dithyrambs, and all songs in Greek drama (see **chorus, verse**). It was also used in orgiastic music (Plate IIIb), and is called Phrygian at Eur. *Bacch.* 127 because of its association with **Cybele**.

Autonoe [awto'nō-ē]   Daughter of **Cadmus**; mother of **Actaeon** (Fig. 3).

Axius [a'ksius]   A river of Macedonia; see **Lydias**.

B

Bacchae [ba'kē]   Another word for **Maenads**. In English it sometimes appears as Bacchants [ba'kants] or Bacchantes [baka'ntēz]. 'Bacchae' should mean 'female Bacchuses', and so suggests a strong identification between the votaries and their god.

For the content of Euripides' play see **Dionysus, Pentheus**. He apparently wrote it while staying at the court of Archelaus, King of Macedon. He died when it was still unperformed, and it was then produced at **Athens** by his son or nephew, together with Eur. *IA* and other plays. It is uncertain whether it was primarily intended for performance at Athens or in Macedonia; for allusions to Macedonia see **Lydias, Pieria**. For the gaps in the play's text see **text, Agave**.

Bacchus [ba'kus], Bacchius [ba'kius] and Baccheus [ba'kūs]   All names of **Dionysus**.

Bactria [ba'ktria]   A remote province of the Persian Empire, between the Oxus and the Hindu Kush.

barbarians   The word *barbaros* simply meant non-Greek. Although the Greeks tended to assume that they were superior to other peoples, *barbaros* is not in itself derogatory, as is shown by the fact that Persians in Aesch. *Pers.* use it of themselves.

Barca [bar'ka] (adjective Barcaean [barsē'an])   A Greek settlement in **Libya**.

Beacon Speech   It is convenient to discuss in one place the geography of **Clytemnestra**'s speech at Aesch. *Ag.* 281-316. (The details are in any case less important than the general picture of the beacon fire as a creature of demonic energy leaping ever closer to **Argos** at the Queen's command.)

From Mount **Ida** (presumably a foothill near **Troy** rather than the main summit) the signal travels (1) to the Rock of **Hermes**, an unknown site on **Lemnos**, about 70 miles; (2) to Mount Athos, sacred to **Zeus**, on the eastern promontory of Chalcidice, about 50 miles; (3) to Mount Macistus (or Macistum), said to be on **Euboea** — if so, at least 100 miles; (4) across the **Euripus** to Mount Messapium on the coast of **Boeotia**, at most 40 miles if Macistus is in the north of Euboea; (5) across the **Asopus** valley to Mount **Cithaeron**, about 23 miles; (6) across the Gorgopian (**Gorgon**-Faced) Lake, which might mean the sea to the north of Aegina, to Mount Aegiplanctus (Goat-Wandered), which might be the peak on Aegina itself — if so, about 35 miles; (7) across the **Saronic** Strait, probably between Aegina and the **Peloponnese**, to Mount Arachnaeum between **Epidaurus** and Argos, about 28 miles if Aegiplanctus is on Aegina; (8) to Argos itself, about 17 miles. It is thought, however, that something is missing from the **text** after line 287, so there may have been another stage between Athos and Macistus.

At 312-14 the passing on of the beacon fire is described in terms of a relay race in which a torch is passed between members of a team; the runner of the first lap contributes as much to victory as the runner of the last. Such a race was held annually at **Athens**.

Bia [bi'a]   Force or violence, *biā*, personified as a goddess; see **Strength**.

Bibline [bi'blin] **Mountains**   See **Io's wanderings**.

Boeotia [bēō′shia]   Part of central Greece, north-west of **Attica**, dominated by **Thebes**.

Boreas [bo′rēas]   The North Wind. Personified as a god, he dwells in **Thrace** (the land from which he blows) with his storm-winds and horses, and was the father of **Cleopatra** ('Boread' means 'child of Boreas').

Borrhaean [bore′an] **Gate**   One of the seven gates of **Thebes**. The name means 'northern'.

Bosporus [bo′sporus] (less correctly 'Bosphorus')   The name of two straits.

(i) The Thracian Bosporus, joining the Propontis (Sea of Marmara) to the Black Sea (see **Clashing Rocks**); but sometimes in poetry the Hellespont (Dardanelles), joining the Propontis to the **Aegean**, is meant.

(ii) The Cimmerian (Crimean) Bosporus, north of the Black Sea, joining it to Lake **Maeotis** (the Sea of Azov).

Both Bospori were considered to separate Europe from **Asia**, and both were associated with **Io**, since the name suggests 'Ox Passage' or 'Cow Passage'. At Aesch. *Supp.* 544-6 she crosses from Europe to Asia by the Thracian Bosporus (the usual version), but at *PV* 729-35 she does so by the Cimmerian Bosporus (see **Io's wanderings**).

Bromius [bro′mius]   A name of **Dionysus**.

Bybline [bi′blin] **Mountains**   See **Io's wanderings**.

C

Cadmus [ka′dmus]   Son of **Agenor** (Fig. 3); founder of **Thebes**. Hence Thebes is often called the Cadmea [kadme′a] , City of Cadmus, etc., and its citizens are the Cadmeans.

He left his native **Phoenicia** in quest of his sister Europa, whom **Zeus** had abducted, and after various adventures he was commanded by the gods to settle in Greece and to found his new city. First he had to kill a snake or dragon, which guarded a local spring, sacred to **Ares**. He then sowed the snake's teeth in the ground, and a host of armed men sprang up from them. By flinging stones among the men he made them fight one another until only five were left. These five were called the Spartoi or Sown Men, and they and their descendants formed the Theban nobility (though at Soph. *OC* 1534 the word is applied to the Thebans in general); they included **Pentheus**'s father **Echion** and ancestors of **Creon** and **Melanippus**.

Cadmus then married Ares' daughter **Harmonia (ii)**, by whom he had several children (Fig. 3), including **Semele**, the 'Cadmean bride' of Soph. *Ant.* 1115. When we see him in Eur. *Bacch.* he is too old to rule, and, since he has no sons (see **Polydorus (i)**), the kingship has passed to his grandson Pentheus.

Various accounts are given of his later fate, and the very curious prophecy at *Bacch.* 1330-9 is an attempt to combine several of these. The transformation into snakes may be a relic of a cult in which Cadmus and Harmonia were worshipped in this form. The barbarian tribe which they will lead against Greece is the obscure Encheles of Illyria, far to the north; their sack of **Delphi** was prophesied in an oracle known to **Herodotus** (9. 43; see also 5. 61). The ox-cart of 1333 was apparently supposed to explain the name of a certain Illyrian town. Cadmus's translation to the land of the blessed is a more orthodox fate for a **hero** honoured by the gods (see **death and burial**), though in the bitter context of the play he can regard even this as a punishment (1360-2).

Calchas [ka'lkas]   A **seer** who served with the Greek expedition to **Troy**.

Canobus [kanó'bus] or Canopus   See **Io's wanderings**.

Capaneus [ka'panŭs]   One of the **Seven against Thebes**. He climbed the wall of the city boasting that he would sack it whether **Zeus** was willing or not, and was at once dashed to his death by a thunderbolt, as is related at Soph. *Ant.* 134-7.

Caphereus [kafē'rŭs]   A cape (Eur. *Tro.* 90 talks of 'Capherean [-ē'an] headlands' in the plural) in the south-east of **Euboea**. When the Greek fleet was returning from **Troy**, some of the ships were lured to their destruction on this cape by Nauplius, who was seeking revenge for the death of his son Palamedes (see **Odysseus**).

Cassandra [kasa'ndra]   A daughter of **Priam** and **Hecabe**, rarely mentioned by **Homer**. According to the tragedians, she was desired by

Apollo and promised to yield to him, and he therefore granted her the gift of prophecy (see **seers**). She then broke her promise, however, and the god, unable to withdraw his own gift, turned it into a punishment by decreeing that her prophecies should never be believed.

During the sack of **Troy** she took refuge at an image of **Athena** (see **supplication**) but was dragged away by **Ajax (ii)**. **Agamemnon** then took her as his concubine. When he brought her back to Greece, she was murdered with him by **Clytemnestra**.

She is a character in Aesch. *Ag.* and Eur. *Tro.*

Castalia [kastă′lia]   A sacred stream flowing past **Delphi** from a spring on **Parnassus**.

Castor [kah′stor]   Son of **Leda** either by her husband **Tyndareus** or by **Zeus**; hence either brother or half-brother of Polydeuces, **Helen** and **Clytemnestra** (Fig. 2). Castor and Polydeuces are commonly spoken of together as the Dioscuri, i.e. Sons of Zeus, but sometimes also as sons of Tyndareus; and mythical accounts usually assign one son to each father.

After heroic lives Castor and Polydeuces were translated to the heavens as star-gods, who specialise in rescuing sailors from shipwreck. As gods closely related to Clytemnestra and Helen they appear at the end of Eur. *El.* and *Hel.* (see *deus ex machina*).

catastrophe   A word used by some ancient writers to mean the ending of a play, and by some modern ones to mean the last turn of its plot causing the final ruin or salvation of its characters. Comparable (though not necessarily synonymous) terms are 'dénouement', 'climax', and **Aristotle**'s *lysis* (*Poetics* 18; translated as 'resolution', 'unravelling' or 'dénouement') and *peripeteia*. Naturally all these words can more easily be applied to some tragedies than to others; the murder of **Agamemnon** is the catastrophe of Aesch. *Ag.* and **Oedipus**'s discovery of the truth is that of Soph. *OT*, but Aesch. *Pers.* and Eur. *Tro.*, for instance, are constructed on different principles.

catharsis (or *katharsis*; but the adjective can only be 'cathartic')   The word can be used of physical cleaning; of purification in a religious sense (see **pollution**); and of purgation in a medical sense (see below). It is applied to tragedy by **Aristotle** in Chapter 6 of his *Poetics*, where, in the course of defining what a tragedy is, he says that it 'effects through pity and fear the catharsis of such emotions'. A greater amount of ink than any non-specialist could possibly be induced to believe has been spilt in attempts to elucidate these words. It is hoped that the following attempt is no worse than most.

Aristotle, it seems, is concerned about the paradoxical fact that, while the purpose of all art is to give pleasure (this is taken for granted), tragedy does so by arousing emotions that are in themselves distressing. He may also wish to rebut **Plato**'s charge (*Republic* 10. 605C-606B) that tragedy encourages us to indulge emotions which we normally think it manly to suppress, and that this must weaken our resistance to them in our daily lives. For these reasons Aristotle wishes to claim that, by arousing our pity and fear, tragedy rids us of these emotions; we leave the theatre *less* subject to them than we were before we entered it.

This he expresses by the word catharsis, used in its medical sense. Greek physicians believed that illness, physical or mental, was normally caused by an imbalance between the four 'humours' of the body (blood, phlegm, yellow bile and black bile), and the 'purgation' of a humour that was present in excess was a standard form of medical or psychiatric treatment. As a rule, however, the treatment was not homoeopathic; for a patient with an excess of a wet humour, for instance, a physician would naturally recommend a diet of dry food. So the medical metaphor does not by itself explain how tragedy can rid us of the emotions that it arouses.

For such an explanation we must refer to *Politics* 8. 7, a passage quoted by many translators of the *Poetics*. Here Aristotle is discussing the functions of different kinds of music, including the 'enthusiastic' music performed in the rites of the **Corybantes** and in other religious cults. This was believed to be capable of curing madness and what we would call neurosis, but it did so in a paradoxical and homoeopathic way, by temporarily arousing the same passions which, in the longer term, it relieved. Aristotle calls this process catharsis, using the word as an explicitly medical metaphor (though in such a context it must have carried some religious associations also), and referring the reader to the *Poetics* for a fuller discussion (which may have been provided in the lost second book). And he singles out pity and fear as emotions to which this musical catharsis ministers.

This, then, shows how Aristotle could have believed that pity and fear are purged through pity and fear. But the application of the term catharsis to tragedy still rests on an analogy (almost on an analogy to an analogy); we cannot know whether Aristotle ever gave, or could have given, a psychological explanation of how tragedy (or for that matter music) achieved its cathartic effect, nor whether he recognised the considerable differences in this regard between music performed to the sick and plays performed to people in normal health. Nor do attempts by modern authors to reconstruct the account that Aristotle *might* reasonably have given seem particularly fruitful.

Those who use the word catharsis in English generally wish to import some notion which is certainly alien to Aristotle. In earlier centuries it was commonly used with reference to the moral uplift afforded by poetic justice; we are purged of excessive passions by seeing how such passions are punished on stage. Nowadays the notions imported are generally derived, more or less remotely, from **Freud**; we tend to harm ourselves by repressing emotions (or the need for emotions) which we find no opportunity to express (or to feel) in our daily lives, and tragedy provides such an opportunity in an innocuous way. Since this would not necessarily be true even if Aristotle had said it, there is perhaps not very much point in pretending that he did.

Caucasus [kaw'kasus]   The name usually refers to the high mountain range between the Black Sea and the Caspian, as it presumably does at Aesch. *PV* 422 (see **Arabia**). In some versions of the **Prometheus** legend this was the site of the rock on which he was bound, but the scene of *PV* is an anonymous mountain in the far North. For the Caucasus of *PV* 719 see **Io's wanderings**.

Cecrops [ke'krops]   An ancestor of **Theseus** and the Athenians. So the Cecropian [kekrō'pian] Land is **Athens**, and the Cecropian Rock is its **Acropolis**.

Centaurs [se'ntorz]   Fabulous creatures, part man and part horse, who were sometimes depicted as wild and savage but sometimes as wise and benevolent. For the most famous of them, Chiron, see **Achilles**, **Prometheus**.

Cephallenia [sefalē'nia]   An island close to **Ithaca**. **Homer** regards it as part of the kingdom of **Odysseus**, and, since it is the largest island of its group, the inhabitants of the whole group, including Ithaca, are sometimes called Cephallenians.

Cephalus [se'falus]   See **Eos**.

Cephisus [sēfī'sus]   A stream flowing past **Athens**. Unlike most Greek streams, it did not dry up in summer.

Cerberus [ser'berus]   The many-headed hound who guards the gate of the **Underworld**. It is Cerberus who is described at Soph. *OC* 1568-73.

Cerchnia [serknī'a]   Known only from Aesch. *PV* 676, but apparently a stream near **Argos**.

Chalcis [ka'lsis]   A city on the south-west coast of **Euboea**, opposite **Aulis**.

Chalcodon [kalkō'don]   A king of **Euboea**, whose son Elephenor served in the Trojan War.

Chalybes [ka'libēz] or Chalybians [kali'bianz]   An eastern race, whose home was usually located south of the Black Sea; but it is apparently north of the Black Sea and east of **Scythia** at Aesch. *PV* 714-16 (see **Io's wanderings**), and the Chalybes are implicitly identi- fied with the Scythians at *PV* 301-2 (the land of **Prometheus**'s rock is 'the mother of iron') and in Aesch. *Sept.*

The Chalybes were the first to use iron, which can therefore be referred to as Chalybian or Scythian. Hence the riddling **imagery** at *Sept.* 727-33, where the iron with which **Eteocles** and **Polynices** have killed each other is described as a Chalybian stranger from Scythia who has come as an arbitrator to divide the property of **Oedipus**. It is uncertain how much of this imagery is supposed to derive from the words of Oedipus's **curse**; Oedipus might have said that a Chalybian stranger would divide his property, or simply that his sons would divide it with iron (as at *Sept.* 788-90).

character   The word is used in two relevant senses. It can mean a per- son's nature, the set of qualities which distinguish him from other people; or it can mean any person portrayed on stage, whether or not he is endowed with any 'character' in the former sense. In what follows (though not elsewhere in this book) the word will be used in the former sense only, and will be replaced in the latter sense by the term '*dramatis persona*'.

Anyone approaching Greek tragedy with expectations derived from the modern novel, and from drama which the novel has influenced, will be struck by something that he may be tempted to call crudity of characterisation. Characterisation by language, for instance, in the sense that particular *dramatis personae* use particular mannerisms, dialects or barbaric or uneducated forms of Greek, is almost entirely absent. Characterisation by style can certainly be said to exist in the limited sense that, for instance, the victim pleading for his life will use a different style from the tyrant condemning him; but it is possible to feel that such differences in style are dictated much more by the differences in situation than by any personality that the *dramatis personae* possessed before the situation arose. If the victim became the persecutor (as in fact happens in some of Euripides' plays), he would take over the persecutor's style. We are seldom allowed to know of any individual traits that would give us a sense of a *dramatis persona*'s continued existence outside the play in which we see him; he says only what he has to say in order to impart information, or to persuade others (see **rhetoric**), or to arouse the emotions of the audience. There are exceptions, or partial exceptions, not least among minor *dramatis personae* (the Nurse in Aesch. *Cho.* and the Guard in Soph. *Ant.* come across more as individuals than many more important figures); but they stand out as such.

Again, the way in which prominent *dramatis personae* in certain plays (e.g. **Orestes** in Aesch. *Eum.*, **Antigone** in Soph. *Ant.*, **Phaedra** in Eur. *Hipp.*) drop out of view well before the end may disappoint a reader who expects plays to be about particular individuals, rather than about the actions in which they are involved; he may then recall **Aristotle**'s insistence (*Poetics* 6) that 'tragedy is an imitation [*mimēsis*] not of men but of action and life'. (Later, in *Poetics* 15, Aristotle does discuss character, *ēthos*, in its own right; the discussion is conducted in typically moralistic and restrictive terms, but reveals much about Greek attitudes.) And the fact that **actors** wore **masks** may suggest a view of human personality as something to be projected outward to onlookers, rather than something to be probed for within an individual consciousness.

All this has been said in recent years by critics impatient with their predecessors, who had obtained implausible and often conflicting results by insisting on finding a character as complete and individual as possible within every figure on stage. But other critics have continued to argue that tragedy must in a straightforward way be about people; that we must somehow believe in the *dramatis personae* if we are to take the plays seriously; that the behaviour of *dramatis personae* in Greek tragedy is in practice recognisably that of human beings; and that downright inconsistency of characterisation seldom occurs.

Evidently each of these groups of critics has some justice on its side. Some of the disagreement between them no doubt arises from the assumption that 'character' must always mean something that can be analysed in terms of modern psychological theories — an assumption which, where Greek tragedy is concerned, is certainly false. The Greeks seldom attempted to explain differences of personality through, for instance, different experiences in early childhood, and none of the tragedies invites us to do so. Antigone and **Ismene** undoubtedly have different characters in Soph. *Ant.*, but, for all we know, their up-bringing and experience have been identical, as their parentage was. Any critic who attempts (as some have done) to explain **Hippolytus's** puritanism through the psychological stigma of his illegitimate birth is exploring in a direction in which Euripides' text wholly fails to point (besides giving 'illegitimacy' a significance that is barely Greek). See also **Freud**.

When Greek philosophers and other theorists did discuss human character, they frequently classified it into a limited number of fixed stereotypes, which might be arranged in order of merit, or explained in physiological terms as being caused by different combinations of the four 'humours' of the body. And an approach to characterisation in terms of stock 'types' works well for later Greek comedy. It is worth noting, therefore, how *badly* it works for tragedy. A few stock 'types' do exist, at least in Euripides; one can easily learn to recognise the blustering tyrant (Lycus in *HF*, Thoas in *IT*, Theoclymenus in *Hel.*), the noble, self-sacrificing virgin (Macaria in *Heracl.*, **Polyxena** in *Hec.*, **Iphigenia** in *IA*), and perhaps a few others. But this approach fails us as soon as we try to extend it beyond the obvious cases. **Pentheus** in Eur. *Bacch.* and **Creon (i)** in Soph. *Ant. are* blustering tyrants, and the stereotype con-tributes something to them, but more interesting things can be said about them than this. And it would be an insensitive critic indeed who saw no more in Sophocles' Antigone than a 'noble virgin type' (see also **women**).

Antigone may well serve as a token of what characterisation in Greek tragedy *can* achieve. We are told nothing about her background, or about her life and behaviour in normal times; her part is short, even by Greek standards; the range of situations in which we see her is strictly limited; the text quite fails to answer numerous questions which we should wish to ask if we hoped to gain an understanding of a person's character in real life. And yet she resists pigeon-holing as effortlessly as she resists explanation; what reader does not feel, from her first line to her last, that he is being presented with a figure who is complex, interesting, and wholly, even unnervingly, individual?

Individuality is (to write paradoxically) something that all Sopho-clean 'heroes' have in common; so is pride, nobility, and above all a refusal to compromise with the demands of prudence and common sense. But the differences between them are equally striking; nothing, for example, could less resemble the self-centredness of **Ajax (i)** in *Aj.* than **Oedipus**'s benevolent concern for his subjects in *OT*. Again, the demands of prudence and common sense are often put into the mouths of *dramatis personae* who act as foils to the 'heroes', but these figures too differ considerably from one another; the function of **Chrysothemis** in *El.* is in many respects identical with that of Ismene in *Ant.*, but her cold complacency is far removed from Ismene's passionate devotion to her sister.

It is perhaps not surprising if this discussion has failed to reach any neat and simple conclusion. All *dramatis personae* in any dramatic tradition are stylised to some extent, and those of Greek tragedy, if more stylised than those of Ibsen or Shakespeare, are less so than those of **Seneca** or the Noh play. To say that the tragedians were not interested in character-drawing *for its own sake*, beyond what emerges from, and is needed for, the action, is not to deny that many figures in tragedy are in fact strongly and interestingly characterised, for the tragedians did not make a point of writing plots to which character was of little relevance. In the event the terms in which we discuss different *dramatis personae* must be very flexible, as it is impossible to generalise beyond a certain point about the practice of the three tragedians, or even of any one of them. Euripides' **Medea** could not have been created by Aeschylus, nor Sophocles' **Philoctetes** by Euripides; within Aeschylus's work there is perhaps no other *dramatis persona* who can be discussed in the same terms as **Clytemnestra**; and so on.

Charites [ka′ritēz]   See **Graces**.

Charybdis [kari′bdis]   A mythical whirlpool that sucked down ships. In order to avoid it, **Odysseus** was forced to sail close to the monster **Scylla (i)**, who seized six of his men; see **Homer**, *Odyssey* 12. 234-59.

Chimaera [kĭmē′ra]   A fire-breathing monster, part lioness, part goat and part snake. It was killed by the hero Bellerophon riding the winged horse Pegasus, which he had caught and bridled when it came to drink at the spring **Pirene**.

Chiron [kī′ron]   See **Achilles, Centaurs, Prometheus**.

Choephori [ko-ē′forĭ] or *Choephoroe* [ko-ē′forē]   The word means libation-bearers. Aeschylus's play derives its title from the occupation of its Chorus when they first appear (see *Cho.* 15). It is the second play of the **tetralogy** the *Oresteia*, and concerns the return of **Orestes** to **Argos** and the killing of **Aegisthus** and **Clytemnestra**; see also **Electra**.

choregus [kore'gus] A wealthy citizen who paid for the **chorus** of an Athenian play (or **dithyramb**) and for most other aspects of its production, though not for the **actors**. He might either have volunteered for the office, in the hope of gaining prestige and publicity, or have been nominated by a magistrate (archon).

chorus The chorus of Greek tragedy is a group of singers and dancers, always male and always wearing masks, who collectively take on a role within a play (usually the role of women or old men) but are not given any identity as individuals. A member of a chorus is a choreutes [korū'tēz] (plural choreutae [korū'tē]) or choreut. Its leader is the **coryphaeus**. The word 'chorus' is also used by some writers to mean a choral song.

The number of the chorus is generally thought to be twelve in the extant plays of Aeschylus and fifteen in those of Sophocles and Euripides, but neither figure is quite certain. A chorus can refer to itself, or be referred to by actors, as either singular or plural, more or less indifferently.

The chorus's main task is to deliver songs and 'recitative' (see **verse**) and to take part in *amoibaia*. Its songs in any play comprise the *parodos* (i), the *stasima*, and sometimes shorter songs within an 'act'. They were accompanied by a single *aulos*-player. It is remarkable that a chorus was able to dance as it sang, but the dance, including expressive movements of the arms and body as well as the feet, was an important element in its performance; indeed the word *choros* primarily means 'dance', and the place where a dramatic chorus performed was the *orchēstrā*, 'dancing area'. We know few details about the movements, except where it is clear from the text that the chorus are beating their heads in **lamentation**, marching in a procession, running in fear, or the like, and we cannot be sure how far formal symmetry could be abandoned in order to suit the gestures to the words being sung.

As a rule the chorus seems to have sung and danced in unison; but most songs *can* be divided between semichoruses or individual chorus-members (translators are fond of doing this), and a few *must* be so divided. A few plays have a second chorus, which may (as in Aesch. *Eum.*) or may not (as in Eur. *Hipp.*) be present at the same time as the first.

The chorus can also take part in spoken dialogue, though it is assumed that in this case it is represented by its leader alone, and the word 'chorus' in the margin of texts and translations should here be taken to refer to him. He very rarely delivers continuous speeches of more than a few lines, but he may take part in **stichomythia**, announce the entrances of characters, and comment briefly on their speeches (especially in an *agōn*).

The modern reader wonders why Greek plays have a chorus at all. The question would probably not have occurred to anyone in the fifth century, when performances by a chorus and no actors were a common and traditional part of Greek life, while performances by actors and no chorus were unknown (apart, perhaps, from certain undignified and non-Athenian genres). Choruses were employed to celebrate victory in battle (see **paean**) or in athletic competitions, to mourn the dead (see **lamentation**), and for various other social and religious purposes, and by the fifth century such 'functional' songs reached a high level of literary sophistication in the hands of such poets as **Pindar**. Whether or not tragedy developed from the **dithyramb**, it is certain that the style, the metre and even the dialect employed in its choral songs were much influenced by the non-dramatic choral tradition (even though non-dramatic choruses were unmasked and usually sang to the **lyre**, not the *aulos*). Indeed many songs in tragedy *are* dirges, paeans, **hymns** and so forth, functioning within the plays much as they did in the real world. And the gradual decline in the chorus's importance in tragedy after the middle of the fifth century corresponds with a decline in its importance in Greek life generally.

The convention of the tragic chorus being once established, it could be used for various purposes. Perhaps the only function common to all tragic choruses is that of marking out the play into distinct divisions or acts (the Greek theatre having no curtain with which to do this). Most choral songs are preceded by the exit of one or more characters and followed by the entrance of one or more (though it is not unusual for an actor to remain visible during a song), and this underlines their structural function.

We happen to have two plays by Aeschylus (*Supp.* and *Eum.*) in which the chorus is an essential party to the action and the events of the play simply could not take place without it (in a sense this is true of Eur. *Supp.* also, though this chorus is much less active). But this cannot have been common at any period. Normally the chorus is in some degree detached from the action, commenting on it from the point of view of ordinary men or women and broadening the focus of the drama beyond the narrower concerns of the characters.

Choral songs in Aeschylus (though not in *PV*; see **Prometheus**) are often long and elaborate, containing complex **imagery** and carrying much of the significance of the plays. And there are few Aeschylean scenes in which the chorus, or its leader, does not take some part. Actors generally take account of its presence, and often address it where we might expect them to address each other. It serves as a counterpart, within the drama, of the audience outside it, enabling — and compelling — the characters to be constantly aware that their actions are on public display, and to project their speeches outward to that public.

Euripides, in contrast, often deals with intrigues and domestic disputes of a kind that would most naturally take place behind closed doors, so the chorus is often ignored for long periods, and sometimes has to be rather self-consciously sworn to silence (*Med.* 259-68, *Hipp.* 710-14). The 'broadening of focus' in choral songs, especially in late Euripides, often takes the form, not of comments on the action's significance, but of charming evocations of an ideal world remote in time or space from the characters' sufferings (e.g. *Hipp.* 732-51, *El.* 432-86). These should not be dismissed as mere light relief, for the characters' sufferings may appear all the more poignant by contrast, but in such places we can see Euripides moving in the direction of fourth-century tragedy, in which choral songs were mere *entractes* unrelated to the play in which they occurred (**Aristotle**, *Poetics* 18; see also **Agathon**). Throughout *Bacch.*, however, the chorus has the exceptional and highly pertinent function of exploring the religion of **Dionysus**.

It is impossible to generalise about Sophocles' practice. In two plays, *Aj.* and *Phil.*, where the chorus has the unusual role of men of action, its singing part is comparatively short, and it does not see far beyond the immediate situations in which it finds itself. Elsewhere, especially in *Ant.*, Sophocles exploits all the possibilities of a chorus with great resourcefulness. One common function is to underline dramatic **irony** and the fallibility of human predictions, as when a chorus sings a song of jubilation immediately before disaster strikes (e.g. *Ant.* 1115-52, *OT* 1086-109; see *peripeteia*).

It is always dangerous to assume that a tragic chorus is the mouthpiece of the dramatist; indeed it may never be so in any straightforward sense. On occasion, as we have just seen, it is proved positively wrong, and always its vision is limited. Even when it draws an acceptable moral from the action that it has witnessed, this is generally too simple and commonplace to be regarded as *the* moral of the play. The chorus's reflections are there for the sake of the drama, not vice versa; they set the play's action against a background of Greek proverbial wisdom, but leave it to us to judge how far that wisdom meets the individual case. At Soph. *El.* 860-3 a choral platitude is immediately exposed as inadequate by **Electra**'s sharper perception of a particular event, and, if the immediate exposure is unusual, the inadequacy is not.

Chryse [krī'sē]   The name of a small island (perhaps purely mythical) near **Lemnos**, and also of the goddess who presided over it; see **Philoctetes**.

Chryseis [krīsē'is]   Daughter of a Trojan priest of **Apollo**. She was captured by the Greek army at **Troy** and awarded to **Agamemnon** as his concubine. As **Homer** tells in *Iliad* 1, Agamemnon had to return her to her father in order to appease Apollo's anger, but seized **Achilles'** concubine Briseis in compensation, thus bringing about the Wrath of Achilles.

Chrysothemis [krīso'themis]   Daughter of **Agamemnon** and **Clytemnestra**; sister of **Electra** and **Orestes** (Fig. 2). She is a character in Soph. *El.*, but is unmentioned in Eur. *El.* and by Aeschylus.

Cilicia [sīli'sia]   A coastal region of Asia Minor, opposite **Cyprus**.

Cilissa [sīli'sa]   The name of **Orestes'** nurse according to Aeschylus. It means 'Cilician woman'; slaves were often called after their country of origin in this way. The poets **Stesichorus** and **Pindar** had earlier given her more heroic names.

Cimmeria [simē'ria]   See **Io's wanderings**; **Bosporus (ii)**.

Circe [ser'sē]   A witch encountered by **Odysseus** in his wanderings. She turned his companions into swine, but he forced her to return them to human form (**Homer**, *Odyssey* 10). In Homer her land is a purely mythical Aeaea, but at Eur. *Tro.* 437 it is identified with **Liguria**.

Cissia [si'sia]   The district round Susa, the capital of **Persia**; see **Arians**.

Cisthene [sisthē'nē]   See **Io's wanderings**.

Cithaeron [sithē'ron]   A mountain on the border of **Attica**, **Boeotia** and the territory of Megara, its northern foothills being about eight miles south of **Thebes**. It is the site of the exposure of the infant **Oedipus** and of the deaths of **Actaeon** and **Pentheus**; see also **Beacon Speech**. The claim, at Eur. *Bacch.* 661-2, that snow falls (or perhaps lies) on Cithaeron throughout the year is a considerable exaggeration.

city   In the classical period Greece was divided into a great many city-states, completely independent of one another (except where weaker states were dominated by stronger), often at war (see **Peloponnesian War**), and each having its own social and religious institutions. The word for such a city-state is *polis* (plural *poleis*), generally translated as 'city'.

In **Homer** the *polis* is a much more primitive community, ruled over by a 'king' or chieftain, and lacking most of the institutions of the classical city-state, including a code of laws. The kings, however, act almost as independently as classical city-states did (see **Agamemnon**).

The tragedians veer between the classical and the Homeric conception, sometimes with slightly incongruous results. Thus **Theseus** can be presented as a champion of **democracy**; conversely the **Athens** of Aesch. *Eum.* seems to have no king at a time when **Argos** has, and the **Areopagus**, which is apparently representative of the legal institutions of the mature *polis*, is founded in the course of the play. See also **politics**.

Clashing Rocks   Two mythical rocks which clashed together to crush any ship that tried to pass between them. They are usually located in the Thracian **Bosporus (i)**. **Jason** managed to pass them safely in the Argo on his way to, or from, **Colchis** by letting a dove fly between them to make them clash and then speeding through as they rebounded. In Greek they are called the Cyaneae, 'dark (blue)', or Symplegades, 'clashing together', or both names combined.

Cleopatra [kleopah'tra]   The unnamed subject of perhaps the most obscure mythical allusion in Greek tragedy, at Soph. *Ant.* 966-87. It is difficult even to make out what the Chorus are saying here, and no one has ever convincingly explained why they are saying it.

She was the daughter of **Boreas**, the North Wind, and of the Athenian princess Oreithyia, who was a daughter of **Erechtheus** and whom Boreas had carried off to his home in **Thrace**. Cleopatra married **Phineus**, King of **Salmydessus** in Thrace, and bore him two sons. He later abandoned her (unless she died) and married a woman called Eidaea or Eidothea, who blinded these two sons in her jealousy.

In some versions of the story Cleopatra and her sons were later avenged. According to one late writer Cleopatra's sufferings included imprisonment, and if only Sophocles had mentioned this, and had laid some stress on it instead of emphasising the blinding of her sons, the relevance of the story to **Antigone**'s case would be clear enough. Sophocles wrote at least two plays on the subject, and is doubtless alluding to one of them in this song; if we knew what version of the myth that play followed, the difficulties might be resolved.

Clytemnestra [klĭtemne'stra] Daughter of **Tyndareus** and **Leda**; half-sister of **Helen**; wife of **Agamemnon** (Fig. 2). According to **Homer** (*Odyssey* 11. 404-34; see also 4. 524-37) the murder of Agamemnon was committed by her lover **Aegisthus** with her help, and she then murdered **Cassandra**. **Pindar**, however (*Pythian* 11. 17-25), probably writing before Aeschylus's *Oresteia* and perhaps following **Stesichorus**, makes Clytemnestra commit both murders, and speculates whether her motive was revenge for the sacrifice of her daughter **Iphigenia** or lust for Aegisthus.

The tragedians then follow this version, relegating Aegisthus to the background. According to Aeschylus, when Agamemnon was in his bath, she trapped him in a kind of robe (probably one which lacked holes for the head and arms and much resembled that seen in Plate IIa, judging by *Cho.* 997-1004), and killed him with Aegisthus's sword (*Cho.* 1011). According to Sophocles and Euripides, however, the murder weapon was an axe, an idea perhaps suggested by *Cho.* 889 (compare Plate IIb).

Clytemnestra is herself killed after Aegisthus in Aesch. *Cho.* and Eur. *El.*, but before him in Soph. *El.*; see **Electra**, **Orestes**. She is seen as a ghost in Aesch. *Eum.*; and Euripides is able to present her sympathetically in *IA*, where her crimes have not yet been committed. See also **women**.

Cocytus [kōki'tus] A river of the **Underworld**. The name means 'wailing', as in **lamentation** for the dead.

Colchis [ko'lkis] A land generally located at the eastern end of the Black Sea; the kingdom of **Medea**'s father Aeetes (see also **Jason**), and also a home of the **Amazons**. The Amazons of Aesch. *PV* 723-8 apparently live in Colchis (compare *PV* 415-16), but this must be a

Colchis north, not east, of the Black Sea; see **Io's wanderings.**

Colonus [kolŏ'nus] The name of a village about a mile and a half north of **Athens** (sometimes called Colonus Hippius, 'Equine Colonus', to distinguish it from a Colonus within Athens); also the name of a local hero.

The village was the birthplace of Sophocles, and its legends and cults (described at *OC* 39-43, 54-63; see also 668-719, 1590-7) were probably little known outside the district until *OC* was performed. Although it in fact means simply 'hill', the name was supposed to derive from the hero Colonus the Horseman, an image of whom was perhaps visible during the performance of *OC*. There was a sanctuary of **Poseidon** the horse-god (it was here, according to *OC* 714-15, that he had shown men how to tame horses) and **Athena** the horse-goddess, and **Prometheus** was worshipped at a nearby village.

There was also (in myth, if not in reality) a rift in the ground which was apparently supposed to be the route by which **Theseus** and **Pirithous** descended to the **Underworld**. A memorial to them stood beside this rift, which was supposed to contain bronze steps (*OC* 1591) and caused the whole neighbourhood to be known as the Bronze Threshold (*OC* 57), **Homer** having spoken of a bronze threshold to the Underworld (*Iliad* 8. 15). It was doubtless because of this entrance to the Underworld that a nearby grove was sacred to the **Eumenides**; and the edge of this grove is the scene of Sophocles' play. No other Greek tragedy gives as much sense of being set in a real and individual place.

For the plot of *OC* see **Oedipus.** The usual story was that Oedipus died and was buried at **Thebes**, but small towns often claimed to be the burial places of famous heroes, and the tragedians liked to invest the myths of other cities with Athenian connections (see **Athens**).

'Coloneus' [kolŏnē'us] in the Latin title of Sophocles' play is an adjective meaning 'connected with Colonus' or in effect 'at Colonus'.

comedy See **Aristophanes, tragedy.**

Corinth [ko'rinth] A city in the north-east **Peloponnese**, close to, and controlling, the **Isthmus**. It played an important part in Greek history, and in the late fifth century it was one of **Sparta**'s most useful allies (see **Peloponnesian War, politics**). In myth it is rather less prominent, though it was the city of **Sisyphus**, the city of **Polybus** in which **Oedipus** was brought up, and the city of **Creon (ii)** in which **Jason** and **Medea** lived in exile and the events of Eur. *Med.* occurred. At the time of the Trojan War it was part of **Agamemnon**'s realm according to **Homer**, but the reference to it at Eur. *Tro.* 205-6 seems to have more to do with fifth-century conditions than with those of Homeric Greece.

Corybantes [koriba′ntēz]   Deities originally associated with **Cybele** (the 'mountain mother' of Eur. *Hipp.* 144) and originally oriental, though their cult could be found in fifth-century **Athens**. The rites paid to them included ecstatic dancing to the music of the *aulos* and **tympanum**, which was thought to be capable of inducing madness but also of curing it (see **catharsis**). At Eur. *Bacch.* 125 they are equated with the Cretan **Curetes**, whose music was said to have been similarly frenzied; it is not clear why they are 'triple-helmeted'.

Corycian [kōri′sian] **Cave**   A large cave high on Mount **Parnassus**, sacred to, and haunted by, the local **nymphs**. The Corycian Peaks are those near the cave.

coryphaeus [korifē′us]   The word means 'chief, leader', and is applied to the leader of the **chorus** in drama.

Cranaus [kra′nā-us]   A shadowy ancestor of the Athenians. The name means simply 'rocky', a standard description of **Athens**.

Crathis [krā′this]   A river in the south of **Italy**, whose water was said to dye the hair golden. It flowed close to Thurii, a Greek colony founded under Athenian leadership in 444/3. There had been other Greek colonies in the neighbourhood earlier, though certainly not as early as the Trojan War; see **Sicily**.

Creon [krē′on]   **(i)** Son of **Menoeceus (i)**; brother of **Jocasta** (Fig. 3); ruler of **Thebes** after the fall of **Oedipus**, and again after the death of **Eteocles** and **Polynices**. His children are **Megareus** at Aesch. *Sept.* 474, Megareus and **Haemon** in Soph. *Ant.*, Megara (wife of **Heracles**) at Eur. *HF* 9, **Menoeceus (ii)** and Haemon in Eur. *Phoen.* Very different impressions of his character are given by the four plays in which he appears, Soph. *OT*, *OC* and *Ant.* and Eur. *Phoen.* In the end he was killed by the usurper Lycus (Eur. *HF* 33).
    (ii) The king of **Corinth** killed by **Medea**.

Crete [krēt]   The long island to the south of the **Aegean**. A civilisation had flourished there in the Bronze Age, but in classical times it was something of a backwater. In myth it was the birthplace of **Zeus** and land of the **Curetes**, and also the home of King **Minos** and his family (see **Theseus, Phaedra**, Fig. 4).

Crisa [krī'sa] (adjective Crisaean [krīsē'an]) A town below **Delphi**; also the small plain between this town and the sea, which was left untilled as sacred to **Apollo**, and on which the chariot races of the Pythian Games were held.

Cronus [krō'nus] A **Titan**; son of **Uranus** and **Earth**; father by **Rhea** of **Hestia, Demeter, Hera, Hades, Poseidon** and **Zeus**. For his birth and overthrow of **Uranus** see **Hesiod**, *Theogony* 137-210. Knowing that he in his turn was destined to be deposed by a child of his, he swallowed all his children until Rhea tricked him into letting the youngest, Zeus, survive (*Theogony* 459-91). Zeus later defeated him and the other Titans in battle, forced him to vomit up the children whom he had swallowed, and, according to Aesch. *PV*, imprisoned the Titans in **Tartarus**. The *Prometheus Unbound* presumably had Cronus released from bondage with the other Titans (see **Prometheus**), and this release is implied also at Aesch. *Eum.* 645.

Curetes [kūrē'tēz] Mythical Cretan beings who, when **Zeus** was born, or hidden, in a cave on **Crete**, drowned his cries with loud music so that **Cronus** would not discover and swallow him. In this way they invented the **tympanum**. At Eur. *Bacch.* 120-5 they are identified with the **Corybantes**.

curses The victim of crime hates the criminal and wants him punished. For the criminal such hatred is fearful and disturbing, especially when it is that of a close relation who would normally wish him well. So the curse, *arā*, is thought of not just as an expression of emotion but as an active force bringing the accursed man to destruction. It generally operates through the 'natural' events of human life (see **fate**), but it may require direct intervention from supernatural beings. In either case it can be personified, and the personified curse can be equated with an **Erinys**; the Erinyes call themselves *Arai*, Curses, at Aesch. *Eum.* 417.

The curse works blindly and automatically, even if the person cursed is as innocent as **Hippolytus** (see **pollution**). It can be passed down from one generation to another, and undeserved misfortune can thus be accounted for by saying that the unfortunate individual is a member of an accursed **house**. In tragedy, however, curses tend to renew themselves in each generation by making each member of the family commit some fresh crime (see *ātē*) and so bring about his own downfall; see Aesch. *Sept.* 720-91, *Ag.* 750-71, Soph. *Ant.* 582-625. The old conception of automatic liability attaching to a family has not yet been fully replaced by that of moral responsibility attaching to an individual, but the two are combined in a vision whose complexities and ambiguities contribute much to the power of the *Oresteia* and other tragedies.

Cyaneae [sīa'nē-ē]   See **Clashing Rocks**.

Cybele [si'belē]   A mother-goddess, originally from **Phrygia** but worshipped elsewhere in **Asia** (in talking of the **Pactolus** at Soph. *Phil.* 393 the Chorus has her cult at **Sardis** in mind) and also in fifth-century Greece, where she was identified with **Earth** and with **Rhea**. She was pictured as riding upon lions, or in a chariot drawn by them. She was worshipped in orgiastic rites similar to those of the **Corybantes** and (in legend, at least) of **Dionysus**.

Cyclops [sī'klops] (plural Cyclopes [sīklō'pēz])   The Cyclopes were a race of one-eyed cannibal giants. *The* Cyclops was Polyphemus, who imprisoned **Odysseus** and his men on their way home from **Troy**; see **Homer**, *Odyssey* 9, on which the **satyr** play Eur. *Cycl.* is based.

The 'Cyclopean [-ē'an] walls' were walls of huge blocks of stone surrounding **Mycenae**, **Argos** and neighbouring cities. They were built in the Bronze Age and attributed to the Cyclopes by later Greeks.

Cyllene [silē'nē]   A mountain in north-east **Arcadia**, birthplace of **Hermes** and sacred to him.

Cypris [sī'pris] or the Cyprian   A name of **Aphrodite**.

Cyprus   The island, on the fringe of the Greek world; a haunt of **Aphrodite**. Mention of it at Eur. *Bacch.* 402 seems to be due purely to this association with Aphrodite, which enables the island to be described in idyllic and enticing terms.

D

Danaans [da'nā-anz]   A poetic name for the Greeks (see **Hellas**), supposedly from King Danaus (see **Danaids (i)**).

Danae [da'nā-ē]   A princess of **Argos**. Her father Acrisius was warned that he was destined to be killed by a son born to her, so he imprisoned her in a bronze-walled chamber. **Zeus**, however, was able to impregnate her from on high by means of golden rain (this is what Soph. *Ant.* 950 seems to imply, though in later versions Zeus himself takes the form of the rain), and she became the mother of **Perseus**. Acrisius then put mother and child in a chest and set them adrift on the sea, but Zeus rescued them; and eventually Perseus killed his grandfather by accident. Danae was the subject of plays by Sophocles and Euripides.

Danaids [da'nā-idz]   **(i)** The fifty daughters of Danaus, an Egyptian descendant of **Io** (see Aesch. *PV* 853-69). They were desired in marriage by their cousins, the fifty sons of Aegyptus, but fled with their father to **Argos**, where they obtained, by **supplication**, the protection of King Pelasgus, as Aesch. *Supp.* relates. The story was continued in the other plays of the trilogy (see **tetralogy**), almost certainly called *Egyptians* and *Danaids*, but the details are obscure. Somehow the Egyptians managed to marry the Danaids, but all the brides except one (called Hypermestra) murdered their husbands on their wedding night (Aesch. *PV* 860-8); the final outcome is quite uncertain. The **satyr** play of the tetralogy was the *Amymone*, dealing with a separate myth about one of the Danaids.

  (ii) Sometimes 'Danaids' means the same as **Danaans**, i.e. Greeks.

Dardanus [dar'danus]   An ancestor of **Priam** and the Trojans.

Daulia [daw'lia] or Daulis [daw'lis]   A town in **Phocis**, a little to the north of the direct route from **Thebes** to **Delphi**.

Dawn   See **Eos**.

death and burial   Death can bewilder anyone, and Greek attitudes to it were no less confused and contradictory than those of other peoples. The force which gave a man life has left his body, so it must have gone off somewhere else; it has become a twittering, insubstantial ghost in the **Underworld**, as **Homer** tells. But a body that was powerful in life cannot have quite lost its power in death, and it must be feared, especially if the dead man has reason to be angry; so dead **heroes** exert a potent force from their graves, as can be seen in Aesch. *Cho.* and Soph. *OC* (also Aesch. *Eum.* 767-74), and a murderer might mutilate his victim's corpse (*Cho.* 439, Soph. *El.* 445) in an attempt to make it harmless. The dead can also walk from their graves in visible form as ghosts, which can be conjured up by **rituals** (Aesch. *Pers.* 598-680) or appear spontaneously in **dreams** (Aesch. *Eum.* 94-139). But again, a man who achieved great things in his life — an **Achilles** or a **Cadmus** — must have been loved by the gods, so they cannot have deserted him in death; such men have been transported to the Islands of the Blest, to live in eternal happiness, or in a few cases (**Heracles**, **Castor**) have become gods themselves. And great sinners against the gods, such as **Ixion**, **Sisyphus** and **Tantalus**, are being correspondingly punished in the Underworld or in **Tartarus**.

By the fifth century yet more ideas had come to exist side by side with these: the soul is subject to reincarnation, or eternal bliss can be purchased for it by initiation into an exclusive mystery religion (see **Eleusis**, **Orpheus**), or it floats up to the sky. But these modern ideas do not often impinge on tragedy.

To acknowledge and assimilate the fact of death we need rituals, and even today we tend to project our need onto the dead and to see the rituals as a last favour to them. Among the Greeks this emotional impulse was crystallised into actual belief, and funeral rites in Greek tragedy are always something more than an expression of the survivors' feelings (see **lamentation**). For a virtuous but helpless girl like **Cassandra** to die without such rites was deeply pathetic, and Cassandra's need to sing her own dirge, since no one else will sing it (Aesch. *Ag.* 1322-3), can be taken quite literally. For a great king and general like **Agamemnon** to die so was a monstrous perversion of the natural order (*Ag.* 1541-50), and in Aesch. *Cho.* the health of the House, which depends on continuity between the dead and the living, cannot be restored until the rites owed to Agamemnon have been paid. For an **Ajax (i)** or a **Polynices**, whose status in life had been more doubtful, it was the presence or absence of honourable burial that finally established that status; to deny such burial was to pay a man the ultimate humiliation of declaring his life and achievements worthless (note also Soph. *El.* 1487-90, which seems to imply that **Aegisthus** will lie unburied). It seems, in fact, to have been quite usual in the fifth century for the state to forbid the burial of a public enemy, though the corpse would normally have been cast beyond the borders, as at Aesch. *Sept.*

1014, rather than left where it might bring **pollution** on the city, as in Soph. *Ant.*

In Homer the dead are cremated, and their ashes are buried in an urn. In the fifth century burial without cremation was common, but the older practice also persisted, and men who had died abroad might be cremated so that their ashes could be sent home for burial (Aesch. *Ag.* 437-44, Soph. *El.* 757-60). At any period female relatives and other women would perform ritual laments while the corpse was laid out, during the procession to the pyre or grave, and at the tomb. **Sacrifices** might be carried out at the tomb, and it might be marked with a mound or a stone. The dead might then continue to be honoured in subsequent rituals, perhaps monthly (as in the parody of them at Soph. *El.* 277-81), and these could include sacrifices, the pouring of **libations** over the tomb, and the dedicating of locks of hair by the dead man's descendants to establish a link with him.

Death is often personified as a god; he is a character in Eur. *Alc.*

Deiphobus [dē-i′fobus]   A son of **Priam**, briefly married to **Helen** between the death of **Paris** and the fall of **Troy**.

Delos [dē′los]   A small island among the Cyclades; birthplace of **Apollo** and **Artemis**, and one of the main centres of their worship. Famous features of the island included a ridge (Mount Cynthus) and a sacred lake.

Delphi [de′lfī]   A town in **Phocis** on the slopes of Mount **Parnassus**, above the **Pleistos** Gorge; also called **Pytho**. It is very important in both myth and history as the site of the principal oracle of **Apollo**; for details see **oracles**. Apollo's **temple** contained a perpetually burning fire and also a sacred stone, called the Omphalos or Navel, which was supposed to mark the centre of the earth; it is to this stone that **Orestes** clings in **supplication** at Aesch. *Eum.* 40. Beneath the temple there was believed (falsely) to be a cavern from which prophetic influence ascended; this is probably mentioned at Aesch. *Cho.* 807-8, 953-4.

Other gods, especially **Dionysus**, were worshipped at Delphi also; see Aesch. *Eum.* 1-29. It is probably historical fact that the oracle belonged to an earth goddess before Apollo took it over, though the details of the succession, as given by Aeschylus, will be purely mythical, and its ordered, peaceful character may well be an innovation; the account at Eur. *IT* 1234-83, which makes **Earth** and **Themis** more reluctant to give up the oracle, is probably more conventional.

Certainly the role of the Athenians in bringing Apollo to Delphi (*Eum.* 12-14) is a purely Athenian invention.

For the Pythian Games see **Pytho**.

Delphus [de'lfus]   A king of **Delphi** who was supposed to have given the town its name.

Demeter [dēmē'ter]   Daughter of **Cronus** and **Rhea**; a goddess of vegetation, especially corn. With her daughter the Maiden (*Korē*, identified with **Persephone**) and **Iacchus** she presided over the Mysteries at **Eleusis**; two Eleusinian titles of Demeter and the Maiden together are the Queens and the Great Goddesses. The passage at Eur. *Bacch.* 275-7, where she is equated with **Earth** and associated with dry food as opposed to the liquid of **Dionysus**, is sophistic rationalising (see **sophists**) rather than popular belief.

Deo is a shorter form of her name. The Hill of Demeter Euchlous (i.e. goddess of young plants) is close to that of **Colonus**.

democracy   In fifth-century **Athens** all decisions concerning legislation and public policy were taken by vote of an Assembly consisting of all adult male citizens who chose to attend. Public offices were filled, normally for a year at a time, by the drawing of lots among those willing to serve (except for generalships, which were elective), and were paid for out of public funds. Mass juries for legal cases were also normally appointed by lot (but see **Areopagus**), and paid. In practice the wealthy and aristocratic retained much influence (see **rhetoric, sophists**), but this influence was not in any way enshrined in the constitution, and all politicians were fully accountable to the Assembly.

A few other cities, such as **Argos**, evolved more or less democratic constitutions in the same period, and many more acquired such constitutions under Athenian influence or pressure. The usual alternative to democracy in the fifth century was oligarchy; this meant that the right to vote was limited to citizens with a certain property qualification, and that public offices were elective and unpaid.

In tragedy there are few direct references to democracy (see **politics**). At Soph. *OC* 66-7 we are expressly told that Athens is not a democracy but a monarchy (though clearly a benevolent and popular one) in the time of **Theseus**. In the *agōn* at Eur. *Supp.* 399-455, however, Theseus himself champions democracy as opposed to tyranny (see *tyrannos*, **city**), and the terms of the debate reveal much about Greek political attitudes. For the politics of Aesch. *Eum.* see **Areopagus, Argos**.

Deo [dē′ō]   See **Demeter**.

deus ex machina (feminine *dea e.m.*, plural *dei e.m.*)   The God from
the Machine was proverbial in Latin, and in Greek from the fourth
century on, as a facile device used by dramatists to get them out of
difficulties with the plot, like the Good Fairy of pantomime. The
Machine (*mēchanē* in Greek) was a sort of crane which could convey
an actor through the air to give an impression of flying.
  It is true that a god appears at the end of Soph. *Phil.* and of many
of Euripides' plays. But it is unlikely that the Machine was used for
this purpose in the fifth century (it doubtless *was* used at Eur. *Rhes.*
885-9, but for the date of this play see **Rhesus**); more probably these
gods simply appeared on the roof of the scene-building. On the rare
occasions when fifth-century dramatists did use the Machine it was
for other purposes; the only probable example in surviving tragedy is
the entry and exit of **Oceanus** in Aesch. *PV* (the entry of the Chorus
in that play being wholly problematic).
  Nor are gods at the ends of plays used in the illicit way which the
term *deus ex machina* suggests. In Euripides they do tie up loose ends
in the *myth*, by predicting later events which the play could not have
included, but the essential action of the *drama* is usually over before
they arrive. The god's main function is always to allow the mortal
characters and the audience to see the action that has occurred from
his own position of perfect knowledge, so that no mysteries remain;
and there is often, as in *Hipp.* and *Bacch.*, a bitter and pathetic contrast between the gods' untroubled lives and the mortal characters'
sufferings.
  In Soph. *Phil.* **Heracles** does in a sense resolve an *impasse* in the
plot, but the fact that only divine intervention can bring **Philoctetes**
to **Troy** is not an awkwardness which Sophocles should have avoided
but an essential feature of his play. Something similar can be said of
Apollo's intervention in Eur. *Or.*

dianoia   'Thought, mind, intellect'; see **rhetoric**.

Dictynna [dikti′na]   A Cretan goddess of wild animals, identified
with **Artemis**.

dikē   See **justice**.

Diomedes [dīomē′dēz]   Son of **Tydeus**; prominent in **Homer** as the

King of **Argos** who fought at **Troy**. For his role in the story of Philoctetes see **Philoctetes**. The Thracian Diomedes (Eur. *Alc.* 483, *HF* 382) is a different character.

Dionysus [dioniˊsus]   A god, son of **Zeus** and **Semele** (Fig. 3). When Semele, while pregnant with Dionysus, was consumed by lightning, Zeus snatched his child from the ashes and hid him in his own thigh, where the jealous **Hera** could not find him. He was then born for a second time from Zeus's thigh, and so can be called 'twice born'; see **dithyramb**. (At Eur. *Bacch.* 286-97 **Tiresias** provides a curious and obscure rationalisation of this myth, turning on the resemblance between the words *mēros*, 'thigh', and *homēros*, 'hostage'.)

The child Dionysus was nursed by the **nymphs** of Mount **Nysa**, somewhere in the orient. When fully grown he established a cult in **Phrygia**, and then travelled to Greece by way of **Thrace**, bringing his worship with him. Various mortals impiously refused to recognise his divinity and were duly punished, notably **Lycurgus** of Thrace and Semele's nephew **Pentheus** of Thebes.

Although his name is thought to occur on a Bronze-Age Greek tablet, Dionysus is barely mentioned by **Homer**, and the later Greeks thought of him as younger than the other major gods (apart from deified mortals such as **Heracles**). It is possible, though not certain, that the legends of his coming from **Asia** or Thrace preserve memories of historical truth. In appearance he is usually pictured as young and graceful (Plate IIIc; later painters make him beardless and even effeminate).

By the fifth century he was worshipped throughout Greece as an accepted and popular member of the Olympian pantheon. At **Athens**, besides being a fertility god in general, he was in particular the benevolent giver of wine (this is allegorically treated by Tiresias at Eur. *Bacch.* 278-85; see also **Demeter**). He therefore presided over parties and festivities, as described in the First *Stasimon* of Eur. *Bacch.* (376-85, 417-32). In this capacity he was escorted by nymphs and drunken **satyrs**; and he was the patron of **tragedy** and comedy, which were performed at festivals of Dionysus, especially at his most important festival, the **Great Dionysia**. It is doubtful whether the connection between Dionysus and tragedy was ever more intimate and essential than this (see **ritual**); certainly in the fifth century there is no discernible tendency for tragedians to pick Dionysiac myths in preference to others for their subject matter.

Myths told of another, less civilised way of worshipping Dionysus:

wild bands of women, called **Maenads**, **Bacchae** or **Thyiads**, roamed the mountains clad in fawn skins and crowned with ivy, brandishing **thyrsi** and performing ecstatic, uncontrollable dances to the music of the *aulos* and **tympanum** (Plate III). They handled fire or snakes without being harmed, and might wear snakes in their hair; and they tore animals apart to eat them raw, though they might also be fed miraculously by the god. The Dionysus whom they worshipped was sometimes imagined in the form of an animal, especially a bull, rather than a man.

There is little or no evidence for such hysterical Maenadism in the fifth century, although it was commemorated in more organised rituals at certain places, notably on Mount **Parnassus** where a party of women from **Delphi** danced in a biennial winter festival (*Bacch.* 132-4) in Dionysus's honour. Among Athenians, at any rate, the need for orgiastic religion seems to have been satisfied at this period by the rites of other divinities, such as **Cybele**, the **Corybantes** and Sabazius, who had more recently been imported from the orient.

It is this kind of Dionysiac religion, however, that is portrayed throughout most of Eur. *Bacch.* (the First Stasimon being rather different, as noted above). The Chorus of Asiatic Maenads are sane but deeply value the liberating experience that the ecstatic rites provide, while the Theban Maenads on **Cithaeron**, whom Dionysus wishes to punish, are wholly possessed by the god. The spirit, and many of the details, of this religion can be paralleled from other cultures by anthropologists and historians. It is uncertain, however, how far the play's undoubted realism derives from survivals of Maenadism somewhere in fifth-century Greece, how far from myth (which could have preserved authentic details of early cult practice), and how far from Euripides' imagination (which could have drawn on the orgiastic rites of other gods).

At Eur. *Bacch.* 298-305 Tiresias claims that Dionysus's power to cause frenzy makes him a god of prophecy and of war, but these are not his usual functions.

Among other names of Dionysus are Bacchus, Bacchius and Baccheus (of non-Greek origin), Bromius (the Roarer), Dithyrambus (see **dithyramb**), Euhios or Evius (from the cry *euhoi* that was uttered in his rites). He is also identified with **Iacchus**. Soph. *OT* 210 refers to a connection between a name of Dionysus and a name of Thebes, probably 'Bacchic Thebes'.

The 'wife of Dionysus' at Eur. *Hipp.* 339 is **Ariadne**.

Dioscuri [dioskū′rī]   See **Castor**.

Dirce [der'sē]   One of the two rivers of **Thebes**, the other being
Ismenus.

dirge   See **lamentation**, *kommos*, **death and burial**.

dithyramb [di'thiramb]   A type of song associated with **Dionysus**.
The form underwent a radical transformation during the fifth century,
but it is likely that early dithyrambs were wild and exuberant songs in
the god's honour, performed by a **chorus** and accompanied on the
aulos. The **Great Dionysia** at **Athens** included performances of dithyrambs as well as tragedies and comedies, and **Aristotle** claims in *Poetics*
4 that **tragedy** itself developed 'from those who led off the dithyramb'.
Scholars differ greatly in their interpretation of this phrase (**actors**
developed from the leaders of dithyrambic choruses?) and the value
they place on it.
   Dithyrambus [-a'mbus] (the same word) was also a title of Dionysus.
The title was probably derived from the name of the type of song,
rather than vice versa; but at Eur. *Bacch.* 526-9 the Chorus try to
explain the word in terms of Dionysus's double birth (from **Semele**
and from **Zeus**'s thigh), fancifully taking it to mean 'he who came twice
(*dis*) to the door (*thurā*)'.

divination   See **omens**, **seers**.

Dodona [dōdō'na]   A town in the far north of Greece; site of an
oracle of **Zeus**, second in importance only to **Apollo**'s oracle at **Delphi**.
The priestesses were apparently believed to hear the god's voice in the
rustling leaves of sacred oak trees. See **Io's wanderings**.

Dorians [dor'rianz]   Doris was a small region of central Greece, north
of **Parnassus**, and 'Dorian **Merope**' (Soph. *OT* 775) perhaps came from
there. Two kinds of knife are called Dorian and Phthian at Eur. *El.*
819, 836, the Phthian being evidently the heavier.
   More often, however, 'Dorian' is used in a much wider sense, of one
of the major divisions of the Greek people (compare **Ionians**). The
inhabitants of Megara, most of the **Peloponnese** (including **Corinth**,
Argos and **Sparta**), the southern islands of the **Aegean** (including
Crete), south-west Asia Minor, and various colonies, all called themselves Dorians, shared certain social and religious institutions, claimed
a common ancestry, and (with a few exceptions) spoke the dialect
called Doric Greek. They numbered **Heracles** among their ancestors,

believing that descendants of his had returned to Greece from exile shortly after the Trojan War to found the Dorian cities and tribes. The tragedians, however, are not scrupulous about the chronology and describe Peloponnesian cities as Dorian in earlier times.

dramatic irony See **irony**.

dreams The idea that dreams are mere illusions barely existed in the fifth century, and it was assumed that anything seen in sleep reflected some supernatural reality. Dreams often foretold the future; it was known that they could do so deceptively, but this might mean that some god was deliberately tricking the dreamer, and at Aesch. *PV* 485-6 we learn of an art by which men may recognise those dreams which will be fulfilled. In literature from **Homer** onward the dream tends to be pictured in terms of a visitant – usually a god or a ghost – who comes and stands by the sleeper and reveals his will, as the Ghost of **Clytemnestra** stands by the **Erinyes** and rebukes them at Aesch. *Eum.* 94-139. But we also hear of more symbolic and (to us) more psychologically plausible dreams, such as Clytemnestra's own at Aesch. *Cho.* 523-50 and the 'Oedipal' dreams of Soph. *OT* 981-2 (see **Freud**).

Like other forms of **omen**, dreams may have to be interpreted and accepted in the correct sense if the prophecy is to be fulfilled; hence the importance of the words of **Orestes** and the Chorus at Aesch. *Cho.* 540-52. On the other hand, if a dreamer fears the import of his dream, the way to exorcise it is to tell it to the sun (see **Helios**) or sky in the open air the next morning (Soph. *El.* 424-5, Eur. *IT* 42-3).

Dryas [drī′as] Father of **Lycurgus**.

E

eagle The sacred bird of **Zeus**, and an emblem of sovereignty.

Earth *Gē* or *Gaia* in Greek, often personified, or semi-personified, as a goddess or Titaness. Usually, as in **Hesiod**, she is the consort of **Uranus**, the Sky, and the mother of **Cronus** and the other **Titans**. But she can also be identified with **Themis**, with **Rhea**, the mother of **Zeus**, and with other mother-goddesses such as **Cybele**; so at Soph. *Phil.* 391-402 the goddess addressed is named as Earth, but is described as 'mother of Zeus himself', and is then given the attributes of Cybele for the rest of the stanza.

Since crops grow from Earth, she is the benevolent giver of nourish-
ment to mankind; but she is also named in prayers to the dead and the
deities of the **Underworld**, since they dwell in her keeping. She is often
the mother of Underworld powers, such as the **Erinyes** (in **Hesiod**)
and the **Eumenides**; at Soph. *OC* 1574 the son of Earth and **Tartarus** is
probably Death (see **death and burial**). **Giants** and Spartoi (see **Cadmus**)
are Earth-born in a slightly different sense. She was believed to have
inspired **oracles** at **Delphi** before **Apollo** took over this function.

Translators commonly misinterpret a purely exclamatory word at
Aesch. *Ag.* 1072 as a reference to Earth.

Echion [ekī'on]   Father of **Pentheus** (Fig. 3). His origin as one of the
Spartoi (see **Cadmus**) is alluded to at Eur. *Bacch.* 540, 995, 1274.

Echo [e'kō]   The personification of echo as a **nymph** is occasionally
found in the fifth century, though the picturesque myths concerning
her are of later date.

Edonians [ēdō'nianz]   A people of **Thrace**, of whom **Lycurgus** was a
legendary king.

Egypt   Soph. *OC* 337-45 recalls **Herodotus** 2. 35: 'Almost all the
customs and habits that they [the Egyptians] have established are the
reverse of other men's. For instance, the women go to market to buy
and sell, while the men stay at home and weave. . . . Sons are not
obliged to support their parents against their will, but there is an
absolute obligation for daughters to do so.' Herodotus exaggerates here,
but **women** probably did have more freedom in Egypt than in Greece.

At Eur. *Tro.* 128 the 'twisted growth of Egypt' means rope, which
was commonly made out of the Egyptian papyrus plant.

See also **Danaids (i)**, **Helen**, **Libya**, **Io's wanderings**, **Proteus**.

ekkyklēma   A low platform on wheels, which could be rolled out of
the scene-building to reveal to the audience what had taken place
within. Most scholars agree that it is alluded to by **Aristophanes** and
was used in fifth-century tragedy, though some deny this.

Its usual function would have been to reveal dead bodies, often
in a kind of tableau with their killers standing over them; for instance,
Agamemnon and **Cassandra** with **Clytemnestra** at Aesch. *Ag.* 1372,
Clytemnestra and **Aegisthus** with **Orestes** at Aesch. *Cho.* 972, **Eurydice**

at Soph. *Ant.* 1293, Clytemnestra with Orestes and **Pylades** at Soph. *El.* 1466, **Phaedra** at Eur. *Hipp.* 811. Occasionally other kinds of tableau were revealed, such as Orestes and the sleeping **Erinyes** at Aesch. *Eum.* 64 (probably), **Ajax (i)** and the slaughtered animals at Soph. *Aj.* 348.

Electra [ele′ktra]   Daughter of **Agamemnon** and **Clytemnestra**; sister of **Orestes**, **Iphigenia** and (in Sophocles) **Chrysothemis** (Fig. 2). She is not mentioned by **Homer**, but her role in Aesch. *Cho.* may well have its origin in the *Oresteia* of **Stesichorus**. It is a secondary role, and she takes no direct part in the killing of Clytemnestra and **Aegisthus**.

In Soph. *El.* and Eur. *El.* she becomes the central character. Sophocles shows great skill in giving her this prominence, and in producing a characteristically Sophoclean drama, while accepting all the essential features of Aeschylus's plot (up to the killings); thus the recognition scene (see *anagnōrisis*) between brother and sister and the pretence that Orestes is dead are both taken over from Aeschylus, and much is made to follow from the simple reversal of their order, so that the pretence deceives Electra as well as Clytemnestra (see **originality**).

Euripides departs more radically from Aeschylus, especially in inventing Electra's marriage to a poor farmer and shifting the scene of the action to his home. The scene that most obviously takes account of *Cho.* comes at 518-44, where Electra criticises the recognition tokens which Aeschylus employs (but the whole passage is most odd and unsatisfactory, and may be spurious). In this play alone she is a full participant in the murder of Clytemnestra; she does not share the **pollution** of matricide in Eur. *Or.* In the end, according to Euripides (*El.* 1249, *Or.* 1658-9, *IT* 695-6, 915), she marries **Pylades**.

It is clear, not only that both Electra plays are dependent on Aesch. *Cho.*, but that one is dependent on the other. Scholars have not, however, been able to establish for certain which is the earlier. It is now generally agreed that Eur. *El.* dates from before 415, and recent scholarship is inclined to date Soph. *El.* rather later than this; but anyone who (like the present writer) subjectively feels that Sophocles' play should be the earlier cannot be proved wrong.

Electran [ele′ktran] **Gate**   The southernmost of the seven gates of **Thebes**; nothing to do with the **Electra** above.

Eleusis [elū′sis]   A town in **Attica**, on the Bay of Eleusis opposite **Salamis**. It was sacred to **Demeter**, **Persephone** (there usually called the Maiden) and **Iacchus**; Demeter and the Maiden are the Queens referred to at Soph. *OC* 1050, and at Soph. *Ant.* 1119-21 **Dionysus** haunts the plain of Eleusis because of his identification with Iacchus. These divinities presided over the Eleusinian [elūsi'nian] Mysteries, a widely respected cult which promised life and happiness after death to those who were initiated into it (see **death and burial**). The shores of Eleusis are 'torchlit' at Soph. *OC* 1049 because of an annual torch-bearing procession from Athens and similar rituals. See also **Eumolpidae** and pp. 21-2.

Enetoi [e'netoi]   See **Veneti**.

Ennosis [e'nosis]   A goddess personifying earthquake.

Enyo [eni'ō]   A goddess of war.

Eos [ē'os]   Goddess of the dawn. In more than one myth she falls in love with a mortal youth and carries him off; two of these youths are Cephalus of **Athens** and **Priam**'s brother Tithonus. Tithonus is the husband referred to at Eur. *Tro.* 854, where the point is that Dawn ('the light of white-winged day', 848-50) looked on the destruction of **Troy** with indifference even though married to a Trojan.

Epaphus [e'pafus]   Son of **Zeus** and **Io**; ancestor of the people of **Egypt**, including the **Danaids (i)**. His name suggests *epaphē*, 'touch'; hence the story that Zeus begot him by merely touching Io with his hand.

Epeus [epē'us]   A man from **Phocis** who served with the Greek army at **Troy** and built the Wooden Horse.

Epidaurus [epidaw'rus]   A city on the east coast of the **Peloponnese**, famous for its cult of **Asclepius**.

episode (*epeisodion*)   'The complete section of a tragedy between complete choral songs', according to **Aristotle**, *Poetics* 12. In practice this definition is rather too narrow, for when two sections of a tragedy are separated, not by a choral song, but by an *amoibaion*, a passage of choral anapaests (see **verse**), or even a **monody**, and also by the entrance or exit of one or more characters, it is reasonable to regard them as distinct 'acts'; and indeed there can also be strong breaks in the action at points where no singing or chanting occurs.

Erechtheus [ere'kthŭs]   An early earth-born king of **Athens**, sometimes regarded as a god. The 'children of Erechtheus' are the Athenians,
who, because of their descent from him, are literally autochthonous,
born from the soil of their land.

Eridanus [eri'danus]   A river in the far West, believed to be the source
of amber (see **Phaethon**). By the time when Eur. *Hipp*. was written it
had probably become identified with the Po in northern **Italy**, which
was not far from the actual amber route from the Baltic.

Erinys [eri'nis]   (plural Erinyes [eri'ni-ēz])   Erinyes   are   female
demons of vengeance and punishment dwelling in the **Underworld**. In
English they often appear as Furies, from the Latin *Furiae*. In **Hesiod**
and elsewhere they are children of **Earth**, but Aeschylus makes them
children of **Night** and so sisters of the Moirai (see **fate**), with whom
they are often associated.

They are invoked in **curses**, especially by those who have been
wronged by blood-relations, and they ensure that these curses are
fulfilled; indeed they are identified with personified curses at Aesch.
Sept. 70, *Eum*. 417. The Erinys who enforces the curse of a particular person is often called the Erinys *of* that person. They may also
punish breaches of **justice** and of the natural order in general; at Aesch.
Cho. 283-4, 925, they will punish a son's failure to avenge his father,
though this is unusual. Because of their concern with justice they often
help to fulfil the will of **Zeus**, although they are quite unlike the
Olympian gods in their nature (for the exceptional relation between
Zeus and the Erinyes at Aesch. *PV* 516 see **fate**).

As a rule they remain invisible and act through the 'natural' misfortunes of human life, including madness, disease (see **pollution** and
Aesch. *Cho*. 278-96) and the work of human avengers. At Aesch.
Ag. 1188-9, *Cho*. 577-8, they are pictured as drinking the blood which
human avengers have shed. In Aesch. *Eum*., however, they assume
visible form as the Chorus (a most remarkable role for a chorus to
take) and act more directly. It is uncertain how many of the vivid
details which Aeschylus gives of their appearance (*Cho*. 1048-58,
Eum. 46-59) and behaviour (*Eum*. 307-96 and elsewhere) are traditional, but most may well derive from the dramatist's imagination; the
idea that they drink their victim's blood, for instance (*Eum*. 183-4,
264-6, 302, 305), is almost unknown outside Aeschylus.

At the end of *Eum*. **Athena** persuades the Erinyes to accept a
place of honour at **Athens**. There they will retain their terrifying

appearance (990-1) and their function of punishment, even including the punishment of inherited guilt (934-7), but it seems that they will now exercise their powers within the framework of the **city** in order to enforce its laws, and will thus ensure the justice and prosperity of its citizens.

In historical times Erinyes, under this name, are largely confined to literature, cults of them being rarely attested. They are sometimes identified, however, with similar beings who did receive worship. The end of *Eum.*, where they are to be honoured with **sacrifice** (834-6) and inhabit a cave beneath the **Acropolis** (854-5, 1008, 1022-6), implies an identification with **Semnai Theai**; and in Eur. *Or.* they are sometimes called **Eumenides**.

In a difficult sentence at Soph. *Ant.* 603 'the Erinys of the mind' seems to mean *ātē* or madness such as the Erinyes send. An Erinys has 'bent feet' or legs (in running) at Aesch. *Sept.* 791, 'bronze feet' at Soph. *El.* 490; in both places tireless pursuit of her victim is indicated.

Eris [e′ris]   Strife or discord personified as a goddess.

Eros [ē′ros]   The ordinary word for sexual love, personified as a god, who then duplicates the main functions of **Aphrodite**. The whimsical Piccadilly Circus conception of him is in general later than the fifth century, though his darts are mentioned at Eur. *Hipp.* 530-4 and his wings at *Hipp.* 1270-5. In tragedy he is celebrated more for his power, often destructive, over human minds than for the pleasure he gives, and the 'odes to Love' at Soph. *Ant.* 781-800, Eur. *Hipp.* 525-64 are not exactly songs of praise (though *Hipp.* 1268-82 is more favourable). The statement at *Hipp.* 538-41 that Eros is not worshipped is an exaggeration, since a few actual cults are known, but only a slight one. Poets give various accounts of his parentage; 'child of **Zeus**' at *Hipp.* 534 seems to be an innovation, designed to emphasise his power. The point of Eur. *Tro.* 841-5 is that Eros formerly exalted **Troy** by making Zeus and **Eos** fall in love with the Trojans Ganymede (see **Laomedon**) and Tithonus.

The plural Erotes [erŏ′tēz] of Eur. *Med.* 844, *Bacch.* 405 are more decoratively conceived and seem to have little to do with sex; in *Med.* they are concerned with the beauty and emotional effect of art, in *Bacch.* with the beauty and peace of nature.

Erythrae [eri′thrē]   A town on the northern slopes of **Cithaeron**.

Eteocles [e'teoklēz]   Son of **Oedipus** and **Jocasta**; brother of **Poly-nices**, **Antigone** and **Ismene** (Fig. 3). Oedipus cursed his two sons before he died, condemning them to die at one another's hands. Different authors give different reasons for this **curse**. In Soph. *OC* the reason is the sons' neglect of their father, but difficulties of text and inter-pretation at Aesch. *Sept.* 785-7 make it uncertain what Aeschylus's version was; it may be that here the sons were cursed simply because they were the offspring of an incestuous union. For the wording of the curse according to Aeschylus see **Chalybes**.

The sources differ also on the rights and wrongs of the quarrel between the brothers and on whether Eteocles was the elder or the younger. In Soph. *OC* he is the younger and has unjustly expelled Polynices from **Thebes**; in Eur. *Phoen.* he is the elder, but has broken an agreement to let Polynices rule in alternate years; in Aesch. *Sept.* there is no proof that he has done anything wrong, and Polynices, while claiming to have been unjustly banished (637-8, 644-8), certainly stands condemned for attacking his own city (576-86). All authors agree, however, that Eteocles remained at Thebes while Polynices went to **Argos** and raised the army of the **Seven against Thebes** in order to expel him.

In one way or another the brothers came face to face in battle, and the curse of Oedipus was fulfilled. In Aesch. *Sept.* Eteocles does not learn that Polynices will attack a gate in person until 632, when defenders have already been assigned to the other six gates; thus a divinely ordered coincidence, coupled with the logic of his own pre-vious decisions, makes Eteocles the natural opponent for Polynices, and, seeing the curse at work, he rushes to accept his fate. *Sept.* 632-8, however, hints at an alternative version, in which the brothers fight a duel after the main battle is over, and this is what happens in Eur. *Phoen.*

The name Eteocles suggests 'truly famed'; it is usually thought (perhaps wrongly) that a play on the name has dropped out of the text before the play on Polynices' name at Aesch. *Sept.* 830.

Eteoclus [e'teoklus]   An Argive; the most shadowy of the **Seven against Thebes**.

Etna [e'tna]   The volcano, highest mountain in **Sicily**. Its eruptions were explained by saying either that the monster **Typho** was buried beneath it or that it contained the forge of **Hephaestus**. Aesch. *PV* 363-72 combines both explanations, in a passage which derives from

Pindar, Pythian 1. 15-28; this in turn is inspired by an eruption in 479 or 475.

The district of Etna was famous for its horses. At Eur. *Tro.* 220-1 the 'Etnean [etnḗ'an] Land of Hephaestus' means Sicily.

Etruscans   See **Tyrrhenians**.

Euboea [ūbē'a]   The long island off the north-east coast of **Attica**, **Boeotia** and Locris. At Eur. *El.* 442 the **Nereids** probably pass the capes of Euboea on their way to **Thessaly** from **Hephaestus's** forge on **Lemnos**.

Euchlous [ūklō'us]   A title of **Demeter**.

Euhios [ū'hios] or Evius [ē'vius]   A name of **Dionysus**.

Eumenides [ūme'nidēz]   Female deities honoured at certain places in the **Peloponnese** and, as we learn from Soph. *OC*, at **Colonus**. The play tells us all we know about their attributes there. They are daughters of **Earth** and Darkness, inspire fear among the local people, and expect the kind of **libations** proper to deities of the **Underworld**. On the other hand they dwell in an idyllic grove, are much revered by **Oedipus** (he calls them 'sweet' at *OC* 106), and protect him as their suppliant (see **supplication**), being connected in some mysterious way with his miraculous and merciful death. The name Eumenides, meaning 'kindly ones', is perhaps conferred more in the hope of propitiating them than as a description, but the play on the name at *OC* 486 shows that they may live up to it. At *OC* 89-90 they are called **Semnai Theai**, the title of similar goddesses at **Athens**. It seems evident, however, to the present writer (if to few others) that in this play they are *not* identified with the **Erinyes** (mentioned at *OC* 1299, 1434, with reference to the curse of Oedipus), even though such an identification does occur in Eur. *Or.* and in later authors.

Aesch. *Eum.*, the third play in the **tetralogy** the *Oresteia*, concerns the pursuit of **Orestes** by the Erinyes of **Clytemnestra**, his trial and acquittal before the Council of the **Areopagus** at Athens, and the propitiation of the Erinyes by **Athena**. The word Eumenides does not occur in the play as we have it; a scrap of ancient scholarship claims that Athena in this play, having tamed the Erinyes, addressed them as Eumenides, but this is probably no more than a mistaken inference from the play's title. In any case that title can hardly be

Aeschylus's own, and must have been conferred by someone who believed that the Erinyes were called Eumenides during their pursuit of Orestes, as they are in Eur. *Or.*

Eumolpidae [ūmoʹlpidē]   An aristocratic Athenian family, in which a hereditary priesthood at **Eleusis** was handed down (see **priests**).

Euripus [ūriʹpus]   The strait between **Euboea** and the mainland, only 40 yards wide at its narrowest point.

Europe   See **Asia**, **Io**'s wanderings.

Eurotas [ūroʹtas]   The river of **Sparta**.

Eurydice [ūriʹdisē]   Wife of the Theban **Creon** (i) (Fig. 3).

Eurytus [ūʹritus]   King of **Oechalia**; see **Heracles**.

exodus   The word means 'departure, exit'. As a structural term in tragedy it should refer to the part of the play in which chorus and actors leave the *orchēstrā* for the last time. **Aristotle**, *Poetics* 12, however, defines it as 'a complete section of a tragedy which is not followed by a choral song', and some modern writers attempt to follow this definition; but to do so literally leads to very curious results in some cases (e.g. the 'exit' section of Aesch. *Eum.* would begin at line 566 and take up nearly half the play). See also **episode**.

extras   Although Greek tragedy was usually restricted to two or three speaking **actors**, a number of mute persons (*kōpha prosōpa*, singular *kōphon prosōpon*) or extras could also be used. Sometimes these portray named characters, such as **Hermes** in Aesch. *Eum.* (perhaps), Force in Aesch. *PV* (see **Strength**), **Pylades** in Soph. *El.* and Eur. *El.*, and Polydeuces in Eur. *El.* (see **Castor**). Pylades' three portentous lines at Aesch. *Cho.* 900-2 should probably be seen as a unique case in which such an extra is allowed to speak for special effect. It has sometimes been thought that six Theban champions appear as extras after Aesch. *Sept.* 374, but, since their entrance is not announced, this seems clearly wrong. Children perform in several plays, and are given brief singing parts at Eur. *Alc.* 393-415, *Andr.* 504-36; two children speak off stage at Eur. *Med.* 1271-8.

More often extras function simply as **attendants**, bodyguards and the like, a few of whom are probably present most of the time in most tragedies. Stage crowds (not necessarily of any great size) are seen in the *orchēstrā* at the beginning of Aesch. *Sept.* and Soph. *OT*, when it is not yet occupied by the Chorus; and in Aesch. *Eum.* a number of Jurors (perhaps twelve; see **Areopagus**) are present from line 566 on, though these are probably identical with the chorus which sings lines 1032-47.

F

family See **house**.

fate Several Greek words are commonly translated as 'fate', 'destiny' or the like, notably *moira* and its synonym *aisa*. This 'fate' is often personified as a goddess, and we hear also of a plurality of Moirai, 'the Fates'. It must be emphasised, however, that references in Greek tragedy to 'fate', 'the Fates', or the like do not imply any systematic determinism. The events that unavoidably befall a man are, in a straight-forward sense, given to him as his 'portion' by forces outside himself; the most obvious of these is his death, and it is in the context of death that such words as *moira* are most often used. But to talk of a man's 'portion' or 'destiny' in this sort of context is very different from, and far more natural than, saying that he is 'fated' to commit his own delib-erate actions. It is not surprising, then, that a man can be held to account for his own deeds, as though he had 'free will' in choosing to commit them, while still being thought of as subject to *moira* in other respects. The word *anankē*, 'necessity', which often comes close to *moira*, is used in a similarly unphilosophical way. Nor does the fact that an event has been prophesied mean that it is predetermined; see **oracles**.

Men like to think that one aspect of the natural and inevitable order of things is the punishment of crime, and so Moira comes to be much concerned with retributive **justice** (e.g. Aesch. *Ag.* 1535-6). Hence she is often linked with the **Erinyes** who enforce justice; the Moirai are the Erinyes' 'sisters by one mother' (namely **Night**) at Aesch. *Eum.* 961-2.

In determining what must be, Moira tends to duplicate the functions of other gods, especially **Zeus**, and the same events are often attributed to both agencies (e.g. Soph. *Phil.* 1466-8, where Zeus is the 'all-subduing god'; Eur. *El.* 1248). Where the relation between the two is specified,

Moira is usually the instrument or expression of Zeus's will (e.g. Aesch. *Cho.* 306-8). At Aesch. *PV* 511-20, where the point is that even Zeus cannot escape the consequences of his own actions, the Moirai (here three in number, as in **Hesiod**) and the Erinyes are said to be stronger than he; but this is exceptional. (Similarly Hesiod is uncertain whether the Moirai are daughters of Night and so older than Zeus, as at *Theogony* 217-22, or daughters of Zeus and **Themis**, as at *Theogony* 901-6.) Conversely, the personification of the Moirai is occasionally carried so far that, like other gods, they can be tricked; see **Alcestis**. Aesch. *Eum.* 1045-6 is often thought to refer to a fresh alliance between Zeus and Moira, as though they had previously been at variance, but this must surely be a mistranslation; what is said is that Zeus and Moira have allied themselves with the citizens of **Athens** (so as to ensure their prosperity).

flute   See *aulos*.

Force   See **Strength**.

fragments   In addition to the 32 tragedies and one **satyr** play that survive more or less complete (see **text**), we possess numerous fragments of lost plays, ranging in length from a single word (or less) to some hundreds of lines. With very few exceptions, these fragments are preserved either as quotations in the work of later Greek writers and anthologists or on portions of ancient papyrus books unearthed in **Egypt**, where the dry climate has preserved them. Quotation fragments often consist of moral maxims or other generalisations, but one must beware of assuming, without knowledge of the contexts in which they occurred in the plays, that these represent the dramatists' opinions. Papyrus fragments provide a truly random sample from those plays which were popular in antiquity, but often present scholars with severe problems of restoration and interpretation.

The fragments of Aeschylus, though brief, are often of particular interest (the numbering here is that of the Loeb Edition; see p. 199). In fr. 25, from the *Danaids* (see **Danaids (i)**), **Aphrodite** claims to be the cause of a marriage between Heaven and **Earth**, which leads to the Earth's fertility. Fr. 34 is notable for its 'pantheism', as is fr. 199 for its 'fatalism' (see **fate**). Fr. 107 is a valuable extract (or adaptation) from the *Prometheus Unbound* (see **Prometheus**). The fragments of satyr plays, notably 274-5 from the *Dictyulci* (*Net-Haulers*), show how successfully Aeschylus could adopt a light and humorous tone. Fr. 277, from the *Niobe*, includes some much-quoted lines, for which see *āte*. In fr. 282 the personified **Justice** explains how she acquired her privileges from **Zeus**.

Fragments of Sophocles include extensive portions of his satyr play *Ichneutae* (*Trackers*); see **satyrs**. Those of Euripides are very numerous, and allow us to reconstruct the plots of some lost plays, such as *Phaethon* and *Hypsipyle*, in a good deal of detail (see also **Paris** for the *Alexander*). Fragments of other tragedians are much more scanty.

Freud, Sigmund (1856-1939)   The founder of psychoanalysis. When Freud wished to give a name to a boy's fantasy of killing his father and marrying his mother, it was natural for him to call it the **Oedipus** Complex, after the mythical figure who did both these things. Freud believed that the myth reflected the presence of the Oedipus Complex among the Greeks, and as evidence he was able to cite Soph. *OT* 981-2, where **Jocasta** remarks that many men have slept with their mothers in **dreams**. He did not claim that the character of Oedipus in Sophocles' play could be explained in psychoanalytic terms, but he did claim that the play's powerful effect on audiences was due to their having felt 'Oedipal' desires in their own childhoods. This seems to involve supposing that the play's effect is due to the myth and not to Sophocles' treatment of it (see **originality**), and that it cannot be fully experienced by women.

Attempts have been made by some critics to apply Freudian ideas to other plays. The only play for which such attempts have won much support is Eur. *Bacch.*, where there are certain attractions in saying that **Pentheus** has repressed, in a Freudian sense, his need for Dionysiac experience.

Fury   See **Erinys**.

G

Gaea [gē′a]   See **Earth**.

Ganymede [ga′nimēd]   See **Laomedon**.

Ge [gē]   See **Earth**.

Geryon [jē′rion]   A monster with three heads and three bodies, killed by **Heracles**.

ghosts   See **death and burial**.

Giants   A race of monstrous beings, born of **Earth**, whom the gods defeated in battle on the **Phlegraean Plain**. See also **Zephyr**.

Glauce [glaw′sē]   A name sometimes given (but not by Euripides) to the daughter of the Corinthian **Creon (ii)**, killed by **Medea**.

gods   The Greeks in the fifth century had no sacred books (or none whose authority was recognised outside certain specific cults) and no centrally organised priesthood (see **priests**) to prescribe correct religious belief. Nevertheless, almost all Greeks believed in gods, and believed that it would be both wrong and dangerous to treat them with disrespect or to neglect traditional forms or worship. **Myth**, poetry, painting and sculpture told them what these gods were like; they resembled human beings in form but were larger, usually finer (though some were ugly), much more powerful, and above all immortal.

But any god who is to be seriously worshipped must be something more than this, and the Greek gods, like those of other peoples, embodied or presided over forces that affected men's lives. Indeed at their simplest, gods might merely be personified abstractions, such as Love (see **Eros**), Death (see **death and burial**), **Strength**, Madness. Even such 'abstract' gods could be portrayed by a dramatist (or a painter) in a fully anthropomorphic way, but they were not usually worshipped (though there are exceptions), and they could be invented for a particular occasion; an extreme example is Eur. *Hel.* 560, 'even to recognise friends is a god'. Such an *ad hoc* personification would be used to make a point about the abstract quality in question rather than a point of theology.

Then there were the various gods and **nymphs** that haunted, tended or embodied features of the landscape, such as springs, rivers, caves and groves, and were objects of purely local cults, though no doubt taken very seriously by their worshippers. And fearful spirits such as **Eumenides** and **Semnai Theai** lurked beneath the earth's surface and required appeasement at particular sites.

Finally there were the great gods of **Olympus**, each worshipped in numerous cults throughout the Greek world: **Zeus**, **Hera**, **Poseidon**,

Demeter, Apollo, Artemis, Ares, Aphrodite, Hermes, Athena, Hephaestus, Dionysus, Hestia. Not every Olympian was the god of a *single* aspect of life; certainly Ares was devoted to war and Aphrodite to love, but such figures as Apollo, Athena and Hermes appear in a variety of roles, and different roles could be emphasised in different local cults. Myths, often shifting and inconsistent (but to some extent systematised by **Hesiod**), described the gods' origins and relationships, and other myths told of their exploits and their dealings with men in the Heroic Age. Throughout much of Greek history and prehistory there was a tendency to supplement the Greek pantheon by importing foreign gods; see **Dionysus, Cybele, Corybantes.**

Gods (other than Zeus) are often presented on stage by Aeschylus and Euripides, but not on quite the same footing as mortal characters. In the surviving work of Aeschylus there is a distinction between plays set on the divine plane (*PV* if genuine, *Eum.*), in which most of the characters are supernatural, and plays set on the human plane, in which gods do not appear at all. In Euripides, apart from the disguised Dionysus of *Bacchae*, gods are confined to positions in which they are somewhat detached from the human action; they appear in **prologues**, where they are useful for setting the scene and foreshadowing the plot, and in epiphanies from the roof of the scene-building (see *deus ex machina*), normally occurring at the ends of plays, but are not seen elsewhere. In the surviving tragedies of Sophocles there are only the epiphany of Athena at the beginning of *Ajax* and that of **Heracles** at the end of *Philoctetes*.

Throughout most of tragedy, then, we see the gods not directly but through their influence on the lives of men, and, since human life is depicted with a certain amount of realism, this precludes divine interference of a purely arbitrary and miraculous kind. When characters and choruses explain the events of the plays in religious terms, they are doing no more than Greeks would regularly have done in real life. In life, as in tragedy, gods revealed their will to men through **oracles, omens, dreams** and the inspired visions of **seers**; and men hoped to influence gods, so as to have some control over the world around them, by prayer and **ritual**, especially **sacrifice**.

One function of gods that is often alluded to in tragedy (as in **Homer**) is to define by contrast the limits imposed on humanity. Their immortality is set against men's mortality, their perfect knowledge against men's ignorance, and their untroubled ease against the inevitable tribulation of men's lives. Every man must accept this contrast, whether with bitterness or with resignation; although myths do tell of certain exceptional mortals (Heracles, **Castor**) who crossed the boundary between the human and the divine, the human characters of tragedy, however great (including even the Heracles of Soph. *Trach.* and Eur. *HF*), have to come to terms with the limitations of their mortal status. At times it is felt to be the active jealousy of the gods that punishes extremes of prosperity and attainment among men, though this is a less common idea; see ***hybris***.

There are other ways, however, in which Greek gods can themselves seem human and limited by comparison with those of some other cultures. The Greek tendency towards anthropomorphism militated against any tendency to conceive the gods in transcendental or mystical terms, and poets were able to take this anthropomorphism to its logical conclusion. Each god has a will of his own, and their wills may conflict (though such conflict is strikingly absent from Sophocles' work, where the individual gods are seen rather as representatives of a single divine purpose). Even Zeus is subject to the laws of nature, and so, on occasion, to the Moirai (see **fate**), who, on other occasions, can themselves be deceived (see **Alcestis**).

From early times gods were seen as the source of traditional laws of **justice**, hospitality and the like, and any mortal who broke these laws would be liable to suffer for having slighted the gods' power (see **Zeus**). But this did not mean that the gods were themselves bound by any moral principles; and goodness, or even justice, forms no part of the essential definition of a god. The various forces that affect our lives seem, after all, to take little enough account of our deserts; and Greek myths represented the gods as all too human in their behaviour towards each other as well as towards mankind. At an early stage of Greek culture gods hardly needed to deserve worship for their virtue as long as they could enforce it by their power, especially when power was more admired than virtue among men.

In the fifth century, however, the idea was beginning to gain ground that any god worthy of the name ought to be morally better than men, and such an idea is expressed by certain characters in Euripides (e.g. *Hipp.* 120, *Bacch.* 1348 and, most remarkably, *HF* 1340-6). The gods presented in his plays, on the other hand, are obviously *not* better than men, and such lines as *Bacch.* 1348 serve only to draw attention to their failings (note also *El.* 1245-6). It is doubtful whether Euripides personally believed in the gods of the myths, though he was prepared to take them seriously for dramatic purposes.

Golden Fleece   See **Jason**.

Gorgons [gor'gonz]   Three female monsters with snakes for hair, who dwelt in some remote region — the far West at **Hesiod**, *Theogony* 274-5, **Asia** at Aesch. *PV* 799 (see **Io's wanderings**), **Libya** at Eur. *Bacch.* 990. They were so hideous that the sight of them turned men to stone. One of the three, Medusa, was killed by **Perseus**, who cut off her head and used it (since it continued to petrify those who saw it) to destroy his enemies.

Gorgons' heads were often represented on shields and elsewhere; the 'Gorgon-faced circle' of Eur. *El.* 1257 is **Athena**'s **Aegis**, here pictured as a round shield. For the Gorgon-Faced or Gorgopian [gorgo' pian] Lake see **Beacon Speech**; the reason for the name is unknown.

Graces   The English name for the Charites, goddesses of beauty, whether that of nature, art or human beings. They are often associated with **Aphrodite**, sometimes with **Dionysus**.

Great Dionysia [dioni'zia] or City Dionysia   The festival of **Dionysus** for which most Athenian plays, and perhaps all surviving Greek trage-dies (see **Athens**), were written. It was held every year in late March, and centred on the Temple and Theatre of Dionysus, at the foot of the **Acropolis**. It included joyful processions, **sacrifices**, and contests between choruses performing **dithyrambs**, as well as contests between three tragic poets and between five (at times perhaps three) comic poets.

Each tragic poet competed with four plays (see **tetralogy**), which were all performed on one day and normally comprised three tragedies and one **satyr** play (but in 438 BC the tragedy Eur. *Alc.* was performed in place of a satyr play, and there were probably other exceptions of this kind). The poets competing in any year were selected in advance by one of the archons (magistrates). The prizes were awarded by a panel of ten judges, selected by lot, one from each of the ten tribes into which the Athenians were divided.

By the late fifth century plays were being performed also at the Lenaea (a festival held in the same place but about the end of January) and at the Rural Dionysia (minor festivals held in other parts of **Attica**).

See also **actors, choregus, ritual**.

Great Goddesses   A title of **Demeter** and the Maiden **(Persephone)** at **Eleusis**.

griffins or gryphons   Mythical monsters of uncertain form; see **Io's**

wanderings. The 'four-legged bird' on which **Oceanus** rides in Aesch. *PV* (see *PV* 395) may be a griffin.

guilt   See **pollution.**

H

Hades [hā′dēz]   God of the **Underworld**; consort of **Persephone**; brother of **Zeus** and **Poseidon**, but never found on Mount **Olympus** and practically never worshipped. He is a grim and fearful being who keeps the dead in his power and in certain cases punishes them for crimes (see **death and burial**), but he is not positively evil or malevolent.

Since he dwells at the opposite extreme to Zeus, he can be called 'the Zeus below the earth' by anyone who is paradoxically thinking of him as kindly and helpful. In the blasphemous context at Aesch. *Ag.* 1386-7 the expression is clearly meant to shock, but the effect is different at e.g. Aesch. *Supp.* 156-8; and with reference to the thunder and the merciful death of **Oedipus** at Soph. *OC* 1606 we should perhaps think rather of Zeus himself in an Underworld capacity.

Aidoneus is a lengthened form of Hades' name, and suggests, perhaps rightly, that it means the Unseen One. He is often identified with **Pluto**. At Soph. *OT* 178 he is the god of the West or the evening (the Greek is ambiguous) because his shadowy realm was sometimes located in the far West, where the sun sets.

The usual term for his realm is 'the House of Hades', but with the word 'House' very often omitted to leave only the possessive form of 'Hades'. When modern writers call the place 'Hades' this is a simplification, but one occasionally practised by the Greeks themselves. Sometimes the name is used to mean 'death', as at Aesch. *Ag.* 667, Eur. *Hipp.* 1047; this may be the point when **Clytemnestra** is called a 'raging mother of Hades' at Aesch. *Ag.* 1235, but meaning and **text** are doubtful here.

Haemon [hē′mon]   Son of the Theban **Creon (i)** and **Eurydice** (Fig. 3); betrothed to **Antigone** before the action of Soph. *Ant.* begins.

Halirrhothius [haliro′thius]   A son of **Poseidon** who raped a daughter of **Ares** and was killed by him in revenge; see **Areopagus.**

hamartiā   The word means a failure or failing of various kinds, ranging from an innocent mistake of fact to a moral crime. It is found from time to time in tragedy, usually in a moral sense.

Its use as a technical term in English, however, derives from a famous passage in **Aristotle**, *Poetics* 13, where Aristotle is trying to establish the best type of tragic plot. He has rejected the alternative of 'decent men passing from good fortune to bad', which would be 'revolting'; that of 'depraved men passing from bad fortune to good', which would be unfit for tragedy in every respect; and that of 'the thoroughly wicked man passing from good fortune to bad', which would satisfy our human sympathy but would not arouse pity and fear. 'There is left the person between these. He is someone not outstanding in virtue and justice, and not passing to bad fortune through badness and depravity but through some *hamartiā*; a person in high esteem and good fortune, such as Oedipus and Thyestes and the famous men of such families.' A little later we learn that it should be 'a great *hamartiā*'.

The whole passage is obscure in the extreme and has been the subject of endless argument. At one time it used generally to be assumed that a *hamartiā* was a moral flaw − a pardonable defect of character which saved the 'ideal tragic **hero**' from being so good that his fall was merely shocking and not tragic − and the 'tragic flaw' became a well-known cliché of literary criticism. But this view, at least in its simple form, has been universally abandoned, partly for technical reasons to do with Aristotle's ethical vocabulary in other works, partly because of the difficulty of seeing how a 'great defect of character' can be pardonable, and partly because of the example of **Oedipus**, which Aristotle gives; whatever defects of character Oedipus may have in Soph. *OT* (the play which Aristotle certainly has in mind), they do not bring about his downfall.

Many scholars have therefore taken *hamartiā* to be a mistake of fact, so that it lies outside the moral categories in which the chapter is mainly dealing. (The word, indeed, bears no great emphasis, and we need not assume that it is essential to Aristotle's argument.) This will fit the case of Oedipus, whose fall is brought about by ignorance of his parents' identity, a *hamartiā* quite unrelated to his moral character. But it will not fit many other plays.

It has recently been strongly argued that the word is used with its full range of meaning; it refers to a mistake of fact in the case of Oedipus, but to a flaw of character in the case of, for instance, **Pentheus** in Eur. *Bacch.* So taken, *hamartiā* can in fact be applied to most of those tragedies which show a fall from good fortune to bad, and it often corresponds to what, in the poetic and religious language of

Aeschylus and Sophocles, is called *átē*. The only ways in which a fall
from good fortune to bad could now occur *without* a *hamartiā* would
be through sheer wickedness or through some fortuitous cause lying
entirely outside the person who suffered the fall, and we may well
agree with Aristotle that a play on either of these themes, if it possessed
no other redeeming features, would probably seem trivial.

Aristotle's *separate* requirement that tragedy should not depict the
fall of 'decent men' is harder to defend; surely Oedipus and **Hippolytus**, for example, are thoroughly decent, and, if they are not saints,
their faults are not such as to diminish any sense of moral outrage
that we might otherwise feel at their fall. Perhaps the best that can be
got from this is that a dramatist would seem gratuitously sadistic if he
delighted in portraying the downfall of good men purely for its own
sake. In that case Soph. *OT* and Eur. *Hipp.* are saved from being 'revolting', not because their central characters are not 'decent', but because
they are far more complex plays than Aristotle's classification allows
for.

Harmonia [harmoˈnia]   (i) Harmony or concord, personified at Eur.
Med. 834, where some translators think that she is the mother of
the **Muses**; but more probably it is the Muses who, by their concord,
'begot Harmonia', only lightly personified.

(ii) Daughter of **Ares** and **Aphrodite**; wife of **Cadmus** (Fig. 3).

Harpies [harˈpiz]   See **Phineus**.

Hecabe [heˈkabē]   Wife of **Priam**; mother of 19 sons, including
Paris and **Hector**, and some daughters. In Eur. *Tro.*, set outside **Troy**
after its capture, it appears that all her children except **Cassandra** are
dead, her daughter **Polyxena** having recently been sacrificed at the
tomb of **Achilles** (622-3). In the course of the play Hecabe also learns
(277) that she has been allotted as a slave to **Odysseus**.

Eur. *Hec.*, written earlier than *Tro.*, deals with some of the same
events, but the two plots are not reconcilable. In *Hec.* the Greek
fleet, attempting to return from Troy, has been forced back to the
coast of **Thrace**, and it is here that Polyxena is sacrificed. Hecabe also
learns that her youngest son **Polydorus (ii)** (unmentioned in *Tro.*),
who had been sent to Thrace for safety, has been murdered by his host
Polymestor, and she takes revenge by blinding Polymestor and his sons.

Hecate [heˈcatē]   A sinister goddess who presides over witchcraft, and is therefore chosen by **Medea** as her patroness (Eur. *Med.* 395-7). She haunts road-junctions, and is the 'Wayside Goddess' mentioned at Soph. *Ant.* 1199, where she is invoked because of her concern with corpses. She can also be a source of madness. She is sometimes pictured as a torch-bearer, and this is apparently why she is invoked at Eur. *Tro.* 323, though there is effective incongruity in associating her with the torches of a marriage ceremony.

Hector [he'ktor]   Son of **Priam** and **Hecabe**; husband of **Andromache**; greatest of the Trojan warriors. He is one of the most sympathetic characters in **Homer**, and his death at the hands of **Achilles** in *Iliad* 22 forms the climax of the poem. He is also a character in Eur. *Rhes.*

Helen [he'len]   Daughter of **Zeus** and **Leda**; half-sister of **Clytemnestra**; wife of **Menelaus** (Fig. 2). Her abduction by **Paris** provoked the Trojan War, after which Menelaus brought her back to Greece. In tragedy (though not in **Homer**) it is generally implied, and sometimes clearly stated, that she was a wicked woman who voluntarily deserted her husband. The *agōn* between her and **Hecabe** at Eur. *Tro.* 860-1059 is partly inspired by a story (Plate IV) that Menelaus intended to kill her after the fall of **Troy** but dropped his sword on seeing her beauty (for the influence of Gorgias see **sophists**).

Eur. *Hel.* follows a different version of the legend, derived from **Stesichorus**, and also mentioned at Eur. *El.* 1280-3. In this version it is only a phantom duplicate of Helen, constructed by the gods, that goes to Troy with Paris, while she herself is transported to **Egypt** and stays there with King **Proteus**. In the play Menelaus visits Egypt on his way home from Troy and so meets the real Helen, and they both escape from Proteus's wicked son Theoclymenus. Helen is also a character in Eur. *Or.*

At Aesch. *Ag.* 681-98 the Chorus plays on Helen's name (*Helenā*), which suggests 'ship-destroying' (*helenaus*) and 'destroying' (*hele-*) in general.

Helenus [he'lenus]   A Trojan **seer**, son of **Priam**, captured by **Odysseus** shortly before the events of Soph. *Phil.*; see **Philoctetes**.

Helicon [he'likon]   A mountain in south-west **Boeotia**.

Helios [hē'lios]   The sun, regarded as a god. Because he sees all that happens on earth, he is often called upon to witness oaths and the like; see also **dreams**.

I The Theatre at **Epidaurus** from the air. The building dates from the middle of the fourth century BC, and is the best-preserved example of the type of theatre for which the surviving tragedies were written; note the circular **orchēstrā** in the centre. At the bottom of the plate the **parodoi (ii)** pass through gateways, and the foundations of the **skēnē** are largely covered by modern staging. Photo by courtesy of the Rev. Professor Raymond V. Schoder, SJ.

II The deaths of **Agamemnon** and **Aegisthus**. This Athenian vase has usually been dated slightly earlier than the *Oresteia* of Aeschylus (458), but it is possible that it may be later.

In (a) Agamemnon is trapped in just such a robe as the text of Aeschylus implies, but is killed by Aegisthus, not **Clytemnestra**. Clytemnestra backs up Aegisthus to the left, and three girls (one invisible here) make horrified gestures; one or other of them is presumably **Cassandra**.

In (b) Aegisthus is killed by **Orestes**, while Clytemnestra tries to save him with her axe, and **Electra** is seen to the extreme right. By courtesy of the Museum of Fine Arts, Boston, William Francis Warden Fund (63.1246).

III **Maenads**, a **satyr**, and **Dionysus**, on a vase painted about the middle of the fifth century. Dionysus carries a wine-bowl and a branch, wears a leopard skin, and has long and elegant hair. His followers advance to the music of a double **aulos** and a **tympanum**, and carry **thyrsi** and branches; most are crowned with ivy. One of the Maenads handles a snake; another has torn an animal apart; a third wears a fawn skin. By courtesy of the Bibliothèque nationale, Paris (Cab. Méd. 357).

IV **Menelaus**, intending to kill **Helen**, drops his sword on seeing her beauty (a nameless girl balances Helen to the left). The vase, painted about the middle of the fifth century, illustrates the legend which inspired the **agōn** of Eur. *Tro.* By courtesy of the Trustees of the British Museum (E 263).

V The infant **Oedipus** (labelled OIDIPODAS) is carried by a traveller (labelled EUPHORBOS), who must be an equivalent of the Corinthian shepherd in Soph. *OT*, towards a bearded man (not shown here), who may be **Polybus** or an equivalent. The vast was painted about the middle of the fifth century (almost certainly earlier than Soph. *OT*) by the same artist as Plate III. By courtesy of the Bibliothèque nationale, Paris (Cab. Méd. 372).

In myth he is **Medea's** grandfather, and he therefore provides the chariot seen at the end of Eur. *Med.* The companions of **Odysseus**, while returning from **Troy**, stole cattle belonging to Helios; in punishment for this they were shipwrecked and drowned, only Odysseus himself escaping (**Homer,** *Odyssey* 12. 260-450).

Hellas [he'las]   The normal Greek name for Greece. Hence Hellenic [hele'nik or hele'nik] means Greek, and the Hellenes [he'lenz] are the Greeks. These words, however, are not used by **Homer**, and the words that he does use for Greeks — **Achaeans**, Argives (see **Argos**) and **Danaans** — often occur in tragedy. The Panhellenes are the Greeks combined, as opposed to individual **cities**.

Hephaestus [hefe'stus]   God of smith-craft and fire; husband of **Aphrodite**. His forge is located on **Lemnos**, on Mount **Etna**, and in other volcanic places. His creations included the arms of **Achilles**. He is a relative of **Prometheus** (Aesch. *PV* 14) because both are descendants of **Uranus** and **Earth**, and, since Prometheus was also connected with craft and fire, the two were often associated in cult. The Athenians claimed descent from Hephaestus through his son Erichthonius. His name sometimes means simply 'fire'.

Hera [he'ra]   Daughter of **Cronus**; sister and wife of **Zeus**; a goddess of women and marriage. Her marriage to Zeus is the archetype of all marriage, and in this context she is called Teleia, 'Accomplisher', like her husband. She was a patroness of **Argos**, a famous temple of hers being situated between Argos and **Mycenae**. On the **acropolis** of **Corinth** there was a temple of Hera Acraea, 'Hera on the Height', and an annual ceremony that was held here was said to commemorate, in one way or another, the death of **Medea's** children.

In myth she spends much of her time persecuting the paramours of Zeus, such as **Io** and **Semele**, and his children by them, such as **Heracles**. She took the Greek side in the Trojan War because of the Judgement of **Paris**.

Heracles [he'raklez]   Son of **Zeus** and **Alcmene**; greatest of the Greek **heroes**. Unlike other heroes he received fully divine honours, and his worship was not confined to a local cult but extended all over Greece.

His mother Alcmene was of Argive ancestry and a descendant of **Io**, but she and her husband Amphitryon were living at **Thebes** when Heracles was born. Throughout his life he was pursued by the jealousy of **Hera**, who was responsible for most of his troubles. He was depicted as an archer, clad in a lion-skin and carrying a club as well as a bow.

Only a few of the numerous tales about him are relevant to tragedy. His most famous exploits were the Labours which he had to perform for Eurystheus, King of **Mycenae**; some are listed at Soph. *Trach.* 1091-100, Eur. *HF* 359-435. It was on his way to one of these Labours that he rescued **Alcestis** from death.

Another exploit was shooting the eagle which tormented **Prometheus** (Heracles is the descendant of Io prophesied at Aesch. *PV* 771-4, 871-3). It appears that in the *Prometheus Unbound*, after the shooting of the eagle, Prometheus prophesied Heracles' wanderings in the far West, in quest of the Golden Apples of the **Hesperides**, just as he prophesies **Io's wanderings** in the far East in *PV*.

During another Labour (fetching **Cerberus** from the **Underworld**) he was reported to be dead, and his supposed father Amphitryon, his wife Megara and his children were therefore persecuted by Lycus, tyrant of Thebes. In Eur. *HF* Heracles returns just in time to save his family and kill Lycus, but is then visited with madness at Hera's instigation so that he kills Megara and the children. At the end he is befriended by **Theseus** of **Athens**.

For the sacking of **Troy** by Heracles and **Telamon** see **Laomedon**.

Heracles fell in love with Iole, daughter of **Eurytus**, King of **Oechalia**, but Eurytus would not give the girl to him. Heracles then treacherously killed her brother Iphitus; in punishment for this crime he was compelled to work for a year as a slave of Omphale, Queen of **Lydia** (this is the servitude mentioned at Aesch. *Ag.* 1040-1). On returning to Greece he sacked Oechalia and took Iole by force.

In Soph. *Trach.* this episode is linked with Heracles' death. His second wife, Deianira, is waiting for him at **Trachis** when she learns the truth about Iole. In the hope of regaining his love she sends him a robe anointed with what she believes to be a love potion; realising that it is in fact a deadly poison, she commits suicide. Heracles, tormented by the poisoned robe, insists that his son Hyllus should take him to a pyre on Mount **Oeta** to die.

The only person who could bring himself to light the pyre and release Heracles from his pain was **Philoctetes**, son of the local king **Poeas**. In gratitude, before he died, Heracles gave Philoctetes his famous bow. He was then burnt and received among the gods; and it is as a god that he miraculously appears at the end of Soph. *Phil.* (see *deus ex machina*).

'Heraclidae' [hērakliˊdē] means children or descendants of Heracles.

In Eur. *Heracl.* his children by Deianira, his mother Alcmene and his friend Iolaus are menaced by Eurystheus but rescued by Demophon, son of Theseus (see **supplication**). See also **Dorians**.

Hermes [her'mēz]   An important and friendly god, son of **Zeus** and **Maia**, born on Mount **Cyllene**. He presides over flocks and over the fertility of animals and men. As Hermes Dolios he is the god of guile and trickery, even theft. He is responsible for lucky accidents (and mentioned for this reason at Aesch. *Sept.* 508). He is the herald of the gods, and therefore the god of heralds.

As Hermes Pompaios or Pompos he is the Guide or Escort; and he not only guides travellers on earth but also conducts the dead to the **Underworld** (the 'goddess below' with whom he is linked at Soph. *OC* 1548 is **Persephone**), or, in exceptional circumstances, back again. Thus he can also be called Hermes Chthonios, 'Hermes of the Underworld', but even here he usually remains benevolent (though he represents death itself at Aesch. *Cho.* 622). The meaning of Aesch. *Cho.* 1 has been disputed ever since **Aristophanes** (*Frogs* 1138-49); probably 'Hermes of the Underworld, you who watch over your father's realm', Hermes acting as Zeus's deputy below ground.

He is a character in Aesch. *PV* (where he is given an unpleasant personality in keeping with that of Zeus in this play) and in Eur. *Ion*. It is uncertain whether he is seen as an **extra** at **Apollo**'s side at Aesch. *Eum.* 64-93.

For the Hermaean [hermē'an] Rock (or Mount of Hermes or the like) on **Lemnos** see **Beacon Speech**.

hero   A confusing word, which occurs very seldom in Greek tragedy but often in criticism of it. At least three senses need to be distinguished.

1. In Greek religion a hero is a man who, because he was powerful (or marked out by the gods in some other way) during his life, is believed to retain some power in the grave (see **death and burial**), and is worshipped on this account. **Libations** were poured, and other offerings made, at the supposed or actual tombs of numerous mythical and historical figures. Because a hero is dead and dwells beneath the earth, his power is somewhat sinister and his anger is to be feared. Each city, however, has its protective heroes (Aesch. *Ag.* 516), and the bones of a hero can act as a talisman for the city in whose soil they are buried. Thus the dead **Amphiaraus** will benefit **Thebes** (Aesch. *Sept.* 587-8), the dead **Orestes** will do good or harm to **Argos** (Aesch. *Eum.*

762-74), the dead **Oedipus** will defend **Athens** (Soph. *OC* 459-60, 576-82, 1518-35), and the dead **Hippolytus** will be honoured at **Trozen** (Eur. *Hipp.* 1423-30). Although the word 'hero' is not used in any of these passages, all these figures were the subject of actual hero-cults (with the possible exception of Oedipus, who is untypical in that he has no grave which can receive offerings). The dead **Heracles** became not simply a hero but an Olympian god.

2. **Homer** applies the word 'hero' to various characters during their lives, with no apparent religious implications. Most are warriors, but they are not necessarily outstanding ones. **Hesiod** (*Works and Days* 156-73) thought of the age in which the Theban and Trojan Wars were fought, and which preceded his own Iron Age, as an Age of Heroes – men partly descended from gods, and better than the men of his own day. Similarly modern writers use the term Heroic Age to refer to the period which Greek myth and epic describe – partly the historical Bronze Age, but mainly the timeless past of legend. But, because the most memorable characters of myth and epic are the great warriors – men of supreme strength and courage with a simple but stern code of honour – it is such men that the word 'hero' in this sense chiefly suggests.

Senses 1 and 2 are clearly connected, but they do not correspond exactly, and the relation between them is a matter of dispute.

3. In modern literary criticism the hero means the central character of a play or novel; and much has been written about the nature of 'the Sophoclean hero', 'the tragic hero', and the like. This is not a Greek use of the word; and indeed there is no single Greek word that can be translated by 'hero' in this sense. Some therefore argue that the word is misleading when applied to Greek tragedy; but it is, after all, the case that certain characters – Orestes in Aesch. *Cho.*, Oedipus in Soph. *OT* and *OC*, and **Medea** in Eur. *Med.*, for instance – play a dominant role in their plays. There is probably no harm in calling such characters the heroes of plays, provided that the different senses of the word are not confused, and provided that it is not felt to imply that all tragic heroes must resemble each other, or that every tragedy must have a hero, or that a major function of any play which does have one must be to explore his **character**. Generalisation about 'the Sophoclean hero' can be useful in practice, as long as it does not seek to impose a rigid pattern; whether the same is true of generalisation about 'the Greek tragic hero', let alone 'the tragic hero', is another question (see also *hamartiā*, tragedy).

Herodotus [hero'dotus]   A native of Halicarnassus in Asia Minor, who probably lived from the 480s to the 430s; the earliest of the Greek historians. His work is a history of the Persian Wars (see **Persia**), including numerous digressions on earlier history and on foreign lands. Though shrewd and often sceptical, he believed profoundly in traditional Greek religion, frequently seeing the hand of a god in the events that he describes, and drawing attention wherever possible to the fulfilment of **oracles** and the punishment of wickedness or presumption. His work thus provides an excellent guide to the beliefs of a conventional but intelligent Greek of the fifth century. His outlook is often compared to that of Sophocles, who appears to have written a poem in his honour, and who echoes his work at *Ant.* 905-12 (a passage derived from Herodotus 3. 118-19, but often thought not to be the genuine work of Sophocles) and elsewhere (for *OC* 337-41 see **Egypt**). Some of the stories which Herodotus tells as fact read very much like tragedies, e.g. the whole story of Croesus (1. 26-91), especially the death of his son Atys (1. 34-45), and the story of Polycrates (3. 39-43, 120-6).

Hesiod [hē'siod]   A Boeotian didactic poet of, perhaps, the early seventh century BC. He wrote in the same epic metre as **Homer** and in similar language, but in a rougher style. His poems are the *Theogony* and the *Works and Days* (several others were ascribed to him in antiquity, but the attribution is wrong in most cases, if not all). The *Theogony* tells of the origin of the world and the genealogy of the **gods**, including not only beings traditionally worshipped but various mythical monsters and personified abstractions. The parentage assigned to these beings must be partly traditional but largely the invention of Hesiod himself in accordance with various criteria of appropriateness; his scheme became to some extent canonical for later poets, although no one ever felt bound by it. The *Works and Days* consists of a variety of precepts, mainly relating to **justice** and farming. The myth of **Prometheus** appears in both poems (*Theogony* 521-616, *Works and Days* 42-58), and Aesch. *PV* is greatly influenced by them.

Hesione [hesī'onē]   Daughter of **Oceanus**; wife of **Prometheus**.

Hesperides [hespe'ridēz]   Goddesses dwelling in the far West, who sing sweetly and tend the garden of the gods, where **Zeus** first slept with **Hera** and **Earth** brought forth the Golden Apples of the Hesperides as a bridal gift to her.

The Lord of the Sea mentioned at Eur. *Hipp.* 744 is a sea-god who prevents ships from sailing beyond the Pillars of **Heracles** (Straits of Gibraltar), near which the Garden of the Hesperides is situated. At *Hipp.* 747 **Atlas** is mentioned as another neighbour.

Hestia [he'stia]   The hearth, as centre of family life (see **house**), personified as a goddess, daughter of **Cronus** and **Rhea**. It is uncertain whether it is the goddess or simply the hearth of the palace that is mentioned in a corrupt context (see **text**) at Aesch. *Ag.* 1056.

Hippolytus [hipo'litus]   Son of **Theseus** and an **Amazon** (Fig. 4). His story is of a type that is found attached to various mythical characters (see **Acastus** for the story of **Peleus**). The essentials of the myth before Euripides seem to have been that his stepmother **Phaedra** fell in love with him; he resisted her advances; she denounced him to Theseus with a false accusation of having tried to rape her; Theseus cursed his son, who was therefore killed by **Poseidon**; the truth was discovered, and Phaedra committed suicide.

The surviving *Hippolytus* is the second play that Euripides wrote on the subject. The first seems to have been a straightforward dramatisation of the legend as set out above; Phaedra was a wicked woman who tried to seduce Hippolytus, then lied to Theseus and did not commit suicide until she was found out. The play was apparently unsuccessful because the audience was offended by Phaedra's immoral character, and Euripides therefore took the unusual step of writing a second version (perhaps influenced by the *Phaedra* of Sophocles, of which little is known). Here Phaedra struggles honourably against her passion; it is revealed to Hippolytus not by her but by her Nurse; and it is at this stage that she commits suicide, her denunciation of Hippolytus being contained in a suicide note and intended to preserve her reputation and protect her children.

We are to understand from the play that Hippolytus was brought up by his great-grandfather **Pittheus** at **Trozen** (*Hipp.* 11), while Theseus reigned at **Athens**, though Theseus has now taken control of Trozen also. Phaedra first saw Hippolytus, and fell in love with him, when he visited Athens to attend the Mysteries (24-8), i.e. to be initiated at **Eleusis**. He returned to Trozen, while she dedicated a temple at Athens (29-33; see below). Theseus and Phaedra are now spending a year at Trozen, so that Theseus can expiate a fairly minor **pollution** (34-7), but at present Theseus is away for a few days consulting an **oracle** (281, 792, 807).

For Hippolytus's chastity and misogyny see **Artemis, women**. There is some dispute among critics as to whether the Athenian audience would have regarded these traits as flaws in his character.

Hippolytus was honoured as a **hero**, a minor one at Athens and a major one at Trozen; both cities claimed to possess his grave. On the southern slope of the Athenian **Acropolis** there was a temple of '**Aphrodite** at (?) Hippolytus'; this was normally taken to mean that the temple was beside his grave, but Euripides (*Hipp.* 29-33) gives the preposition a different sense, claiming that Phaedra dedicated the temple to Aphrodite 'because of Hippolytus'. At Trozen girls before marriage cut off their hair and dedicated it to Hippolytus; there was an annual festival in his honour, and **choruses** of maidens sang hymns or laments for him (Eur. *Hipp.* 1423-30). These rituals may well be older than the myth.

Hippomedon [hipo'medon]   An Argive; one of the **Seven against Thebes**.

Homer [hŏ'mer]   The legendary poet to whom the *Iliad* and *Odyssey* are traditionally ascribed. These long epic poems were composed in, perhaps, the late eighth century, and are thus the earliest surviving works of Greek literature, though they certainly had a long tradition of unwritten, orally composed poetry behind them. The *Iliad* relates a single episode, that of the Wrath of **Achilles**, from the tenth year of the Trojan War. The *Odyssey* relates the adventures of **Odysseus** on his way home from that war and on his arrival at **Ithaca**.

In fifth-century **Athens** these poems were constantly recited and deeply revered. The Homeric view of the world — with the **gods** as a quarrelsome and often all too human family, death as a bleak and comfortless end to human existence, and the possibility for great men to achieve a brief glory through courage and martial prowess — had an influence that went beyond mere literary convention. The tragedians seldom took their mythical material from the *Iliad* or *Odyssey*, preferring less well-known sources (surviving exceptions are Eur. *Rhes.*, based on *Iliad* 10, and Eur. *Cycl.*, based on *Odyssey* 9). In the society and way of life that they depict, contemporary elements are constantly mingled with Homeric ones; and the values expressed by their characters (especially by those of Euripides) are often different from those expressed in the Homeric poems. Nevertheless, the very idea of a literature that does not deal in happy endings but contemplates death and suffering seriously and unflinchingly (see **tragedy**) could hardly exist without the *Iliad*; and Homeric attitudes have an

effect on every Greek tragedy even when they serve chiefly as a point
of departure.

A number of later poems were also ascribed to Homer in antiquity.
These included the so-called Homeric Hymns, a collection of poems in
honour of various gods, mostly dating from the seventh and sixth centuries. More important as sources for tragedy were various minor epics
which have not survived, such as the *Trojan Cycle* (dealing with parts
of the Trojan War which the *Iliad* does not cover, and with subsequent
events) and the *Thebais* (dealing with the **Seven against Thebes**).

Homoloean [homolē'an] **Gate**   One of the seven gates of **Thebes**.

Horcus [hor'cus]   The Greek for 'oath' personified as a god, who
punishes perjury and is the servant of **Zeus** in such matters.

house   The Greek words for 'house', like the English, can mean
'household' or 'family' as well as a physical building. The Greeks had
a stronger sense than most of us today of the coherence and continuity of the family, and a correspondingly weaker sense of the auton-
omous individual. The memory of the dead was preserved in family
cults, and the transmission of property from generation to generation
was crucial to the working of society. It was a disaster for a family to
die out, and various precautions were taken in Athenian law to ensure
that it did not. The citizen rights of an individual depended on his
membership of a family (see also **phratry**); and the head of a family
was owed absolute loyalty by his wife (see **women**) and children.

So it was that some Greeks, at least, were content to do without
any idea of reward or punishment for individual souls after death
(see **death and burial**), and to accept that of inherited guilt — or rather,
perhaps, inherited liability to punishment — which is expressed several
times in the older of the surviving tragedies (Aesch. *Sept.* 742-65,
Eum. 934-7, Soph. *Ant.* 582-625; see *ātē*, **curses**, **pollution**). It can be
argued that the *Oresteia*, in particular, is more concerned with the
House or family than with its individual members; certainly the Greek
words for 'house' resound through the trilogy, and the actual palace
represented by the scene-building (see *skēnē*) acquires great symbolic
importance.

Hyades [hī'adēz]   A star-cluster in the same region of the sky as the
Pleiades.

hybris A common Greek word, usually meaning an act of aggression or insult showing disregard of the rights and dignity of others. There was a law against *hybris* in **Athens**, and in legal contexts the word usually refers to physical assault. It is not necessarily a religious offence, except in so far as the gods take account of wrongs done by man to man; indeed it is possible (though unusual) to accuse a god of *hybris* against a mortal, as at Eur. *Hipp.* 445-6, *Bacch.* 9.

Modern literary critics, however, use the word rather differently, to mean the impious presumption of a man who forgets that he is mortal and who challenges the gods by reckless words or deeds so that he incurs divine anger and punishment. Such presumption (whatever name we give it) is certainly a frequent theme of Greek myth and literature; some straightforward examples are provided by **Capaneus** at Aesch. *Sept.* 423-50 and Soph. *Ant.* 134-40 (and the **Seven against Thebes** in general), **Asclepius** at Aesch. *Ag.* 1022-4, **Agamemnon** at Soph. *El.* 566-74, **Ajax (ii)** at Eur. *Tro.* 69-73, **Actaeon** at Eur. *Bacch.* 337-40. The cases which tragedy explores in greater detail are normally more complex than this, but it is often worth discussing how much the standard pattern of presumption and punishment contributes to them; how much of Capaneus is there, for instance, in the Xerxes of Aesch. *Pers.*, the Agamemnon of Aesch. *Ag.*, the **Ajax (i)** of Soph. *Aj.*, the **Creon (i)** of Soph. *Ant.*, the **Hippolytus** of Eur. *Hipp.*, or the **Pentheus** of Eur. *Bacch.*?

The theme is by no means confined to myth; one of the most common doctrines of Greek proverbial wisdom is the danger of over-stepping mortal limits. This doctrine is frequently found when great men are being praised for their achievements; **Pindar**'s poems in praise of his patrons contain numerous parallels to the cautious words of the Priest at Soph. *OT* 31-4. For the Greeks, with their fiercely competitive society and their intense need to excel and to be praised for doing so, any restriction on human achievement was doubtless genuinely irksome. Since all the restrictions imposed by mortality, human weakness and the uncertainty of life are enshrined in the **gods**, we may take it that competition with those gods, even if it seems a rather unreal theme to us, was in fact felt by the Greeks as a particular temptation and danger.

The question remains whether such impious presumption is ever denoted by the word *hybris* in Greek. The usage is rare, but there are probably a few genuine examples in tragedy: Eur. *Hipp.* 474-5 (it is *hybris* to wish to be stronger than the gods); Aesch. *Pers.* 807-8 (those who destroyed Greek shrines will be punished for '*hybris* and godless thoughts'), 820-2 (a mortal's thoughts must not be excessive, for the fruit of *hybris* is *ātē*, 'ruin'); Soph. *OT* 873-9 (*hybris*, which seems to be much the same as the impious pride of 883-96, climbs to a point from which it must fall). This last is a very famous passage, and is doubtless largely responsible for the sense given to *hybris* today, but there is much controversy about its exact meaning and its relevance to the play (see also ***tyrannos***).

In another famous passage at Aesch. *Ag.* 750-81 the Chorus, reject-ing the notion that prosperity in itself leads to ruin (a notion that can probably be found at Soph. *Ant.* 613-14, and certainly in **Herodotus**), states that it is old *hybris* which breeds new *hybris*, leading in time to *ātē*, 'ruin', for the **house**; but the houses of the rich are much more liable to this process than those of the poor, which respect **justice**. Similar ideas had been expressed by **Solon** and others; it was a commonplace that prosperity leads to *koros*, a surfeit of good things, and that this leads to *hybris*, which leads to *ātē*. In such passages, where the word *hybris* has no single reference, it presumably covers a wide range of meaning; the rights of both men and gods may be spurned by the arrogance of wealth, and both may contribute to the ruin that follows.

While the association of *hybris* with *ātē* is not uncommon, its association with ***nemesis***, which was at one time popular with critics, seems to occur only twice, at Soph. *El.* 790-2, Eur. *Phoen.* 179-82. In both places the *hybris* is directed against men, not gods.

Hybristes [hībri′stēz]   See **Io's wanderings**.

Hymen [hī′men]   or Hymenaeus [himenē′us]   God of marriage. Both names appear to derive from ritual cries traditionally uttered in wedding songs.

hymns   Hymns to the gods, sung by **choruses**, were a frequent element in Greek religion; and many of the choral songs in tragedy consist of addresses to gods for one purpose or another. A complete prayer-hymn has a somewhat standardised form, consisting of an invocation of the god (often including an elaborate account of his attributes), a reminder to him of favours that he has bestowed in the past, a request for present help, reasons for this request, and a closing address that echoes the opening. All these features occur at Soph. *Ant.* 1115-54, and selections from them can be found elsewhere.

For the so-called Homeric Hymns see **Homer**.

Hyperbius [hiper'bius]   Brother of **Actor**; one of the seven defenders of **Thebes**.

Hyperboreans [hiperbo're-anz]   A mythical race which lived a life of blessedness and peace in the far North, beyond the home of **Boreas**.

Hypermestra [hiperme'stra]   See **Danaids (i)**.

hyporcheme [hi'porkēm]   A song accompanied by dance. The word is applied by some scholars, ancient and modern, to those choral songs in tragedy for which lively dancing would be appropriate, but this usage probably rests on a misunderstanding and is best avoided (see *stasimon*).

hypothesis   A preface to a play, written by an ancient or medieval scholar. Many manuscripts of Greek tragedies (see **text**) preserve hypotheses, though these vary greatly in age and quality. One of the older examples, if preserved in full, will contain not only a summary of the play's plot but also a note of when it was first performed, what other plays were performed on the same occasion (see **Great Dionysia**), and what prizes were awarded.

Hysiae [hi'si-ē]   A village on the northern slopes of **Cithaeron**.

I

Iacchus [ia'kus]   A god worshipped at **Eleusis** with an annual torch-bearing procession, and often identified with **Dionysus**. The name suggests a word for 'shout', and may be connected with the ritual cries addressed to him.

iambics   See **verse**.

Ida [i'da]   A mountain, or mountain range, to the south-east of **Troy**, noted for its pine-forests. It was here that the Judgement of **Paris** took place. 'Idaean' [idē'an] can be used to mean 'Trojan'. See also **Beacon Speech**.

Ilium [i'lium]   See **Troy**.

imagery   The kinds of figurative language that are used in Greek tragedy vary considerably from one dramatist to another, and also from one type of **verse** to another. In dialogue Sophocles and Euripides (to a much smaller extent Aeschylus) tend to avoid effects that are self-consciously 'poetic' and might risk distracting attention from the large-scale movement of the drama. Sophocles shows great skill in the use of thoughtful but unobtrusive imagery that gently heightens and enriches the style of his dialogue; Euripides is more prepared to risk flatness and poetic cliché; while Aeschylus is less restrained, and admits into his dialogue the kind of bold and difficult imagery which the other tragedians confine to songs.

In lyrics Aeschylus and Sophocles (to a smaller extent Euripides) exploit a wide range of possibilities, ranging from strikingly meta-phorical uses of single words to (occasionally) elaborate conceits sus-tained for several lines; for memorable examples of the latter see Aesch. *Sept.* 854-60 (**lamentation** as the propulsion of the ship of the dead), *Ag.* 437-44 (**Ares** as a 'gold-changer'), Soph. *OT* 873-9 (personification of **hybris**), *OC* 1239-48 (**Oedipus** as a storm-beaten headland). Euri-pides to some extent compensates for the relative scarcity and conven-tionality of his similes and metaphors by skilful use of language that is sensuous and evocative without being figurative, especially in songs describing far-off places or the remote past (see **chorus**).

Patterns of imagery sustained through whole plays have been found in the work of all three tragedians, but in Sophocles and Euripides they are fairly inconspicuous. They are striking and important, however, in Aesch. *Sept.*, where the different themes of the play are linked by the use of imagery taken from the sea and seafaring, and above all in the *Oresteia*, where such recurrent images as the net or robe, the hunt, the light in darkness, and the stain of blood, must be taken into account in any interpretation of the trilogy. The figurative and the literal can become difficult to separate in the *Oresteia*, as image and reality shed light on one another and physical objects – the **House**, the 'carpet', the robe – acquire symbolic significance.

imitation See *mimēsis*.

Inachus [iˈnakus] The main river of **Argos**; personified as a king of Argos, son of **Oceanus** and father of **Io**.

India To the Greeks this was a land on the borders of the known world, and believed to be rich in gold.

Ino [ī'nō]   Daughter of **Cadmus**; sister of **Semele** and others (Fig. 3).
She nursed her nephew **Dionysus** in his infancy, and was therefore
driven mad by the jealous **Hera**; she leapt into the sea and became
a sea-goddess, having first, according to the version followed at Eur.
Med. 1282-9, killed her two children. None of this, however, is compatible with the references to her in Eur. *Bacch.*, where she is one of
the sisters driven mad by Dionysus as a punishment for denying his
divinity.

Io [ī'ō]   Daughter of **Inachus**; an Argive princess who was desired
by **Zeus**. Having been driven from her home by **dreams** and **oracles**,
she was transformed into a cow, either by Zeus, in order to disguise
her from the jealous **Hera**, or by Hera, in order to keep her from
Zeus; in Aesch. *PV*, however, she is merely given a cow's horns, which
must have been more convenient for representation on stage. Hera
also sent the monster **Argus** to watch over her, but he was killed by
Hermes at Zeus's command. Hera then sent a gadfly, which drove Io
in torment over the earth (see **Io's wanderings**), until, still in the form
of a cow, she eventually reached Canobus in **Egypt**. There, made pregnant (either at this point or earlier) by Zeus's touch, she gave birth
to **Epaphus**. Through him she became the ancestress of the Egyptians,
including the **Danaids (i)** (the descendants prophesied at *PV* 853-69),
one of whom (Hypermestra) was herself an ancestress of **Heracles**
(the descendant prophesied at *PV* 772-4, 871-3).
   The myth of Io is not inherently connected with that of **Prometheus**, but she is brought into Aesch. *PV* both to emphasise the cruelty
of Zeus (at Aesch. *Supp.* 524-99 the moral of her story is very different) and because of her connection with Prometheus's deliverer
Heracles (necessarily a remote connection since the deliverance of
Prometheus is to occur so far in the future).

Iolcus [io'lkus]   A city on the slopes of Mount **Pelion** in **Thessaly**.
Jason was its rightful king; see also **Medea, Pelias**.

Iole [ī'olē]   See **Heracles**.

Ion [ī'on]   Ancestor of the **Ionians**; said at **Athens** to be the son of
Apollo and of the Athenian queen Creusa. Euripides' play of this
name tells a romantic story of how the boy Ion, ignorant of his identity, is discovered living at **Delphi**, and how, after various complications,
Creusa's husband Xuthus is made to believe that Ion is his own son.

Ionians [iŏ'nianz]   One of the major divisions of the Greek people
(compare **Dorians**). Ionians, sharing a common dialect and claiming a
common ancestry (see **Ion**), inhabited **Attica** (Attic Greek being a
form of Ionic), **Euboea**, most of the Cyclades, Chios, Samos, several
cities on the east coast of the **Aegean**, and numerous colonies further
afield. Ionia is the name given to the Ionian part of the eastern Aegean;
the Ionian Sea, however, is the sea between Greece, southern **Italy** and
Sicily, supposedly called after **Io** (see **Io's wanderings**), and extended
by poets to include the Adriatic.

Io's wanderings   It is convenient to list in one entry all the geographical names that occur in the accounts of **Io**'s wanderings in Aesch.
PV. The dramatist is eager to display his knowledge about the furthest
regions of the world, but his geography is often vague and perplexing.

From the neighbourhood of **Argos** (*PV* 676-7) Io travelled north
through Greece to **Dodona**, which can be considered to belong either
to Molossis or to Thesprotia (829-35). From there she continued
north-west along the shore of the Adriatic (which was later called
after her the **Ionian** Sea) to the Gulf of **Rhea** at its northern end (836-
41). A storm then drove her back, presumably to the east or north-
east, until she came to **Prometheus**'s rock, in an uninhabited part of
Scythia (2), far to the north of Greece.

From there Prometheus tells her to continue east to the inhabited
part of Scythia (north of the Black Sea), but to skirt that country
by following the sea shore until on her left she finds the **Chalybes**,
who seem to live east of the Scythians (707-16). She will then come
to the river Hybristes, 'Violent', which is otherwise unknown and
seems to be fabulous, and which she must follow to its source in the
Caucasus (717-21).

Interpretation becomes very difficult here, and it seems necessary
to identify this Caucasus, not with the Asiatic range east of the Black
Sea, but with a fabulous range in the far North of Europe, perhaps
the same as the **Rhipae**. After climbing the Caucasus, then, to round
the source of the Hybristes, and doubling back to the south along its
east bank, she will come to the land of the **Amazons** (723) before
leaving Europe. These Amazons live north of the Black Sea, near
Lake **Maeotis**, and the author seems to locate **Colchis** in this region
(415); but, to account for the presence of Amazons *south* of the
Black Sea in other myths, he explains (724-7) that they will later
migrate to the town of Themiscyra on the river Thermodon in Asia
Minor, wrongly identifying this area with that of **Salmydessus** in

Thrace. The Amazons, then, will conduct Io to the Cimmerian **Bosporus (ii)**, which connects the Black Sea to Lake Maeotis, and by crossing this strait she will leave Europe for **Asia** (728-35).

The next phase of the journey takes Io to fabulous places in the far East (790-809). Greek writers are quite vague and inconsistent about the locations of Mount Cisthene and the lands of the **Gorgons**, the **Phorcides**, the **griffins**, and the one-eyed Arimaspian horsemen with their River of **Pluto**; see, however, **Herodotus** 3. 116, 4. 13, 27, from which it appears that some of these details derive from the reports of an early traveller, Aristeas of Proconessus. The Ethiopians, a race burnt black by the sun, were placed far south in Africa by most writers, but *PV* 807-9 places them in the far East, where the sun rises (Herodotus distinguishes two groups of Ethiopians, in Africa and **India**). Nevertheless, their river Aethiops is apparently the source of the **Nile** (the Red Sea must be non-existent or land-locked), and Io must follow this river to where it pours over the Bybline Mountains (presumably hills round the First Cataract) and on to its Delta (810-15), where her journey will end at the city of Canobus or Canopus (846).

Iphianassa [ifiana′sa]   A daughter of **Agamemnon** according to **Homer** (*Iliad* 9. 145). Although **Iphigenia** must originally be an alternative form of the same name, Sophocles makes her a separate character, so that Iphianassa still survives at the time of **Orestes'** return (*El.* 158).

Iphigenia [ifijeni′a]   Daughter of **Agamemnon** and **Clytemnestra** (Fig. 2). Before the Greek fleet could sail for **Troy**, Agamemnon had to **sacrifice** her to **Artemis**; for the reason see **Agamemnon**. According to Euripides she was lured to **Aulis** for the sacrifice by a promise of marriage to **Achilles**.

Eur. *IA* tells the story of the sacrifice. The play was probably left unfinished at Euripides' death, and has suffered badly from later insertions and rewriting (see **text**). In the ending that we have Iphigenia is rescued from death at the last minute by Artemis, but it is doubtful whether this is what Euripides intended.

The idea of a rescue comes from Eur. *IT*, according to which, when everyone thought that Iphigenia was sacrificed, Artemis miraculously transported her to the barbarian land of the Taurians. The play tells how **Orestes** and **Pylades** find her there and how they all escape from the wicked king Thoas.

In other tragedies, however, it is assumed that the sacrifice at Aulis actually took place; there is a classic description of it (or rather of the preparations for it) at Aesch. *Ag.* 218-47. At *Ag.* 242-7 we are told that she had been accustomed to join in the **paean** that accompanied the pouring of the third **libation** at her father's banquets; this is a departure from the custom of fifth-century **Athens**, where banquets were not attended by **women**.

irony   The Greek word means a pretence of ignorance or simplicity, such as was often affected by the philosopher Socrates. In modern literary criticism, however, 'dramatic irony' is an accepted term for the practice of playing on the contrast between the audience's knowledge of what will happen (or has happened) in a play and the characters' ignorance of it. For instance, when **Oedipus** at Soph. *OT* 61 says to the Thebans, 'None of you is as sick as I', he means merely that he feels all the grief of the plague-stricken city, but the audience knows that his words are true in the sense that he is uniquely polluted. When at *OT* 220 he says that he is 'a stranger to the deed' (the killing of **Laius**), the audience, unlike Oedipus, know that this is the precise opposite of the truth.

The shock of being reminded of the truth through the characters' ignorance of it is particularly associated with Sophocles, but it is also common in Aeschylus (e.g. *Sept.* 5-9) and Euripides (e.g. repeatedly in *El.* 220-91), and indeed in tragedy generally. It is connected with the superstitious belief that chance utterances bearing an unintended meaning can be **omens** revealing the future. A variation, also common in Sophocles, is the device of giving a character or chorus a passage of hope or rejoicing immediately before disaster strikes (e.g. Soph. *Ant.* 1115-54, *OT* 1086-109), or of despair immediately before salvation comes (e.g. *El.* 1126-70).

Unfortunately, the word 'irony' is sometimes used more loosely than this. In particular, those critics who believe that a play may have a hidden meaning running counter to its apparent content or moral significance commonly use the word in this context. But the fact that Greek tragedies contain irony in one sense of the word does not mean that they contain it in any other sense.

Ismene [isme'ne]   Daughter of **Oedipus** and **Jocasta**; sister of **Antigone** (Fig. 3). She had a story of her own, but this is ignored in Greek tragedy, where she is treated merely as a foil or partner to her more prominent sister.

Ismenus [isme'nus]   One of the two rivers of **Thebes** (the other being

Dirce). Soph. *OT* 21 refers to an oracular shrine of **Apollo** by the river (perhaps connected with a local **hero** also called Ismenus), where divination was practised by means of burnt offerings (see **oracles, omens, sacrifice**). At Soph. *Ant.* 1125 the 'seed of the dragon' refers to the ground where dragon's teeth were sown; see **Cadmus**.

Ister [i'ster] or Istros   The River Danube.

Isthmus   Sometimes used in a general sense, but *the* Isthmus is that of **Corinth**, and 'Isthmian' means, in effect, Corinthian. The 'Isthmian Peak' at Eur. *Tro.* 1097-8 is that of the Acrocorinth (Corinthian **Acropolis**), overlooking harbours on the **Saronic** and Corinthian Gulfs.

Italy   By the fifth century much of southern Italy (Magna Graecia) had long been colonised by Greeks. Italy is called a home of **Dionysus** at Soph. *Ant.* 1119, apparently because it was famous for its vines (but some scholars alter the **text** here).

Ithaca [i'thaka]   An island to the west of Greece, famous as the home of **Odysseus**.

Itys [i'tis]   Tereus, King of **Thrace**, married Procne, daughter of **Pandion**, but raped her sister Philomela, whose tongue he then cut out to prevent her from revealing the rape. But Philomela managed to tell her sister by weaving a picture of the crime into a tapestry, and Procne, in revenge, killed Itys, her son by Tereus, and served him as food to his father. The gods then turned Procne into a **nightingale**, who always sings 'Itys, Itys' in lamentation for her son, while Philomela became a swallow and Tereus a hoopoe.

Ixion [iksi'on]   A Thessalian who killed his father-in-law and became the first of all suppliants for purification (see **supplication, pollution**). He was purified by **Zeus** himself, but ungratefully attempted to seduce **Hera**. In punishment for this Zeus bound him on a burning wheel and set him spinning for ever in mid air, or in the **Underworld** (Soph. *Phil.* 676-80). Aeschylus and Euripides wrote plays about him.

J

Jason [jā'son]   Son of Aeson; rightful king of **Iolcus**. He was brought up in exile, however, since the kingship had been usurped by his stepfather **Pelias**. When Jason came to claim it, Pelias tried to dispose of him by sending him in quest of the Golden Fleece, a treasure that was kept in **Colchis**, the realm of King Aeetes, and guarded by a serpent.

Jason therefore set sail in the miraculous ship Argo, with a crew of heroes known as the Argonauts, and, after many adventures, including the passage of the **Clashing Rocks**, arrived in Colchis. There Aeetes, not wishing to give up the Fleece, set Jason seemingly impossible tasks — to harness two fire-breathing bulls, sow a field with dragon's teeth, and avoid death at the hands of the armed men who would then spring up. Aeetes' daughter **Medea**, however, who was a sorceress, fell in love with Jason, and with her help he was able to perform these tasks, and also to kill the serpent and win the Fleece. Jason and Medea then escaped in the Argo, and, after further adventures, returned to Iolcus. For events there and at **Corinth** see **Medea**.

Jason died when part of the Argo, which he had hung up in a temple as a dedication to the gods, fell on his head.

Jocasta [joka'sta]   Sister of **Creon (i)**; wife of **Laius** and mother of **Oedipus**; later wife of Oedipus and mother of his children (Fig. 3). For the earliest account of her see **Homer**, *Odyssey* 11. 271-80, where she is called Epikaste; for Sophocles' account see **Oedipus**. Eur. *Phoen.* follows **Stesichorus**, against Homer and Sophocles, in having her still alive at the time of the war between **Eteocles** and **Polynices**, and attempting to mediate between them; she seems to be still alive at Aesch. *Sept.* 926-31 also.

justice   The usual translation of the Greek word *dikē*. The translation is generally a reasonable one, as long as it is realised that in Aeschylus, especially, 'justice' normally involves no more than retribution for crime (see e.g. *Cho.* 306-14); as long as the doer suffers (*Ag.* 1564, *Cho.* 313), so that *in*justice is punished, the order of the world will remain in balance and the requirements of 'justice' will be satisfied. There is no reason, then, why the punishment of a crime should not itself be a crime incurring punishment in its turn, and even such undoubted villains as **Clytemnestra** (*Ag.* 1406, 1432) and **Aegisthus** (*Ag.* 1577, 1604, 1607, 1611) can lay claim to *dikē*, without being contradicted, when they have committed acts of retribution. At *Cho.* 461 we hear that one *dikē* can clash with another, and here 'justice' is hardly a possible translation; perhaps 'plea' or 'legal claim', for the word often has legal associations, and such imagery is common in the *Oresteia*.

It is also true, however, that the Greeks of this period did not possess any *more* moral and enlightened terms for 'right' and 'wrong' than *dikē* and its opposite, so an appeal to *dikē* is an appeal to the highest principle available. It is therefore natural that the **gods**, especially **Zeus** and Moira (see **fate**), should be much concerned with the enforcement of this retributive 'justice', and should ally themselves with the **Erinyes** who preside over vengeance and punishment, while having little interest in the rewarding of virtue or innocence.

Dikē can itself be personified as a goddess, who is often said to be the daughter of Zeus. At *Cho.* 949-51 this idea is reinforced by word-play, her name, in the form *Dikā*, being fancifully connected with *Dios korā*, 'Zeus's daughter'. Soph. *Ant.* 451, however, refers to the 'Justice' who dwells with the gods below, meaning the power that presides over the legitimate claim of these gods that the dead should be properly buried (see **Underworld**). At Soph. *El.* 475 Justice is called a prophetess, perhaps because she has sent the **dream** foretelling the vengeance which she will enforce. She appeared as a character in an Aeschylean play; see **fragments**.

K

k-   See also c-.

katharsis   See **catharsis**.

Ker [kear] (plural Keres [kear′rēz])   A spirit of death, similar to, and sometimes identified with, an **Erinys**. At Aesch. *Sept.* 776-7, however, the 'man-snatching Ker' is the **Sphinx**.

king   See *tyrannos*, **city**.

kommos (plural *kommoi*)   The word means 'dirge'; see **lamentation**. In **Aristotle**, *Poetics* 12, however, the word is defined as 'a dirge shared between chorus and actors', and some modern writers use it to mean *any* lyric exchange between chorus and actors, whether they are lamenting or not. This usage is quite illogical, however, and it is better to call such lyric (or partially lyric) exchanges *amoibaia*. The name Great *Kommos* has come to be used of Aesch. *Cho.* 306-478, which is a *kommos* in any sense of the word.

koros 'Satiety', too much of a good thing; often said to be the parent (less often the child) of *hybris*.

Kratos [kra'tos] See **Strength**.

L

Labdacus [la'bdakus] King of **Thebes**; son of **Polydorus (i)**; father of **Laius** (Fig. 3).

Lacedaemon [lasedē'mon] See **Sparta**.

Laconia [lakō'nia] The land surrounding, and controlled by, **Sparta**.

Laertes [lā-er'tēz] Father of **Odysseus** according to **Homer** and to most other writers (but see **Sisyphus**).

Laius [lā'yus] King of **Thebes**; son of **Labdacus**; husband of **Jocasta**; father of **Oedipus** (Fig. 3). There was a story that he abducted the son of **Pelops** and that the **curse** on his family derived from this crime, but surviving tragedies do not refer to this. They do refer to the **oracle** of **Apollo**, which either commanded him not to beget a child (Aesch. *Sept.* 745-9), or warned him that, if he did, that child would kill him (Soph. *OT* 711-14), or both (Eur. *Phoen.* 13-20). Laius ignored the oracle; for the consequences see **Oedipus**.

lamentation All lamentation for the dead must serve to relieve the feelings of the survivors, and Euripidean characters pay some attention to its subjective benefits, even talking of the 'pleasure' that it brings (Eur. *Tro.* 608-9, *El.* 126). A number of speeches and **monodies** in Sophocles and Euripides are direct expressions of a character's personal grief (e.g. Soph. *El.* 1126-70, Eur. *Tro.* 98-152, 740-79).

It is not these, however, that cause problems for the modern reader, but the highly stylised and purposeful lyric dirges which occur chiefly in Aeschylus. These are often divided antiphonally between semi-choruses (Aesch. *Sept.* 875-1004) or between chorus and actors (Aesch. *Pers.* 908-1077, *Cho.* 306-478, Eur. *Tro.* 1287-332; see *kommos*). They are accompanied by ritual gestures of grief, such as rhythmic beating of the head and breast (*Pers.* 1046-65, *Sept.* 855-6, *Cho.* 425-8, *Tro.* 1235-6), and they are often conceived, not simply as expressing emotion, but as paying the dead a service which they have a right to expect (*Sept.* 854-60, *Cho.* 315-44; see **death and burial**). They are generally performed by women or (in Aesch. *Pers.*) orientals, since Greek men were expected to show more dignified restraint in their grief.

Such ritual dirges are not simply matters of tragic convention, for they are described by **Homer** (e.g. *Iliad* 24. 719-76) and other writers, and their essential features can be paralleled from actual funerals in modern Greece and elsewhere. By the fifth century the lyric dirge, written for occasions of private or public mourning and sung by a **chorus** to the *aulos*, had become an accepted literary form in the hands of such poets as Simonides and **Pindar**. Dirges were sung, not just at funerals and at subsequent ceremonies for those recently dead, but also at the festivals of certain **heroes**, such as **Hippolytus**. Those which are sung in tragedy, then, simply exploit an existing tradition in a dramatic context.

Laomedon [lāo′medon]   King of **Troy**; father of **Priam**, Ganymede and Tithonus. In his time the gods **Apollo** and **Poseidon** were compelled to build the walls of Troy as punishment for a revolt against **Zeus**, but Laomedon refused them payment for their work. Poseidon therefore sent a sea monster, but it was killed by **Heracles**, who thus rescued Laomedon's daughter. Heracles in his turn was cheated of a reward of miraculous horses which Laomedon had promised him, so he sacked Troy, with the help of **Telamon**, and killed the King.

The son of Laomedon referred to at Eur. *Tro.* 821 is Ganymede, a beautiful boy whom Zeus carried off to be the cupbearer of the gods and, so *Tro.* 845-6 hints, for homosexual purposes. For his brother Tithonus, referred to at *Tro.* 853-4, see **Eos**.

Lasthenes [la′sthenēz]   One of the seven defenders of **Thebes**.

Leda [lē′da]   Wife of **Tyndareus**, to whom she bore **Clytemnestra**. **Zeus** seduced her in the form of a swan, and to him she bore **Helen** and Polydeuces. By one father or the other she was the mother of **Castor**. See Fig. 2.

Lemnos [le′mnos]   An island in the northern **Aegean**. In Greek litera-ture it is regarded (oddly) as volcanic, and is associated in various ways with **Hephaestus**. **Philoctetes** was marooned here; and, although the island was inhabited from an early date, and is normally treated as such in literature, it is boldly treated as uninhabited in Soph. *Phil.*, to account for Philoctetes' isolation.

The proverbial Lemnian Crime of Aesch. *Cho.* 631-4 occurred when the women of Lemnos killed their husbands through jealousy of some Thracian concubines.

See also **Beacon Speech**.

Lerna [ler'na]   Site of a spring near **Argos**.

Leto [lē'tō]   A Titaness (see **Titans**); mother, by **Zeus**, of **Apollo** and **Artemis**.

libation   The word means a drink-offering (see **sacrifice**). At feasts it was customary, after the meal and before the drinking, to sing a **paean** and to pour three libations of wine on the ground, the first to Olympian **Zeus**, the second to the **heroes**, and the third to Zeus the Saviour. Aeschylus repeatedly alludes to this third libation in the *Oresteia* (*Ag.* 246, 1386-7, *Cho.* 578, 1073, *Eum.* 759-60), sometimes inverting its usual auspicious significance to shocking effect.

Rather different (and denoted by a different Greek word) were the libations poured on the ground or on tombs to appease the gods of the **Underworld** or the dead, including individual heroes. These might consist of different combinations of milk, honey, wine and water; wine was not poured to **Erinyes** or **Eumenides**. A libation ritual is described in detail at Soph. *OC* 466-90, and one is seen on stage at Aesch. *Cho.* 129-64 (see *Choephori*), *Pers.* 623-80.

The difficult passage at Aesch. *Ag.* 1395-8 probably turns on the distinction (which **Clytemnestra** would like to deny) between the joyful libations poured at banquets and those poured in mourning for the dead.

Libya   The part of Africa closest to Greece. For the reason for mentioning it at Aesch. *Eum.* 292 see **Triton** (some believe that the line also alludes to the fact that Athenian troops were fighting in **Egypt** when the *Oresteia* was produced, but this is unlikely). There were Greek settlements in Libya at Cyrene and **Barca**, and both the Libyans at Soph. *El.* 701-2 must come from these, since non-Greeks could not compete in the games. A kind of *aulos* is described as Libyan at Eur. *Tro.* 544 because it was made from the wood of a Libyan tree.

Liguria [ligū'ria]   A region of north-west **Italy**; see **Circe**.

lotus A magical fruit which made those who ate it forget their homes. For the adventure of **Odysseus** in the land of the Lotus-Eaters see **Homer**, *Odyssey* 9. 82-104.

love See **Eros**.

Loxias [lo'ksias] A name of **Apollo**.

Lycaean [līsē'an] **Precinct** A sacred precinct in **Arcadia**, dedicated to **Zeus** under the local name of Zeus Lycaeus.

Lyceus [līsē'us] A name of **Apollo**. The Lycean Market Place at **Argos** was beside Apollo's temple.

Lycia [li'sia] A region of south-west Asia Minor; home of some of **Troy**'s best allies in the Trojan War. Mention of Lycian mountains at Soph. *OT* 208 must be intended to link **Artemis** with her brother **Apollo Lyceus** (203). The Lycian Spring on **Lemnos** (Soph. *Phil.* 1461) apparently has nothing to do with Lycia but is named after Apollo Lycius or Lyceus; late sources talk of springs of honey and wine provided for **Philoctetes** by Apollo, but Sophocles must be thinking of an ordinary spring of water.

Lycomedes [likomē'dēz] King of **Scyros**; maternal grandfather of **Neoptolemus**.

Lycurgus [līker'gus] Son of **Dryas**; King of the **Edonians** in **Thrace**. Like **Pentheus** he fought against **Dionysus** and his **Maenads** (also, according to Soph. *Ant.* 965, against the **Muses**), and came to a bad end. The legend varies considerably in its details (see e.g. **Homer**, *Iliad* 6. 130-40), and at Soph. *Ant.* 955-65 Lycurgus apparently suffers no worse punishment than imprisonment; this is surprising, but provides a parallel for the imprisonment of **Antigone**. Aeschylus wrote a **tetralogy** called the *Lycurgeia*, which seems to have influenced Eur. *Bacch.*

Lydia [li'dia] Part of western Asia Minor, famous for its gold (see **Pactolus**) and its wealth in general. There is said to be inscriptional evidence for the worship of **Dionysus** there under the name Bacchus.

Lydias [li'dias] A river of Macedonia, a land famous for its horses.

Dionysus would have to cross the **Axius** and the Lydias on his way from **Thrace** to **Pieria**, but the prominence given to these rivers at Eur. *Bacch.* 568-75 is doubtless intended as a compliment to Euripides' host Archelaus (see **Bacchae**), since the capital which he established at Pella was on the Lydias and close to the Axius.

lyre   A stringed instrument (seen in Plate IIb), played with a plectrum, used to accompany many kinds of song, though not dirges (see **lamentation**), **dithyrambs** or the songs of tragedy, which were accompanied on the *aulos*. However, all poetry intended to be sung, whatever the accompanying instrument, is conventionally called 'lyric'. For the 'lyrics' of tragedy see **verse**.

Lyssa [li'sa]   Madness or frenzy, personified as a goddess. She is a character in Eur. *HF*.

M

Macistus [māsi'stus] or Macistum   See **Beacon Speech**.

Maenads [mē'nadz]   The word must originally have meant simply 'mad women', but it was applied specifically to the frenzied female votaries of **Dionysus** (Plate III).

Maeotis [mēō'tis]   The 'lake' now called the Sea of Azov, between the Crimea and the mainland; see **Io's wanderings**.

Magnesia [magnē'zia]   A coastal region of **Thessaly**.

Maia [mi'a]   Mother of **Hermes**.

Malis [mā'lis]   A region to the south of **Thessaly**, on the slopes of Mount **Oeta**; the kingdom of **Poeas** and **Philoctetes**.

masks   These were probably made of wood, linen and other light materials, and covered the whole head. They were worn by all **actors** and **chorus**-members. The few surviving representations of fifth-century masks suggest that they were just as naturalistic as contemporary sculpture; the highly stylised type, with the gaping mouth and high forehead, which is familiar from terra-cotta models and the like, was a later development. Surviving descriptions of masks also come from late and unreliable sources, so it is difficult to determine the range of styles available for different roles. Distinctions of sex, and broad divisions of age, would certainly have been indicated; blind characters doubtless had special masks; it is uncertain whether there were visible differences between gods and men, kings and slaves, or Greeks and barbarians; personalities and emotions were evidently not represented. For the bearing of the use of masks on characterisation see **character**.

The question of their origin is bound up with that of the origin of **tragedy**; see also **Thespis**. By analogy with other cultures, masks suggest religious **ritual**, and there is evidence for their ritual use in various parts of Greece. It does not appear, however, that any religious significance was attached to the dramatic masks of the fifth century, or that they were felt to be anything more than a means of enabling a man to take on a dramatic role. Without masks the convention of sharing parts among two or three actors, and the convention of a chorus whose members lacked individual identities, could not easily have arisen or been maintained.

mēchanē   See *deus ex machina*.

Medea [medē′a]   Daughter of Aeetes, King of **Colchis**; granddaughter of **Helios**; niece of **Circe**. For her role in the quest of the Golden Fleece see **Jason**. At some stage she killed her young brother Apsyrtus; in the best-known version she did so at sea, after fleeing from Colchis with Jason, and scattered pieces of his body in the Argo's wake to delay Aeetes' pursuit, but Eur. *Med.* 1334 implies that the murder took place in the palace at Colchis, and leaves the motive for it unclear.

When Jason and Medea finally reached **Iolcus**, they had to deal with the usurper **Pelias**. In order to trick Pelias's daughters, Medea magically rejuvenated an old ram (or Jason's old father) by boiling it (him) in a cauldron. The daughters were persuaded to repeat the experiment with Pelias, but Medea ensured that this time the magic failed to work. Pelias's son **Acastus**, however, was able to banish Jason and Medea from Iolcus.

They therefore took refuge at **Corinth** as guests of **Creon (ii)**. When Euripides' play begins, Jason has decided to abandon Medea and to marry Creon's daughter. In revenge for this, Medea causes the death of Creon and his daughter and kills her own two children by Jason, finally escaping to **Athens**. These details seem to be Euripides' invention; we hear of earlier versions in which Medea becomes Queen of Corinth and the children are either murdered, for one reason or another, by the Corinthians, or accidentally killed by Medea in an attempt to make them immortal. An annual ceremony, held in the temple of **Hera Acraea**, was explained as an expiation of the children's death.

In another story Medea appears as the wife of **Aegeus**, and attempts to poison her stepson **Theseus**. This is one reason for the importance of Aegeus and Athens in Eur. *Med.*

See also **rhetoric, women.**

Medes [mēdz]   The people of Media, south of the Caspian Sea. Before the middle of the sixth century they controlled the empire which was then taken over by **Persia**, so the Greeks often used the word 'Medes' to refer to the Persians.

Megareus [me'garūs]   Son of the Theban **Creon (i)**; apparently the same character as **Menoeceus (ii)** (Fig. 3). At Aesch. *Sept.* 472-9 Megareus is one of the seven warriors defending **Thebes**; at Soph. *Ant.* 1303 there is a vague reference to his glorious death; and in Eur. *Phoen.* Meneoceus is a boy who commits suicide in order to save Thebes, **Tiresias** having declared that **Ares** demands the death of a descendant of the Spartoi (see **Cadmus**).

Melanippus [melani'pus]   One of the seven defenders of **Thebes**. According to Aesch. *Sept.* 412-14 he is a descendant of the Spartoi (see **Cadmus**), and so in a special sense native to the Theban soil. See also **Tydeus.**

Melos [mē'los]   See **Peloponnesian War** (but note that at least one translator writes 'Melian' for 'Malian', from **Malis**, at Soph. *Phil.* 4).

Menelaus [menelā'us]   Son of **Atreus**; brother of **Agamemnon**; husband of **Helen** (Fig. 2). The usual account makes him King of **Sparta**, but Aeschylus, remarkably enough, makes him share Agamemnon's palace at **Argos**, thus adding to the importance of the **House** and emphasising the crime of **Paris** against both brothers.

When Helen had been abducted by Paris, Menelaus took part in Agamemnon's expedition against **Troy**. For his adventures on his way home see **Proteus. Homer** portrays him as a sympathetic character, though no great fighter, but the tragedians, especially Euripides, tend to treat him more scornfully, in keeping with their moral condemnation of Helen. He is a character in Soph. *Aj.*, Eur. *Andr.*, *Tro.*, *Hel.*, *Or.*, *IA*; see also Plate IV.

Menoeceus [menē'sūs]   **(i)** Father of the Theban **Creon (i)** and of **Jocasta** (Fig. 3). **(ii)** Son of the same Creon; also called **Megareus** (Fig. 3).

Merope [me'ropē]   Wife of **Polybus**, King of **Corinth**.

Messapium [mesā'pium]   See **Beacon Speech**.

messengers   Since changes of scene are usually avoided in Greek tragedy, it is often necessary for events that have occurred some distance away to be reported on stage. There was also a convention that deeds of violence, such as form the climax of most tragedies, were not enacted in the theatre; this may have been not so much from a sense that such deeds were out of keeping with the decorum of tragedy as to provide an opportunity for them to be vividly described in words. Certainly Euripides makes a point of having at least one 'messenger speech' in each play; the form is stereotyped, but the content usually consists of vivid and exciting narrative. In Sophocles such speeches are equally common, but exploited in more varied ways; thus we find 'messenger speeches' that are untrue (*Trach.* 248-90, *El.* 680-763; compare *Phil.* 542-627) and characters who arrive as messengers but then turn out to have some other function (*Trach.*, *OT*). Aeschylus, although he makes frequent use of 'messenger speeches', avoids using them to give a detailed description of the climax of the action; thus in *Sept.* the battle has been so much foreshadowed that a very brief report (*Sept.* 792-821) is sufficient, in *Ag.* **Agamemnon**'s death is described in advance by **Cassandra** and then reported by **Clytemnestra**, and in *Cho.* Clytemnestra's death so nearly happens on stage that no report is needed.

The deliverers of 'messenger speeches' are not often referred to as messengers in the text. Sometimes they are named characters, and here it is often debatable whether a speech counts as a 'messenger speech' or not. More often they are anonymous servants and the like, most of whom are barely characterised, though some explanation is normally given for their presence.

metre   See **verse**.

mimēsis   The word essentially means 'imitation'. In the context of literary criticism some translators prefer 'representation', which often reads more naturally in English but obscures the basic meaning.

In *Republic* 2-3 **Plato** uses the word in a restricted sense to mean 'enactment', as in the performance of drama and the delivery of direct speech in epic. Elsewhere, however, in Plato, **Aristotle** and other writers, it is assumed that every form of art is a *mimēsis* of something. The idea is most plausible when applied to painting, which clearly does 'imitate' real objects, and, when the word is applied to poetry, an analogy with painting is usually explicitly or implicitly present. Aristotle classifies each different form of poetry according to the medium, the object and the mode of its *mimēsis* (*Poetics* 1), though the details are unclear; and it is for this reason that the word is central to the definition of **tragedy** in *Poetics* 6.

Minos [mī́nos]   King of **Crete**; son of **Zeus** and Europa; husband of **Pasiphae**; father of **Ariadne** and **Phaedra** (Fig. 4); see also **Theseus**, **Scylla (ii)**.

Moira [moíra]   See **fate**.

Molossis [molósis]   See **Io's wanderings**.

monody   The word means a solo song. There is probably no example in the authentic work of Aeschylus; actors do sing, but only in *amoibaia*. **Io**, however, sings a monody at Aesch. *PV* 561-608, and the form becomes increasingly common in the later work of Euripides, where there is often a monody preceding the *parodos* (**i**).

Munichus [mū́nikus]   The local hero of Munichia, a bay on the south coast of **Attica**, which was used as the harbour of **Athens** before the bay of Piraeus came into use.

Muses [mū́ziz]   Nine goddesses of music and poetry, born in **Pieria**, imagined as singing before the other gods and as inspiring mortal singers (see **Hesiod**, *Theogony* 1-115). They are often associated with **Apollo**, **Aphrodite** or **Dionysus**. At times 'Muses' is used to mean simply 'poetry'. See also **Harmonia (i)**.

Mycenae [mīsḗnē] (adjective Mycenaean [-ḗan])   A city in the north-east **Peloponnese**; the city of **Agamemnon** according to **Homer**.

Archaeology has shown that it was one of the richest sites in Greece during the Bronze Age (hence the Bronze Age culture of the Greek mainland is called 'Mycenaean'), but it had little importance thereafter. For its final destruction, and for its treatment in tragedy, see **Argos**.

Myconos [mi′konos]   An island in the central **Aegean**, close to **Delos**.

Myrtilus [mer′tilus]   See **Pelops**.

Mysteries   See **death and burial**, **Eleusis**, **Orpheus**.

myth   Numerous ideas concerning the proper definition of myths and their true nature and significance have been put forward by intellectuals and others. Although it is more than likely that not all these ideas are entirely valueless, they need not concern us here.

The term 'the Greek myths' is conventionally applied to the whole of the very large and diverse body of traditional tales which the Greeks told about the legendary and timeless past. Some of these had **gods** as their central figures and concerned the origins of things as they are − of the earth, men and women, agriculture and so forth. Myths of this kind were not usually considered suitable material for tragedy, if only because of the obvious practical problems of staging them; Aesch. *PV* is the only surviving exception.

Most myths, however, concerned mortal **heroes** and were set in a world bearing a recognisable resemblance to the world that we know, despite the prominence of monsters, magic and direct intervention by the gods. Of these heroic myths, again, those which were little more than adventure stories were seldom dramatised directly (the 'adventure story' element in such plays as Eur. *IT* and *Hel*. is Euripides' own contribution). The two great legendary wars of **Troy** and **Thebes**, however, provided the subject-matter for several plays, and many more are concerned with the *aftermath* of great events; it is striking how often the conquest of Troy, the defeat of the **Seven against Thebes** or the **Sphinx**, or the exploits of **Heracles**, **Theseus** or **Jason** lie in the *background* of a play's action, forming a glorious past which contrasts painfully with the harsher realities of the present. (Perhaps it is relevant that all the tragedies we have were written in the generations immediately following the Persian Wars: see **Persia**.)

Myths often provide archetypes of human fortunes, against which a person can measure his own experience; tragic choruses, wishing to make sense of events that they have seen, sometimes cite mythical parallels or contrasts (e.g. Aesch. *Cho.* 603-38, Soph. *Phil.* 676-85, Eur. *Med.* 1282-92), and men must often have done the same in real life. The myths most typically selected by the tragedians gain interest and seriousness from confronting some of the most fundamental rules governing relations between human beings, and so in some sense give expression to (and perhaps provide resolution of) men's curiosity and fear concerning these rules.

Often the rules are ones governing relations within the family, and often the myth explores how they might come to be broken, and what would follow if they were. What if, for instance, a son killed his father and married his mother (Soph. *OT*), or killed his mother (Aesch. *Cho.*, Eur. *El.*), or if a son were killed by his father (Eur. *Hipp.*) or mother (Eur. *Bacch.*), or children by their mother (Eur. *Med.*), or a brother by his brother (Aesch. *Sept.*), or a husband by his wife (Aesch. *Ag.*)? Or again, a rule defining obligations towards kindred, far from being broken, can be carried to its logical conclusion; what might, in extreme circumstances, be entailed by a son's duty to his father (Aesch. *Cho.* again), or a daughter's to hers (Soph. *El.*), or a sister's to her brother (Soph. *Ant.*), or a wife's to her husband (Eur. *Alc.*)? To say that the myths offer answers to such questions is not, of course, to say that this exhausts their significance, let alone that of the plays, and it can be seen even from these brief catalogues that different dramatic treatments can bring out different aspects of the same story.

Another crucial framework of rules making civilised life possible was provided by the **city**, and we see that framework being established (Aesch. *Eum.*), threatened by war (Aesch. *Sept.*), and shattered in defeat (Eur. *Tro.*). Again, the rules governing **supplication**, although they may not capture the imagination of a modern audience, were important enough to the Greeks to need exploring in myth and tragedy. At another level all tragedies are to some extent concerned with relations between men and gods, partly because any important rule by which the human world is regulated tends to be given a religious sanction.

Another common function of Greek myths is to explain the origins of particular social and religious customs and institutions. 'Charter myths' of this kind do not usually receive great emphasis in tragedy (exceptions are the foundation of the **Areopagus**, which is an important theme of Aesch. *Eum.*, and that of the hero-cult of **Oedipus**, which is central to Soph. *OC*), but the endings of most of Euripides' plays conform to a common mythical pattern whereby the origin of a custom or institution is somewhat irrelevantly attached to a story which has otherwise been concerned with other things (e.g. Eur. *Med.* 1381-3,

Hipp. 1423-30, *El*. 1268-75).

The Greeks of the fifth century did not distinguish between myth and history. Historical events might be reduced to patterns of mythical type (see **Herodotus**), and conversely the myths themselves were generally assumed to be true in essence, though it was recognised that their details must have suffered distortion and poetic embellishment. Thus no one doubted that there had been a Trojan War, though it was possible to argue about whether **Helen** actually reached **Troy** (Herodotus 2. 116-18) or about the size and tactics of the Greek expedition (Thucydides 1. 10-11). And if a historian, philosopher or **sophist** found a myth incredible or morally objectionable, he would often seek to modify or rationalise it, in the manner of Eur. *Tro*. 971-82, *Bacch*. 286-97, sooner than reject it altogether.

By the late fifth century there was a firm association in men's minds between myths and poets (see e.g. Eur. *Hipp*. 451-2, *HF* 1346, **Plato**, *Republic* 2-3). It is perhaps unlikely that the process of passing down the old tales in unwritten, non-poetic form had in fact ceased, but it does seem that the tragedians usually, if not invariably, found their source material in the work of other poets, whether epic (see **Homer**), lyric (see **Stesichorus**) or tragic (see **originality**). This does not mean, however, that the myths were 'mere' literary convention or that the period of true and creative myth-making was over. It was in the hands of poets that the myths were passed down, recreated and reinterpreted according to the different needs of each generation, and the tragedians themselves were contributing to a process which clearly played a vital role in Greek society.

The audience must have known the myths well (**Aristotle**, *Poetics* 9, surprisingly denies this, but the denial can hardly be valid for the fifth century). So a tragedian can allude in vague terms to, for instance, the stories of **Danae**, **Lycurgus** and **Cleopatra** (Soph. *Ant*. 944-87), or those of **Pasiphae** and **Ariadne** (Eur. *Hipp*. 337-9), and rely on the audience to supply the details. The audience also knew, however, that there were many versions of the myths and that tragedians were capable of diverging widely from any existing version, so they depended on the words of the plays to give them any necessary information about the stories being enacted (this is one of the main functions of Euripides' **prologues**). And, since the tragedians were not engaged in setting puzzles for the audience, we can assume that any feature of a myth which is omitted from a play was considered irrelevant, if not deliberately suppressed, by its author (the mythical entries in this book may mislead any reader who does not bear this point in mind). Thus, if

Sophocles does not tell us the wording of the **Sphinx**'s riddle, we may assume that its wording is not relevant to the interpretation of Soph. *OT*; and, to take a rather more controversial example, if Aeschylus does not tell us that **Agamemnon** offended **Artemis**, we are presumably not entitled to supply this information from other versions of the myth to account for her anger at *Ag.* 134-45, 198-202. However, while almost all scholars would probably agree in principle that a Greek tragedy provides all the mythical information needed for its interpretation, the application of the principle is not free from difficulty; the action of Soph. *El.*, for instance, does not include the onset of the **Erinyes** (see **Orestes**), and the omission must be significant, but there are those who feel that their onset is foreshadowed (especially at *El.* 1498) in such a way that it cannot be left entirely out of account.

It must finally be emphasised that the significance of a play need not correspond closely with that of a myth expressed in non-dramatic terms, and perhaps can never be fully identical with it. To Eur. *Or.*, indeed, and to large parts of some other plays, the existing myth is almost irrelevant, being little more than a conventional starting point for a freely invented plot. Then there are plays in which the tragedian, while following the outline of a traditional story, deliberately gives it a highly personal treatment which draws attention to its novelty; it is not likely that anyone before the author of Aesch. *PV* had used the **Prometheus** story to depict heroic resistance to overwhelming tyrannical power, or that anyone before Sophocles had used the story of **Philoctetes** to explore a conflict between human feeling, self-interest and traditional loyalties within a young man, or that anyone before Euripides had used **Medea** to present the arguments and the emotions of a betrayed woman. Again, a comparison between Aesch. *Cho.*, Soph. *El.* and Eur. *El.* shows at once how completely each tragedian could make the same mythical material his own. But even if a tragedian appeared to be taking a myth at face value and presenting it for its own sake, the mere fact of dramatic treatment would inevitably make a difference, for a dramatist must provide plausible motives for the actions of his characters, and those characters must arouse our sympathy or dislike far more strongly than is possible in a bare mythical narrative. Thus, while the presence of archetypal themes from the myths was clearly considered necessary to give tragedy its proper power, weight and seriousness, the relation between the effect of the myth and the effect of the play is never a straightforward one.

N

Naiads [nī′adz]   **Nymphs** of springs and rivers.

Nauplia [naw′plia]   The port of **Argos**.

necessity   See **fate**.

Neïstan [nē-i′stan] **Gate**   One of the seven gates of **Thebes**.

nemesis   The word means righteous anger or indignation, as provoked by injustice and the like, and can be applied to men or gods (see *hybris*). The goddess Nemesis [ne′mesis], however, personifies not only anger but divine retribution (see **Adrasteia**), and the Nemesis of a dead man is the goddess who avenges wrong done to him.

Neoptolemus [neopto′lemus]   Son of **Achilles**; also (though not in tragedy) called Pyrrhus. Being too young to accompany his father to **Troy**, he was left on **Scyros** in the care of his maternal grandfather **Lycomedes**. In the tenth year of the war, however, when Achilles had been killed, it was prophesied that Troy could not be taken without Neoptolemus's help, and he was therefore fetched from Scyros by **Odysseus** and **Phoenix**. For his part in the story of Philoctetes see **Philoctetes**.
He was prominent in the sack of Troy, as prophesied, and killed King **Priam**, though the picture of him as savage and bloodthirsty on that occasion (mentioned at Eur. *Hec*. 23-4 and familiar from Virgil) does not square with his character in Soph. *Phil*., which recalls **Homer**, *Odyssey* 11. 506-37. **Andromache** was then assigned to him as his slave and concubine, but, having returned with her to **Phthia**, he married Hermione, daughter of **Menelaus** and **Helen**; hence the events of Eur. *Andr*., leading up to his murder by **Orestes**.

Nereids [nē′rē-idz]   Sea-**nymphs**, daughters of the sea-god Nereus. They were imagined as dancing in the water and escorting ships. At Eur. *El*. 442-51 the Nereids, presumably sent by **Thetis**, bring arms made by **Hephaestus** across the sea to the young **Achilles** in **Thessaly**. The curious epithet 'hundred-footed' at Soph. *OC* 718 seems to mean that there were fifty of them (as in **Hesiod** and elsewhere) with two feet each.

Nestor [ne'stor]   King of **Pylos**. He took part in the Trojan War as a very old man, and in **Homer**'s *Iliad* he often gives advice to the other Greek chieftains.

Nietzsche, Friedrich Wilhelm (1844-1900)   The philosopher Nietzsche was trained as a classical scholar, and his first published work was *The Birth of Tragedy from the Spirit of Music*. In this he claimed that Greek tragedy arose from a combination of an 'Apolline' element, which was calm and rational, and a 'Dionysiac' element, which was savage and frenzied; and he hailed the operas of Richard Wagner as its true successors. The book was badly received by Nietzsche's fellow-scholars, who were able to point out many errors, but, like his later works, it has had a deep influence on German culture.

Night   Often personified as a goddess. In **Hesiod** she is the mother of the Moirai (see **fate**) and of various other beings, and Aeschylus makes her also the mother of the **Erinyes**.

nightingale   The bird whose song was most admired by the Greeks; often mentioned in poetry. At Soph. *El*. 149 she is the 'messenger of **Zeus**' as harbinger of spring, the seasons being in Zeus's charge. For the myth of Procne see **Itys**.

Nike [ni'kē]   Victory, whether in war or in other forms of contest, personified as a goddess, and often identified with **Athena**.

Nile   See **Io's wanderings, Paphos**.

Niobe [ni'obē]   Daughter of **Tantalus**; granddaughter of **Zeus**. She came from **Lydia** to **Thebes** to be the wife of **Amphion**. She had many children (the number is variously given), and boasted of having more than **Leto**; so Leto's children, **Apollo** and **Artemis**, killed all of hers with their arrows. In her grief she was turned to stone, and her stone form was supposed to be visible in a crag on Mount **Sipylus** (she had returned to Lydia at some stage), the water that trickled down the crag being her tears. Aeschylus and Sophocles each wrote a play on the subject (for the former see *átē*, **fragments**).

Nisus [ni'sus]   King of Megara (between **Athens** and **Corinth**); father of **Scylla (ii)**.

nymphs   Minor goddesses who presided over the countryside and natural features, such as springs and rivers (**Naiads**), the sea (**Nereids** and Oceanids; see **Oceanus**), caves, mountains and trees. Offerings were made to them at sites that they inhabited. They were usually benevolent, and could promote fertility, so men might **sacrifice** to them in prayer, or in gratitude, for the birth of children. They enjoyed music and dancing, and were often pictured in the company of **Dionysus**, **Pan** or the **satyrs**, or being amorously pursued by them.

Nysa [nĭ'sa]   A mountain sacred to **Dionysus**, whose name seems to be somehow connected with it. It is variously located by different authors; Soph. *Ant*. 1131 is thought to refer to a Nysa on **Euboea**, Eur. *Bacch*. 556 to one in **Thrace**.

O

Oceanus [ō'se-anus]   The Oceanus, or Ocean, was in early times the name of a mythical river that was thought to flow round the edge of the world. It was sometimes said to be the source of all ordinary springs and rivers; at Eur. *Hipp*. 121 it is the source of a particular spring, probably one that actually existed at **Trozen** and flowed throughout the year. As the Greeks' geographical knowledge increased, Oceanus came to be identified with the sea beyond the Pillars of **Heracles**, i.e. the Atlantic.

Oceanus is also personified as a **Titan**, son of **Uranus**, uncle and father-in-law of **Prometheus**. In Aesch. *PV* we must assume that he did not take part in the war between the Titans and **Zeus** (*PV* 199-221), since he is still free to come and give Prometheus his advice (284-396). For his 'four-legged bird' (395) see **griffins**, *deus ex machina*. The scene appears to have been hastily inserted into the play (though probably by the same dramatist as the rest), since it is awkward in various ways; it is especially strange that there is no contact between Oceanus and his daughters.

These daughters are the Oceanids [ō'se-anidz], **nymphs** of the Ocean, who also come to visit Prometheus and who form the Chorus of the play. They arrive flying through the air, like their father, apparently in some sort of winged chariot, or more than one (*PV* 128-35), in which they remain for some time (until 278-81); it is a mystery how this was staged.

ode   The word simply means 'song'; see **chorus**, **monody**, *parodos* **(i)**, *stasimon*, **verse**.

Odysseus [odi′sūs]   King of **Ithaca**; son of either **Laertes** or **Sisyphus** (the latter is meant at Soph. *Phil*. 625). He was said (though not by **Homer**) to have feigned madness in order to avoid joining the expedition to **Troy**; the man who exposed the pretence and forced him to join was Palamedes, son of Nauplius (see **Caphereus**). In revenge for this, Odysseus treacherously killed Palamedes in the course of the Trojan War; this was the subject of Euripides' *Palamedes*, the second play of the **tetralogy** to which Eur. *Tro*. belongs. In Homer's *Iliad* he is a moderately prominent character, and in particular he and **Diomedes** steal the horses of **Rhesus** in *Iliad* 10 (compare Eur. *Rhes*.). Later the arms of the dead **Achilles** were awarded to him; and he was involved, by most accounts, in fetching **Philoctetes** to Troy. He was one of the warriors in the Wooden Horse, and, after the sack of Troy, **Hecabe** was assigned to him as a slave (according to Eur. *Tro*. 277, but not according to Homer). Homer's *Odyssey* tells the story of his adventures on his way home to Ithaca and on his arrival there (briefly summarised at Eur. *Tro*. 433-43); for Eur. *Cycl*. see **Cyclops**.

In Homer we are invited to admire Odysseus for his resourcefulness, heroic endurance, and other qualities. Later Greeks, however, were sometimes repelled by his tendency to trickery and deception in the *Odyssey*, and hence he is often presented in tragedy as a thoroughly unattractive personality (though there are exceptions, and the Odysseus of Soph. *Aj*. is quite unlike that of Soph. *Phil*.). He is a character in Soph. *Aj*., *Phil*., Eur. *Hec*., *Rhes*., *Cycl*.

Oea [ē′a]   A district of **Attica**. The 'snowy rock of Oea' (Soph. *OC* 1060-1) is probably part of Mount Aegaleus, between **Athens** and **Eleusis**.

Oechalia [ēkā′lia]   The city of **Eurytus**, situated on **Euboea** according to Soph. *Trach*.; see **Heracles**.

Oecles [ē′klēz]   Father of **Amphiaraus**.

Oedipus [ē′dipus] (adjective 'Oedipal' in psychoanalytic contexts only; otherwise 'Oedipodean' [-ē′an])   Son of **Laius** and **Jocasta**; King of **Thebes**; husband of **Jocasta**; father of **Eteocles**, **Polynices**, **Antigone** and **Ismene** (Fig. 3). He is the subject of one of the most famous Greek myths, often dramatised by the tragedians. His name was believed to mean 'swollen-footed', and was explained by the notion that his ankles were pierced when he was exposed in infancy (Soph. *OT* 1034-6). The following is his story as we know it from Soph. *OT* and *OC*.

Before his birth the **oracle** of **Apollo** foretold that he would kill his father. When he was born, therefore, Laius commanded a servant, who tended the royal flocks on Mount **Cithaeron**, to expose the baby there. The servant, however, took pity on the baby, and gave him to a Corinthian shepherd, who gave him in turn to **Polybus**, King of **Corinth** (see Plate V).

Polybus and his wife **Merope** brought Oedipus up as their own son. When he grew to manhood, however, he heard a rumour that he was not their son, and went to the oracle at **Delphi** to learn his true parentage. The oracle, instead of answering this question, declared that he would kill his father and marry his mother. Still assuming that these were Polybus and Merope, he resolved to stay far away from Corinth.

On his way from Delphi, at the junction of three roads, he encountered Laius, travelling with four attendants to consult the oracle again. There was a quarrel, and Oedipus, not unprovoked, killed the King without learning his identity, and also killed three of the attendants. The fourth attendant happened to be the same servant who had failed to expose Oedipus in his infancy, and soon afterwards this man, realising who Oedipus was, insisted on leaving Thebes.

Oedipus came to Thebes, which at this time was being plagued by a monster, the **Sphinx**, destined to prey on the Thebans until someone should succeed in answering its riddle. Oedipus did so, and thus destroyed the monster. He was therefore made King of Thebes, and married Jocasta, not knowing that she was his mother. (The improbabilities in this part of the story will be far more apparent when it is set out in order like this than when its events are revealed piecemeal, as they are in Soph. *OT*.)

Because of the parricide and incest, Oedipus and Thebes were now the victims of a terrible **pollution**. A few years later, therefore, when Jocasta had borne Oedipus four children, Thebes was visited with plague. It is at this point that Soph. *OT* begins, and the play shows Oedipus, the good and conscientious king, making enquiries through the Delphic Oracle, the **seer Tiresias**, Jocasta, and the Corinthian and Theban shepherds, and finally learning the whole truth. This causes Jocasta to hang herself and Oedipus to blind himself.

After the events of *OT* power passed to Jocasta's brother **Creon (i)**, since Oedipus's sons, Eteocles and Polynices, were not old enough to rule. Creon expelled Oedipus from Thebes, and he wandered about Greece as a blind beggar, later ministered to by his two daughters, Antigone and Ismene, but neglected by his sons.

But he was still marked out by the gods for a special fate: he was to be honoured as a **hero** after his death, with power to help or harm men from the grave. Apollo's oracle had at some stage declared that he would end his life and acquire this power when he reached the seat of the **Eumenides**. Later the oracle told the Thebans that the welfare of their city would depend on Oedipus after his death. Meanwhile, however, Eteocles and Polynices had quarrelled over the inheritance, and Eteocles, allied with Creon, had exiled Polynices, who had gone to **Argos** to raise an army with which to attack his own city.

At the beginning of Soph. *OC* Oedipus, guided by Antigone, reaches the sacred grove of the Eumenides at **Colonus**, near **Athens**. He realises that this is where he must die, becomes a suppliant (see **supplication**) at the grove, and wins the friendship of **Theseus**, King of Athens. Creon arrives, wanting to bring him back to Thebes so that he can be buried, not in Theban soil, but near the border where his tomb can be kept under Theban control; but Oedipus sees that Creon is motivated by self-interest, not pity, and refuses to go. Creon's attempt to force him away by abducting Antigone and Ismene is defeated by Theseus. Polynices comes to seek his father's forgiveness, knowing that this would bring him victory over Eteocles, but receives only his **curse**: Polynices and Eteocles are to die at one another's hands. Oedipus is already revealed as wrathful and powerful, as he will be after his death. The gods send for him; he leads Theseus, Antigone and Ismene from the stage and departs from life at a spot known only to Theseus, resolved to help Athens against Thebes in the future.

Many of the details given above will be Sophocles' invention, though it is impossible to say precisely how far this extends (see **myth**, **originality**). Certainly other surviving versions of the story show considerable variations, especially in their later stages. **Homer** (*Odyssey* 11. 271-80, *Iliad* 23. 679-80) seems to have known a version in which Oedipus did not blind himself at all, but died in battle at Thebes. Aeschylus and Euripides each wrote an *Oedipus* which has not survived; that of Aeschylus belonged to the same **tetralogy** as Aesch. *Sept*. (see **Seven against Thebes**). At Aesch. *Sept*. 780-90 the curse on the sons, like the self-blinding, follows directly after Oedipus's discovery of his incest (for the terms of the curse see **Chalybes**). Soph. *Ant*. 49-54 does not mention a period of exile, and suggests (but may not actually mean) that Oedipus died before Jocasta. Eur. *Phoen*. has the blind

Oedipus, as well as Jocasta, still living at Thebes at the time of the war between Eteocles and Polynices.

For the Oedipus Complex see **Freud**.

Oeneus [ē'nūs]　King of Calydon in **Aetolia**; husband of **Althaea**; father of Meleager and **Tydeus**.

Oenops [ē'nops]　Father of **Hyperbius** and **Actor**.

Oeta [ē'ta] (adjective Oetaean [ētē'an])　A mountain dominating **Malis**; the scene of **Heracles'** death.

olive　The olive was an essential part of the Greeks' diet, and its oil was used for various purposes. Although it was a staple crop of most parts of Greece, it was especially associated with **Attica**, and the Athenians liked to believe that it was a gift to them from **Athena** herself; the original olive tree that had sprung up on the **Acropolis** at her command was said to have renewed itself after being burnt by the Persians (**Herodotus** 8. 55). When Soph. *OC* 694-706 was written, however, there had been a Spartan force in Attica for some years, and, if any olive trees were left standing, the Athenians had no access to them (see **Peloponnesian War**).

Olympia [oli'mpia] (adjective usually Olympic)　A town of Elis in the western **Peloponnese**; site of a very important cult of **Zeus**, and of the Olympic Games.

Olympus [oli'mpus] (adjective Olympian)　A mountain to the north of **Thessaly**, believed to be the home or meeting place of the gods. But the gods are often thought of as existing in some invisible place in the sky, and this can be so even when the name Olympus is used. The Olympian gods are the great Panhellenic gods of the upper world, as opposed to those of the **Underworld** and to minor or local deities.

When, however, the Chorus of Eur. *Bacch.* refer to Olympus as a haunt of the **Muses** and **Dionysus** (411, 561), they are thinking of the particular Thessalian mountain and not of the home of the gods in general.

omens　Like **oracles** and the prophecies of **seers**, omens are important in Greek literature as means of foreshadowing future events and making them seem inevitable and aesthetically right when they occur. Many kinds of 'chance' occurrence can be seen as tokens of the gods' will and as pointing to future events in this way; various possibilities are listed at Aesch. *PV* 484-99, where divination is treated as one of the essential skills of civilised life. **Prometheus** here mentions **dreams**; chance-utterances (*klēdones*, remarks which bear a meaning unintended by the speaker; see **irony**); things seen by the wayside while travelling (the sight of a funeral procession or a black animal, for instance, would be unlucky); the flight and behaviour of birds (at Aesch. *Ag.* 104-20 the omen of the eagles and hare, seen by the wayside, comes into two of Prometheus's categories); the appearance of the innards of sacrificed animals (see **sacrifice** and Eur. *El.* 826-9); the way in which the bones and fat burnt after a sacrifice (see Soph. *Ant.* 1005-11); and the appear-ance of flames, probably also in a sacrificial context.

As Prometheus also makes clear, omens require interpretation; and indeed it is often felt to be the act of interpretation − of seeing a certain meaning in a chance occurrence or utterance − that determines what the future will in fact bring. Thus **Eteocles** in Aesch. *Sept.* must interpret the shield-blazons of the **Seven against Thebes** in a sense unfavourable to them if they are to be defeated; and the Chorus at Aesch. *Ag.* 1653 are quick to 'accept the omen' when **Aegisthus** happens to remark that he does not refuse to die.

Omens seen in the flight of birds or in sacrificial rituals are more obscure (though those described in literature naturally tend to be clearer than any that could be expected in real life), and usually need the professional skill of seers, such as **Tiresias** at Aesch. *Sept.* 24-6 and Soph. *Ant.* 998-1022, or **Calchas** at Aesch. *Ag.* 104-59. In two of these passages there is a rather complex and curious relation between omens and events; the harsh cries of birds and the smoky sacrifices in *Ant.* are not merely symbols but direct *results* of the city's **pollution**, while the eagles devouring the pregnant hare in *Ag.* seem to provide not only a symbol of the destruction of **Troy** but a *cause* of the anger of **Artemis**.

A superstition similar to that concerning *klēdones* sees names as revealing the nature or fortunes of the people or things that bear them. Thus the kind of word-play that is found at Aesch. *Ag.* 681-98 (see **Helen**) or Eur. *Bacch.* 367, 508 (see **Pentheus**) draws attention to some-thing that is felt to be significant precisely because it may at first sight seem fortuitous (for other examples see **Eteocles, Polynices, justice**).

Onca [o'ngka]   A goddess of **Thebes**, whose shrine apparently stood outside one of the seven gates of the city. She is sometimes identified with **Athena** (Aesch. *Sept*. 487, 501), but sometimes distinct from her (*Sept*. 164).

oracles   The word is used both of the shrines at which questions are believed to receive divinely inspired answers and of the answers themselves. In what follows it will be restricted to the former sense.

Men in all ages feel a need to know what they should do and what the future holds, and the function that is now performed by horoscopes and the like was performed in the ancient world by oracles, **seers** and **omens** − though these things were taken much more seriously than their modern equivalents, being central to established religion. Scepticism in such matters was possible in the fifth century (see **sophists**), but certainly unusual; the exceptionally shrewd and knowledgeable **Herodotus** treats prophecy of all kinds with the greatest respect.

There were oracles throughout Greece (see **Dodona**, **Abae**, **Ismenus**, **Amphiaraus**), but by far the most important, both in literature and in life, was that of **Apollo** at **Delphi**. There the god spoke through the mouth of a priestess, the Pythia (a character in Aesch. *Eum*. and Eur. *Ion*), who received inspiration while sitting on a sacred tripod in the inmost part of the temple. Many details of the procedure are uncertain, however; some believe that the Pythia was in a trance and uttered incoherent sounds that had to be interpreted by male **priests**, others that she answered questions lucidly and directly. Certainly it was possible to blame the priests for an oracle that was not fulfilled (Soph. *OT* 711-12). It appears from Soph. *OT* 82-3, Eur. *Hipp*. 806-7, that those returning from consulting an oracle might wear garlands in token of a favourable response.

It is likely that most oracular responses in real life were no more than instructions for religious observances. Literature and legend, however, naturally tended to deal in prophecies of the future, spectacularly fulfilled. Everything turned on the actual words, so that, if a prophecy was fulfilled only in a paradoxical and unexpected sense, this was felt to bring credit rather than discredit on the god. Such ambiguous and misunderstood prophecies are a useful way of producing dramatic **irony**, though they are at least as common in Herodotus as in tragedy.

The oracular response could be a statement about the present (e.g. in Soph. *OT*, '**Thebes** is polluted by the murderer of **Laius**'); or a statement about the future, whether unconditional (e.g. '**Oedipus** will kill his father and marry his mother') or conditional (e.g. in Soph. *OC*, 'Thebes will suffer if it does not control the tomb of Oedipus'); or a command (e.g. 'the murderer of Laius must be banished or killed' − all these examples have been simplified for the sake of illustration). These different possibilities show that a belief in oracular prediction did not involve belief in predestination, excluding human freedom of choice (see **fate**); indeed men usually want to know the future precisely *because* they hope to be able to do something about it. Nor should it be assumed, when an oracle issues a prophetic statement (as opposed to a command), that the god necessarily desires the event prophesied or will be responsible for bringing it about. The line between prediction and causation can easily be overstepped, however, especially by people who are looking back after the event, and there are some places in tragedy where Apollo does seem to be felt to have brought about what his oracle first predicted (e.g. Aesch. *Sept.* 689-91, Soph. *OT* 1329-30).

The importance of oracles in Greek tragedy can be explained by their serious and central role in Greek religion; by the usefulness of an oracular command in determining the moral and religious attitude of the audience to an action in a play; and by the usefulness of an oracular prediction in shaping a play by making its dénouement inevitable from an early stage.

orchēstrā   The large circular 'dancing area' in the middle of the theatre (Plate I). For most of the time the **chorus** performed on the floor of the *orchēstrā*, the **actors** (probably) on a raised stage at the back of it, against the façade of the scene-building (*skēnē*), though this did not prevent frequent interaction between chorus and actors.

Oresteia [oresti'a]   See **tetralogy**, **Stesichorus**.

Orestes [ore'stēz]   Son of **Agamemnon** and **Clytemnestra** (Fig. 2). At the time of Agamemnon's murder he was still a small child, and had been sent away (by Clytemnestra according to Aeschylus, by his sister **Electra** according to Sophocles, by his *paidagōgos* according to Euripides) to **Phocis**, where he was brought up by King **Strophius**. When he reached manhood, he returned home with Strophius's son **Pylades** to avenge his father by killing Clytemnestra and **Aegisthus**. For the earliest references to Orestes' revenge see **Homer**, *Odyssey* 1. 40-1, 298-300, 3. 304-10; here the killing of Aegisthus wins strong approval, and that of Clytemnestra is barely hinted at.

After this, according to Aeschylus and Euripides, he was pursued by the **Erinyes** of Clytemnestra until he was put on trial for the matricide before the Council of the **Areopagus** at **Athens**, and acquitted. The various plays, however (Aesch. *Eum.*, Eur. *El.*, *Or.*, *IT*, *Andr.*), while agreeing on these essential points, give very diverse accounts of his fortunes in other respects. In Eur. *Or*. Orestes and Electra narrowly escape being put to death by the people of **Argos**, and become involved in other melodramatic adventures. At one stage (Eur. *El*. 1273-5, *Or*. 1643-7) Orestes went to live in **Arcadia**, which had legends of its own concerning him, and founded the city of Orest(h)eum.

In Soph. *El*., which is less concerned with the moral problem of the matricide, Orestes is not pursued by the Erinyes at all, though the usual version of the story is not positively contradicted, since the play ends too soon after the killings for us to be sure that all is well.

originality   The Greek tragedians did not invent their plots and main characters from scratch, any more than Shakespeare or Racine. But the extent to which their work corresponds to existing **myth** or literature varies greatly from play to play. At one extreme Eur. *Or*. evidently consists of virtually free invention from a mythical starting point, and the same may be almost equally true of Aesch. *Eum*. and Soph. *Ant*. At the other extreme, apart from the special cases of Eur. *Rhes*. and *Cycl*. (based on **Homer**), Soph. *El*. is constructed throughout in such a way as to recall Aesch. *Cho*. and to invite comparison with it (see **Electra**).

Certainly the need to use existing myths did not seriously restrict the range of plots that could be presented. The myths themselves were sufficiently diverse to include most kinds of human conflict or relationship in which the Greeks were interested, and anyway they could be drastically modified where necessary. With **character** the dramatist had a free hand; one of the most familiar figures in pre-dramatic literature was **Odysseus**, but the plays could present him as a scheming villain (Soph. *Phil*., Eur. *Hec*.) or a model of thoughtfulness and decency (Soph. *Aj*.) as required. It follows that the moral emphasis of the stories was equally firmly in the dramatists' control: we are invited to sympathise with **Eteocles** against **Polynices** in Aesch. *Sept*., with Polynices against Eteocles in Eur. *Phoen*.

It is true that, if a dramatist handles a story that already exists, the plot of his play, in its broadest outlines, will be known to the audience in advance (if **Agamemnon** is returning from **Troy**, for instance, he must be killed). But this brings great advantages in terms of the dramatic **irony**, and the sense of foreboding or inevitability, which the dramatist can create or exploit, without preventing him from also creating suspense and surprise in the working out of his plot (it is by no means inevitable that Agamemnon will be killed by **Clytemnestra** and not by **Aegisthus**). Again, the taking over of old stories helps the audience to perceive the distinctive style and vision of the individual dramatists; when critics today want to illustrate the difference between Aeschylus, Sophocles and Euripides, they often pick Aesch. *Cho.*, Soph. *El.* and Eur. *El.*, precisely because all three plays use the same mythical material.

As one ancient critic wrote, 'When we see that Sophocles, Euripides and many others have treated the story of Thyestes and that of Paris and Menelaus and that of Electra and so forth, it is not on this basis that we judge some better than others, but we often rate those who have taken over the material more highly than their predecessors, if they contribute a higher degree of poetic excellence' (Philodemus, first century BC).

Orpheus [or'fūs]   A musician from **Thrace**, who sang so sweetly that even the trees and wild animals followed him. At Eur. *Bacch.* 562 it is probably because of his connection with the **Muses** of **Pieria** that he is placed on Mount **Olympus**. He is sometimes associated with **Dionysus**, though according to one story he resisted the god and suffered the same fate as **Pentheus**.

In the fifth century Orpheus was also believed to have been the founder of certain mystery cults, which promised eternal happiness for the souls of their initiates (see **death and burial**). The sacred writings of such cults, attributed to Orpheus himself, tended to prescribe vegetarianism, periods of sexual abstinence, and perhaps participation in ecstatic rites like those associated with Dionysus. This is the reason for the wording of Eur. *Hipp.* 952-4, where **Theseus**, attacking **Hippolytus** for his supposedly hypocritical display of purity, scornfully treats him as an Orphic and associates him with various Orphic practices.

Ossa [o'sa]   A mountain in **Thessaly**.

Ouranos   See **Uranus**.

P

Pactolus [paktō'lus]   A stream flowing through **Sardis** in **Lydia**, believed to bring down gold dust from Mount **Tmolus**.

paean [pē'an]   The word seems to have originated as a ritual cry addressed to **Apollo**. From this it developed in two directions. Firstly it became a title by which Apollo is invoked in his capacity of Healer by those wanting release from literal or figurative illness; and hence it can mean 'healer' in general. Secondly it came to mean a song of jubilation, of a kind traditionally addressed to Apollo. Paeans were sung to celebrate victory in war, but also to create an auspicious and festive atmosphere on other occasions, as at the pouring of **libations** at a banquet (see also **Iphigenia**). To talk of a paean of the **Erinyes** (Aesch. *Ag*. 645) or of the dead (Aesch. *Cho*. 151) is to use the word in a highly paradoxical sense, reversing its normal associations.

paidagōgos   A trusted slave who was placed in charge of his master's children, giving them elementary education when they were very young and later taking them to school; usually translated 'tutor'.

Pallantids [pa'lantidz] or **Pallantidae** [pala'ntidē]   The sons of **Pallas (ii)**, who was a brother of **Aegeus** (Fig. 4). **Pandion** divided **Attica** between Aegeus, Pallas and two other sons. The Pallantids later disputed the right of Aegeus's son **Theseus** to inherit his father's share; battle was joined, and Theseus killed them all. At Eur. *Hipp*. 34-7 the presence of Theseus and his family in **Trozen** is explained by the need for a year's exile from **Athens** to expiate the **pollution** arising from this killing.

Pallas [pa'las]   (i) A name of **Athena**. (ii) Father of the **Pallantids** (Fig. 4).

Pan [pan]   A god of nature, fertility and animals, wild or domesticated. He is pictured as having the horns and feet of a goat, as playing on reed pipes like a shepherd, and as roaming the countryside in the company, or in pursuit, of **nymphs**. Being a shepherd god, he brought the golden lamb to **Atreus** (see **Thyestes**). He was also responsible for sudden attacks of madness or irrational fear.

Pandion [pandi'on]   King of **Athens**; father of **Aegeus** (Fig. 4); son, perhaps, of **Erechtheus** or **Cecrops** (but the genealogy of these figures is confused and contradictory).

Panhellenes [pa'nhelēnz]   See **Hellas**.

Paphos [pa'fos]   A city on the south-west shore of **Cyprus**, where **Aphrodite** was worshipped. It is not certain how it can be said to be fertilised by the Nile (Eur. *Bacch.* 406-8), but it is possible that water from the Nile was believed to be borne under the sea and to issue in springs near the city.

Paris [pa′ris]   Son of **Priam** and **Hecabe**; often called Alexander. Before he was born, Hecabe dreamed that she had given birth to a firebrand. The baby was therefore exposed on Mount **Ida**, where, however, he survived and was brought up by a shepherd, in ignorance of his own identity.

Either while he still lived there or at a later stage he was appointed by the three goddesses **Athena**, **Hera** and **Aphrodite** to choose which of them was the fairest. Each of the three offered him a bribe (according to Eur. *Tro.* 925-31, contradicted at 971-6), Athena promising military glory, Hera sovereignty over a large empire, and Aphrodite the most beautiful woman in the world. He chose Aphrodite, thus gaining her favour, and the hatred of Athena and Hera, for the future. The Judgement of Paris is often mentioned by Euripides; besides the passages of *Tro.* cited above see *Andr.* 274-92, *IA* 573-81, 1283-309.

After (or before) this came the events portrayed in Euripides' *Alexander*, the first of the plays that accompanied the *Trojan Women* (see **tetralogy, Troy**). Its plot happens to be known in some detail. Paris quarrelled with his fellow-shepherds and was brought by them to Troy, where Priam allowed him to compete in certain games. In these games he defeated his brothers, who were indignant at being beaten by a mere slave; so Hecabe plotted his death, urged on by **Cassandra**, who foretold the destruction of Troy. The murder was prevented; Paris's true identity was at last revealed by the shepherd who had brought him up; and he was accepted by his parents as a Trojan prince.

He then sailed to Greece to claim the reward promised by Aphrodite, and treacherously abducted **Helen** while enjoying the hospitality of her husband **Menelaus**, thus provoking the Trojan War. In **Homer**'s *Iliad* he is ambivalently portrayed, being sometimes a fine warrior but often an indolent and lecherous coward, much inferior to his brother **Hector**. The latter portrayal is generally followed in tragedy. Near the end of the war he managed (according to some authors) to kill **Achilles** with the help of **Apollo**, but he was himself killed by **Philoctetes**.

Parnassus [parna′sus]   A mountain in **Phocis**, dominating **Delphi**. At Soph. *Ant.* 1143-4 Parnassus and the **Euripus** are mentioned as barriers on the routes to **Thebes** from Delphi and **Nysa** respectively.

parodos (plural *parodoi*)   **(i)** The first song of the **chorus**, normally sung immediately on its entry. The *parodos* sometimes consists of an *amoibaion*, but otherwise it does not differ in form from a *stasimon* (as generally defined).

(ii) Either of the two entrance-ramps between the scene-building (*skēnē*) and the seats of the theatre (Plate I; also called *eisodos*). These were used for all entrances and exits to or from the *orchēstrā* other than entrances and exits through the door of the scene-building.

Parthenopaeus [parthenopē'us]   Son of Melanion and of **Atalanta** of **Arcadia**; one of the **Seven against Thebes**. His name suggests 'maiden-faced', and Aesch. *Sept.* 532-7 alludes to this; his face is indeed maidenly but his mood and expression are not. At Soph. *OC* 1321-2, however, the name is explained by the long virginity of his mother before his conception.

Pasiphae [pasi'fā-ē]   Wife of **Minos**; mother of **Phaedra** and **Ariadne** (Fig. 4); mentioned, though unnamed, at Eur. *Hipp.* 337, where Phaedra is hinting at her own guilty passion by mentioning those of her mother and sister. Pasiphae fell in love with a bull and gratified her lust for it by concealing herself within an artificial cow; as a result she gave birth to the Minotaur, half man and half bull (see **Theseus**).

Patroclus [patro'klus]   See **Achilles**; for his death see **Homer**, *Iliad* 16.

Pegasus [pe'gasus]   See **Chimaera**.

Peirene   See **Pirene**.

Peirithous   See **Pirithous**.

peithō   See **persuasion**.

Pelasgus [pela'sgus]   An early king of **Argos**, which is occasionally called Pelasgia [pela'sjia] after him; for Aesch. *Supp.* see **Danaids (i)**.

Peleus [pē'lūs]   King of **Phthia**; husband of **Thetis**; father of **Achilles**; a character in Eur. *Andr.*; see also **Acastus**.

Pelias [pe'lias]   Usurper of the throne of **Iolcus**; father of **Acastus**; stepfather of **Jason**, whom he sent on the quest of the Golden Fleece. For his death at the hands of his daughters see **Medea**.

Pelion [pē'lion]   A mountain dominating **Iolcus**; home of Chiron (see **Achilles**); source of the pine wood from which the ship Argo was made (see **Jason**).

Peloponnese [pe'loponēs]   The part of Greece south of the Corinthian and **Saronic** Gulfs, connected to the mainland by the **Isthmus** of **Corinth**. The name means Island of **Pelops**, and it is sometimes referred to in poetry by other phrases of similar meaning; see also **Achaea**, **Apian Land**.

Peloponnesian War   This was the war that was fought from 431 until the Athenian defeat in 404 between an alliance led by **Athens** and an alliance led by **Sparta**. (The name 'First Peloponnesian War' is sometimes given to an earlier period of conflict, from about 460 to 446.) The allies of Athens included, for most of the war, almost all the islands of the **Aegean** and the cities on its northern and eastern coasts. Those of Sparta, though loosely known as the Peloponnesians, included some cities outside the **Peloponnese**, such as **Thebes** and Megara, while **Argos** within the Peloponnese was neutral for most of the war. There was a partial respite in the fighting from 421 to 415, in which year Athens launched a huge expedition against **Sicily**; the total defeat of this expedition in 413 was the turning point of the war. From 413 on there was a Spartan force continuously encamped in **Attica**, and the whole population was therefore confined within the city walls; but even in these conditions the production of tragedies and comedies continued. The course of the war was recorded by the historians Thucydides and Xenophon.

Considering that most surviving tragedies were produced during this war, it had remarkably little impact on them (see **politics**). No one would be likely to guess, for instance, from Eur. *Med.* that **Corinth** was actively fomenting war with Athens when the play was produced (in 431), or from Eur. *Phoen.* that Thebes would shortly be urging Sparta to raze Athens to the ground. There is, however, some anti-Spartan feeling displayed in Eur. *Andr.*; Eur. *Supp.* probably reflects a dispute over the burial of the dead after a battle between Athens and Thebes (the Battle of Delium) in 424, and certainly advocates alliance with Argos; and the hostility of Thebes is relevant to Soph. *OC*.

Eur. *Tro.* has often been seen as a protest against an episode in 416, when Athens, with very little provocation, attacked the neutral island of Melos, and, having captured it, put the adult male inhabitants to death and enslaved the women and children (Thucydides 5. 84-116). It is unfortunate for this theory that Euripides' **tetralogy** laid great stress on the provocation for the Greek attack on **Troy** (see **Paris**); that the crimes of which the Greeks are accused in *Tro.* (dragging **Cassandra** from a sacred image, sacrificing **Polyxena**, killing **Astyanax**, failing to kill **Helen**) do not correspond at all with any that the Athenians are known to have committed at Melos; and that the Chorus goes out of its way to praise Athens at *Tro.* 208-9, 218-19. The other places named at *Tro.* 205-29 raise more serious problems of contemporary reference; see **Corinth, Thessaly, Sicily, Crathis.**

Pelops [pe′lops] Son of **Tantalus**; father of **Atreus** and **Thyestes** (Fig. 2), and also of **Pittheus**. He gave his name to the **Peloponnese**, which is often called 'Land of Pelops' and the like.

According to a story mentioned by Sophocles (*El.* 504-15) and Euripides (*Or.* 987-94), but not by Aeschylus, the curse on the **House** of Atreus had its origin in a crime committed by Pelops. In order to win the hand of the daughter of a certain King Oenomaus, he had to compete with the King in a chariot race. He bribed the King's servant Myrtilus to remove the lynch-pins of his master's chariot wheels, thus causing the King to fall to his death. Instead of rewarding Myrtilus, however, he flung him into the sea, and Myrtilus cursed the family before he drowned.

Peneus [penē′us] The main river of **Thessaly**, south of Mount **Olympus.**

Pentheus [pe′nthūs] King of **Thebes**; son of **Echion** and **Agave**; grandson of **Cadmus**; cousin of **Dionysus** and **Actaeon** (Fig. 3). The story of how he denied the divinity of Dionysus and was torn apart by the **Maenads** was told in at least one lost play of Aeschylus as well as in Eur. *Bacch.*, and is parallel to stories told of **Lycurgus** and **Orpheus**. His name means 'man of grief (*penthos*)'; hence the word-play at *Bacch.* 367, 508.

Peparethus [peparē′thus] An island off the coast of **Thessaly**, famous for its wine.

Pergamum [per'gamum] and **Pergama** [per'gama]   Names for **Troy** or its citadel.

peripeteia   Aristotle's term (*Poetics* 11) for the 'reversal' which he considers to be a feature of the best type of tragedy, and which he closely associates with *anagnōrisis*, 'recognition'. It is perhaps unnecessary in practice to decide whether he means reversal of the expectation of the audience or reversal of the situation, intention or expectation of the characters; a *peripeteia* will occur as long as events seem, to anyone who does not know the story, to be leading to a certain outcome, but in fact lead to the opposite outcome. Thus in the case of Soph. *OT*, which Aristotle mentions, the natural consequence of the words of the Corinthian messenger would be to comfort **Oedipus**, but they in fact lead to the confirmation of his worst fears. Clear cases of *peripeteia* combined with *anagnōrisis* at the climax of a play occur in Soph. *El.*, Eur. *IT*, *Ion*, and it is doubtless plays like these that Aristotle has principally in mind in talking of 'complex' tragedies (*Poetics* 10); but, as with so many of Aristotle's terms, it is doubtful how far the words *peripeteia* and 'complex' extend.

Perithus [pe'rithus]   See **Pirithous**.

Persephone [perse'fonē]   Queen of the **Underworld**; consort of **Hades**; in tragedy called **Persephassa** [persefa'sa] or **Phersephassa**.

Perseus [per'sūs]   A prominent hero, son of **Zeus** and **Danae**. He acquired winged sandals with which he was able to fly over the sea, escorted by **Hermes** in some versions of the story, and he killed the **Gorgon** Medusa and brought her head back to Greece.

Persia   Persia proper, or Persis, was a land to the north of the Persian Gulf, much smaller than modern Iran. From the middle of the sixth century, however (see **Medes**), it controlled a great empire, including all of Asia Minor (except, from the 470s, for the Greek cities on the **Aegean** coast), **Syria**, **Egypt**, and many lands to the east as far as the Indus.

  A Persian punitive expedition against **Athens** (which had aided an abortive revolt by the Greek cities of Ionia under Persian rule) was defeated at the Battle of Marathon in 490. Later a full-scale invasion of Greece under the Persian King Xerxes was defeated by sea at the Battle of **Salamis** (480), in which Athens played a leading role, and on land at the Battle of Plataea (479). These were the main events of the Persian Wars, recorded by **Herodotus**. Aeschylus fought at Marathon, probably at Salamis, and possibly at Plataea also. In his *Persians*, the only surviving tragedy on a historical theme, the news of the Persian defeat at Salamis is brought to the Queen and elders in the Persian capital, and Xerxes arrives home in rags.

persuasion   The word (*peithō* in Greek) is very prominent in the *Oresteia* and other tragedies, sometimes being personified as a goddess. In a bad sense, as at Aesch. *Ag*. 385, it can come close to 'temptation', not necessarily by words; in a good sense, as at Aesch. *Eum*. 970, it can indicate peaceful persuasion as opposed to the use of force. The prominence of the word reflects the same interest in the ways in which men may be influenced for good or ill, especially through speech, as is seen in the development of Greek **rhetoric** and the concerns of the **Sophists**.

Phaedra [fē'dra]   Daughter of **Minos** and **Pasiphae**; granddaughter of **Zeus**; sister of **Ariadne**; wife of **Theseus** (Fig. 4). For her story see **Hippolytus**.

Phaethon [fā'ethon]   Son of **Helios**. The story of how he tried to drive his father's chariot and crashed to his death was told in Euripides' *Phaethon*, parts of which survive (see **fragments**). His sisters, the Heliades, mourned for him, and were turned into black poplars beside the river **Eridanus**, the tears that they shed becoming beads of amber.

Phanoteus [fa'notūs]   A Phocian, brother of **Strophius**'s father, but an enemy to him and his family, and therefore a plausible ally for **Clytemnestra** and **Aegisthus**.

Phasis [fā'sis]   A river flowing into the eastern end of the Black Sea.

Pheres [fe'rēz]   Father of **Alcestis**'s husband Admetus.

Phersephassa [fersefa'sa]   See **Persephone**.

Philoctetes [filoktē'tēz]   Son of **Poeas** of **Malis**. He was the only man with the courage to set light to the pyre of **Heracles** on Mount **Oeta**, so as to release the hero from his agony. He thus earned the invincible bow and arrows of Heracles as a reward.

Later he joined the Greek expedition against **Troy**. On the way there, however, the Greeks put in at the small island of **Chryse** to sacrifice to a local goddess, also called Chryse. On approaching her precinct, Philoctetes was bitten in the foot by a snake which guarded it. When the wound festered, the other Greeks were unable to bear its stench and Philoctetes' cries, so they abandoned him on the nearby island of **Lemnos** before sailing on.

There he survived by shooting animals with his bow until the tenth year of the Trojan War. In that year the captured Trojan prophet **Helenus** told the Greeks that they could never conquer Troy without the aid of both **Neoptolemus** and Philoctetes (but Soph. *Phil.*, for good dramatic reasons, leaves us uncertain whether the prophecy specified the bringing of Philoctetes himself or his bow or both).

Before Soph. *Phil.* was written, the story of how Philoctetes was brought from Lemnos to Troy had been handled by Aeschylus and Euripides, as well as in an earlier epic poem. In the epic he was fetched by **Diomedes**; in Aeschylus by **Odysseus**; in Euripides by Odysseus and Diomedes; and in Sophocles by Odysseus and Neoptolemus, the role of the latter being a crucial innovation (though Euripides' version is recalled in the False Merchant's story at Soph. *Phil.* 570, 592). In both Aeschylus and Euripides Odysseus confronted Philoctetes face to face without being recognised (he was disguised by **Athena** in Euripides), and both dramatists made Lemnos an inhabited island (as in reality), the Chorus being composed of Lemnians (and not of sailors, as in Sophocles). We know several more details about the lost plays (Euripides introduced Trojan envoys, who urged Philoctetes to take the Trojan side), but we cannot be sure in either case how the fetching of Philoctetes was finally achieved (the intervention of Heracles being doubtless Sophocles' invention).

Phineus [fī'nŭs]   A Thracian king; husband of **Cleopatra**. After the blinding of his sons (see **Cleopatra**), he was himself blinded for some reason, became a **seer**, and was plagued by the Harpies, winged female monsters who used to seize or defile his food whenever it was put before him. They were dealt with by the Argonauts (see **Jason**). The *Phineus* of Aeschylus accompanied his *Persians*; Sophocles wrote two such plays.

Phlegraean [flegrē'an] **Plain**   The site of a battle between the gods and the **Giants**, sometimes located on the promontory of Pallene in the northern **Aegean**. It is mentioned as a possible haunt of **Athena** at Aesch. *Eum*. 295 because she played a prominent part in the battle.

Phobos [fo'bos]   'Rout', personified as a god, son of **Ares**.

Phocis [fō'sis] (adjective Phocean [fōsē'an])   A region of central Greece surrounding Mount **Parnassus**; the kingdom of **Strophius** and home of **Epeus**.

Phoebe [fē'bē]   A Titaness; daughter of **Uranus** and **Earth**; mother of **Leto**; grandmother of **Apollo** and **Artemis**. Her name, the Bright One, is the feminine equivalent of Phoebus; hence at Aesch. *Eum*. 8 Apollo is said to have taken the name Phoebus from her. Her connection with the **oracle** at **Delphi** is probably Aeschylus's invention, designed to enable Apollo to take it over by peaceful succession and not by force.

Phoebus [fē'bus]   A name of **Apollo**.

Phoenicia [fēni'shia]   An eastern country famous for its merchants and colonists; part of modern Lebanon; home of **Agenor**. But the 'Phoenician land' opposite **Sicily** at Eur. *Tro*. 221 must be Carthage (a city near modern Tunis), which was originally a Phoenician colony.
   Eur. *Phoen.* is called after its chorus of Phoenician women, who happen to be visiting **Thebes** on their way to **Delphi**. It concerns the **Seven against Thebes** and the deaths of **Eteocles** and **Polynices**; characters also include **Jocasta**, **Antigone**, **Creon (i)**, **Tiresias** and **Oedipus**.

Phoenix [fē'niks]   A man who was befriended by **Peleus** and who looked after **Achilles** in his childhood and later accompanied him to **Troy** (see **Homer**, *Iliad* 9. 432-95). He is the 'tutor' referred to at Soph. *Phil.* 344.

Phorcides [for'sidēz]   The three daughters of Phorcys, also called the Graeae, grey-haired from birth and having only one eye and one tooth between them. At Aesch. *PV* 795 they are surprisingly called 'swan-shaped', possibly because they are being identified with some swan-women of oriental legend. See **Io's wanderings**.

phratry   A hereditary division of the citizen body at **Athens** and elsewhere, smaller than a tribe but larger than what we would think of as a family. In fifth-century Athens the phratries had ceased to be political or administrative divisions, but retained their religious significance; a man had to be a member of one to take part in various **sacrifices** and other rituals.

Phrygia [fri'jia]   Part of northern and central Asia Minor, considered by poets to include the neighbourhood of **Troy**; hence 'Phrygian' is often used to mean Trojan. The 'Phrygian guest' of Soph. *Ant.* 824 is **Niobe**, who was a guest of the Thebans, having been brought up in **Tantalus**'s realm on Mount **Sipylus** (more properly in **Lydia**, but 'Phrygian' is being used in a wide sense).

Phrynichus [fri'nikus]   A tragedian active in the late sixth and early fifth centuries; the most prominent of Aeschylus's rivals. He is remembered chiefly for two plays on historical subjects: the *Capture of Miletus*, which, according to **Herodotus** 6. 21, so upset the audience that the poet was heavily fined; and the *Phoenician Women* (the title is doubtful), which was on the same subject as Aesch. *Pers.* (see **Persia**) and appears to have influenced it.

Phthia [fthi'a]   A region of **Thessaly**; the kingdom of **Peleus**, **Achilles** and **Neoptolemus**. For a Phthian knife see **Dorians**.

Pieria [pi-e'ria]   A region of southern Macedonia, north of Mount **Olympus**; birthplace of the **Muses**. The emphasis on it at Eur. *Bacch.* 409-16, 565-6, may be connected with Euripides' host Archelaus of Macedon (see **Bacchae**), who is said to have instituted dramatic competitions at Dion in Pieria.

Pindar [pi'ndar]   A Theban lyric poet, active from about 498 to about 445, who brought the tradition of non-dramatic choral song to its highest point of elaboration and grandeur (see **chorus**). His surviving poems were commissioned in honour of athletic victors. His work contains numerous mythical narratives and allusions and statements of proverbial wisdom.

Pirene [pire'ne]   A famous spring at **Corinth**. The 'Pirenaean [-e'an] colt' of Eur. *El.* 475 is Pegasus; see **Chimaera**.

Pirithous [piri'tho-us] or Perithus   A companion of **Theseus**, who accompanied him on his visit to the **Underworld** and was honoured as a **hero** by the Athenians.

Pitana [pi′tana] One of four villages that united to form **Sparta**; hence the 'city of Pitana' means Sparta at Eur. *Tro*. 1112. In the next line the 'goddess of the Bronze Gates' is **Athena**.

Pittheus [pi′t-thŭs] Son of **Pelops**; King of **Trozen**; maternal grandfather of **Theseus** (Fig. 4; see **Aegeus**). He brought up his great-grandson **Hippolytus** at Trozen, and in Eur. *Hipp*. he is imagined as still alive, although the kingship has passed to Theseus.

Plato [plā′tō] (about 429-347 BC) Philosopher; disciple of Socrates; teacher of **Aristotle**. As is well known, although Plato's work constantly displays a deep love, and extensive knowledge, of poetry, he refused to admit poets, and especially dramatists, into the ideal state of his *Republic*. His main objections are: (a) poets attribute immoral behaviour to the gods, and to the heroes whom they invite us to admire, and therefore have a bad influence on the morals of their audiences (*Rep*. 2. 376E–3. 392C); (b) an actor or a reciter of epic sets a bad example by taking on a variety of roles, since singleness and directness of character is to be encouraged (*Rep*. 3. 392C-398B); (c) poets 'imitate' phenomena (see *mimēsis*), which are themselves mere 'imitations' of the higher reality in which Plato believes, and so poetry is at two removes from the truth (*Rep*. 10. 595A-602B); (d) poetry appeals to the emotional part of the 'soul' or personality, which is the lowest, and encourages shameful emotional indulgence (*Rep*. 10. 602C-608B; see **catharsis**). One purpose of Aristotle's *Poetics* is to defend poetry against some of these charges.

Pleiades [plī′adēz] The star-cluster. 'The setting of the Pleiades' normally meant a particular time of year, the time (in early November) when their setting first became visible before dawn. To mention their setting at some *given* time of year, however, could presumably be a way of specifying a particular time of night, and this must be what is intended at Aesch. *Ag*. 826.

Pleisthenes [plī′sthenēz] A shadowy relative of **Agamemnon**, whose family are sometimes called Pleisthenidae [plīsthe′nidē], 'descendants of Pleisthenes'. There is no place for him in the usual account of the genealogy (Fig. 2), but some writers made him a brother of **Atreus** and **Thyestes**, others the son of Atreus and father of Agamemnon.

Pleistos [plī′stos] A river running through a gorge below **Delphi**.

Pluto [plo͞o′tō]   The god of wealth, to whom the gold-bearing river of
Aesch. *PV* 805-6 naturally belongs (see **Io's wanderings**). Often, however, he was identified with **Hades**, since wealth (in the form of crops
and precious metals) comes from beneath the earth; and it is Hades who
is meant at Soph. *Ant.* 1200 (the 'Wayside Goddess' of the previous line
is **Hecate**).

Po   See **Eridanus**.

Poeas [pē′as]   King of **Malis**; father of **Philoctetes**.

Polias [po′lias]   A title of **Athena**.

polis   See **city**.

politics   The *polis* or **city**-state is a prominent feature of many
tragedies (see **myth**), and several confront issues that can be called
'political' in the broadest sense. Thus the absolute demands of a single
ruler (see *tyrannos*) are set against political freedom in Aesch. *Pers.*,
against an individual's refusal to conform in Aesch. *PV* and Soph. *Ant.*,
and against **democracy** in Eur. *Supp.*; the treatment of suppliants is at
issue in a number of plays (see **supplication**); the rights of **women** and
aliens are at issue in Eur. *Med.*; and the conflict between social status
and true worth is remarked on at Eur. *El.* 367-90.
    Specific reference to the particular political issues of the fifth
century, whether by means of prophecy or by 'anachronistic' intrusion
of such issues into the Heroic Age, is less frequent. Mention of **Athens**
in Greek tragedy generally makes some appeal to the patriotic senti-
ments of the audience; mention of other cities that were prominent in
the fifth century *can* allude to contemporary political concerns (see
Argos, Thebes), but such allusion is by no means common, and should
not be assumed where it is not made explicit (see **Peloponnesian War**).
For the politics of Aesch. *Eum.*, which are something of a special case,
see **Areopagus, Argos**.

pollution   The Greeks, like many other peoples, traditionally believed
that certain crimes and (what amounted to the same thing) breaches of
taboo automatically caused a person to be tainted in an almost physical
way. This taint, or pollution, was not the same thing as guilt, though in
some respects it can be seen as a substitute for it. It could be incurred
as easily by an accidental or unavoidable offence as by a wilful one, and

as easily (though not as severely) by a minor breach of taboo (such as contact with a corpse or a pregnant woman) as by homicide. Its existence was independent of the offender's mental state, and even of his knowledge of the offence; nevertheless, it made him unholy in the sight of the gods, and caused them to hate him (Aesch. *Eum*. 40, Soph. *OT* 1341-6) and to punish him (e.g. *Eum*. 307-96). It could be inherited by the offender's children (see *átē*, **curses**, **house**), and it could contaminate his companions (Aesch. *Sept*. 597-614) or his entire city (*OT* 96-101). Those to whom the pollution spread would be liable, like the original offender, to be visited with disease and other misfortunes; so, if a man associated with others and they did *not* suffer for it, this was a sign that he was unpolluted (*Eum*. 284-5). For this reason a man believed to have incurred severe pollution would be shunned (Soph. *OC* 226-36), excluded from the religious and social life of his city (*Eum*. 653-6), and perhaps formally banished (*OT* 233-54). According to some texts even the gods must avoid any contact that could pollute them (Eur. *Hipp*. 1437-9; but see below). Modern scholars often compare pollution to an infectious or contagious disease, although infection and contagion were in fact unknown to fifth-century physicians.

The cure for pollution was ritual purification. Minor cases might merely require washing in water; hence those about to take part in a religious ceremony would wash in any case, to ensure ritual purity (Eur. *El*. 790-4). A crime as serious as homicide, however, would require an elaborate ritual involving **sacrifice** followed by washing in the blood of the sacrificed animal (*Eum*. 282-3, 449-50). A man excluded from the cults of his own city would have to wander abroad until he could obtain, by **supplication**, a protector who was willing to purify him (*Eum*. 447-52). The view is sometimes expressed in tragedy that no purification can suffice for the killing of kindred (e.g. Aesch. *Sept*. 681-2, 734-9, *Cho*. 66-74), though *Eum*. shows that there can be exceptions. (While *Eum*. is a useful source of references to purification, it must be admitted that the purification of **Orestes** is beset with problems; the references are difficult to reconcile either with each other or with Orestes' continued pursuit by the **Erinyes**.)

In fifth-century **Athens** anxiety over pollution evidently remained a powerful force at an emotional and religious level, even though in some respects the Greeks were beginning to outgrow it. Athenian law, although it took account of pollution in various ways, had for some time distinguished fully between deliberate and accidental homicide; and by the time of the surviving tragedies at least one philosopher (Heraclitus) had found it illogical that the stain of bloodshed should be removed by washing in blood.

In tragedy the tension between the older and the newer way of thinking is often detectable, and fruitful. At Eur. *HF* 1214-38, 1399-400, the idea that an involuntary crime leads to a pollution which can then rub off on others is treated with open scorn; in Soph. *Ant.*, however, when **Creon (i)** presumes on the enlightened sentiment that no mortal can pollute the gods (*Ant.* 1044, just like *HF* 1232), he is rapidly proved wrong. In the *Oresteia* the fact that Orestes kills **Clytemnestra** in a spirit of dutiful piety, whereas she killed **Agamemnon** in a spirit of reckless hatred, clearly counts for something, even though he is more polluted than she is, and even though the contrast is never overtly expressed in these terms. In Soph. *OT* **Oedipus** fully accepts that he is horribly polluted (823, 1340-6, 1375-90, etc.), but the audience would be missing the point if it were not at the same time aware of his moral innocence (indeed the realisation of the **myth** in dramatic terms forces that awareness upon us). And in *OC* he vigorously claims to be morally innocent (265-91, 521-6, 538-48, 960-99) and therefore, in some passages at least, unpolluted (287, 548; but contrast 1130-8).

Polybus [po'libus]   The King of **Corinth** who received the infant **Oedipus** from one of his shepherds and brought him up as his own son.

Polydeuces [polidū'sēz]   See **Castor**.

Polydorus [polidor'us]   **(i)** Son of **Cadmus**; father of **Labdacus** (Fig. 3); a shadowy king of **Thebes** providing a link between different chapters of Theban legend. He and his descendants are ignored in Eur. *Bacch.*; indeed *Bacch.* 1305 rules out his existence.

(ii) A son of **Priam** and **Hecabe**, seen as a ghost in Eur. *Hec*.

Polynices [polini'sēz]   Son of **Oedipus** and **Jocasta**; brother of **Eteocles**, **Antigone** and **Ismene** (Fig. 3). For his story see **Eteocles**; for his burial see **death and burial**. His name suggests 'man of much strife', and there are allusions to this at Aesch. *Sept.* 576-9, 658, 829-30, Soph. *Ant.* 110-11.

Polyphontes [polifo'ntēz]   One of the seven defenders of **Thebes**.

Polyxena [poli'ksena]   Youngest child of **Priam** and **Hecabe**. After the sack of **Troy** the ghost of **Achilles** appeared and demanded that she should be sacrificed at his tomb. In Eur. *Tro.* the sacrifice has been carried out before the play begins, but it is a central event in Eur. *Hec.*

Pontus [po'ntus]   The Black Sea. Its 'key' at Eur. *Med.* 213 is the Thracian **Bosporus (i)**.

portents   See **omens**.

Poseidon [posi'don]   God of the sea and rivers; son of **Cronus** and **Rhea**; brother of **Zeus** and others. He is also the god of horses, this being the capacity in which he was worshipped at the inland site of **Colonus** and elsewhere; and the god of earthquakes, sometimes called the Earth-Shaker. Together with **Apollo** he built the walls of **Troy** (see **Laomedon**), and Eur. *Tro.* presents him as a friend of the Trojans, although he is their bitter enemy in **Homer**. He was the principal god of **Trozen**; for his role in the events of Eur. *Hipp.* see **Theseus**. His weapon was a trident, the 'fish-spearing device' of Aesch. *Sept.* 131.

Pothos [po'thos]   Desire or longing, personified as a god similar to **Eros**.

Priam [pri'am]   King of **Troy**; son of **Laomedon**; husband of **Hecabe**; father of fifty sons (including **Paris** and **Hector**) and some daughters (including **Cassandra**). He was killed by **Neoptolemus** in the sack of Troy.

priests   A priest or priestess was a person serving a particular cult of a particular god. In the absence of any religious authority or organisation that was generally accepted, the nature of a priesthood varied widely according to local tradition. It could be anything from a part-time honorary post held for a single year to a lifetime vocation, and its holder could be anything from a mere **temple** administrator to an inspired **seer**, though the most important duty of most priests would be to offer **sacrifice**. Some priesthoods were hereditary (see **Eumolpidae**), others filled by election or the casting of lots, or even offered for sale.

Proetus [prē'tus]   An obscure Theban hero after whom the Proetid Gate of **Thebes** was named.

prologue   This usually means the part of a play which precedes the first choral song or *parodos* **(i)**, in accordance with **Aristotle**'s definition

(*Poetics* 12). Aesch. *Pers.* and *Supp.* and Eur. *Rhes.* have no prologue in this sense, and Eur. *IA* has two alternative ones, both thought to be spurious (see **Iphigenia, text**).

But the word (or the term 'prologue speech') is sometimes used to mean the first *speech* of a play, especially the formal expository speech which begins most plays of Euripides, and which may or may not be immediately followed by the *parodos*. This kind of Euripidean 'prologue', whether delivered by a god or by a mortal, is addressed directly to the audience with little attempt at dramatic motivation. It serves to set the scene, to explain the antecedents of the action, and often to give brief hints as to how that action will develop. Such hints, however, tend to be incomplete and misleading, concealing any innovations that Euripides will make and merely ensuring that all the audience are equipped from the start with the same essential knowledge of the **myth**; thus *Hipp.* 41-8 points to the traditional version of the story rather than Euripides' modification of it (see **Hippolytus**), while *Med.* 42 (if genuine) and *Bacch.* 50-2 refer to possibilities which will not in fact occur (*Ion* 69-73 is still more misleading).

Prometheus [promē′thŭs]   A **Titan**; son of **Iapetus** and **Themis**. His name means 'forethinker', and this is alluded to at Aesch. *PV* 85-7. At **Athens** he was honoured as Fire-Bearer with processions carrying torches, and his altar was close to **Colonus**. His myth is narrated by **Hesiod** at *Theogony* 521-616 and *Works and Days* 47-58; the author of *PV* clearly knew the Hesiodic versions, though he departed from them in many respects. Thus Hesiod, unlike the dramatist, has much to say about the first woman, Pandora, and makes Prometheus seem less a benefactor of men than a cause of their miseries; while the dramatist gives the myths of **Io** and **Thetis** a connection with Prometheus which they do not possess in Hesiod.

According to *PV*, when **Zeus** made war on **Cronus** and the other Titans, Prometheus, having failed to persuade the Titans to listen to his advice, changed sides and aided Zeus, so enabling him to win the war and to cast the Titans into **Tartarus**. Zeus then resolved to destroy the human race, but Prometheus managed to rescue it (it is not clear how); he also gave men 'blind hopes' (to deliver them from foreknowledge of death), stole fire from the gods and bestowed it on men, and taught them all the skills that they possess. (Other versions of the story differ considerably on the extent and nature of the benefits conferred by Prometheus; the one constant feature is fire, and in *PV*, although many other benefits are listed at 442-506, fire still bears the main emphasis.)

In punishment for the theft of fire, Zeus ordered **Hephaestus** to fasten Prometheus to a crag in the far North and abandon him there. This 'binding' occurs at the beginning of *PV*. In the course of the play he is visited by the daughters of **Oceanus**, by Oceanus himself, and by Io, who has also suffered at the hands of Zeus. He tells Io, among other things, that he is destined to be released from his bonds by a descendant of hers (i.e. **Heracles**), and that Zeus, who overthrew his father Cronus, is destined to be overthrown in his turn by his own son if he makes a certain marriage. As we know from other sources, the prophecy which Prometheus has in mind is that the son of **Thetis** will be mightier than his father; Zeus must therefore avoid mating with Thetis, but Prometheus will not reveal her name. **Hermes** comes threatening new tortures if he does not reveal it: Prometheus will be buried for long ages beneath the earth, and then, when he returns to the light, the eagle of Zeus will feast continuously on his liver. Prometheus refuses to give up his bargaining counter whatever tortures Zeus may inflict, and at the end of the play he is accordingly swallowed up by the earth, still shouting defiance.

We know a certain amount about the sequel, *Prometheus Unbound*, also traditionally ascribed to Aeschylus. In this play Prometheus was on the surface of the earth once more, and the Chorus consisted of Titans, now released from bondage. In the course of the play Heracles shot the eagle that devoured Prometheus's liver, and at some stage Prometheus prophesied Heracles' wanderings in the far West. Heracles also freed Prometheus, presumably with the consent of Zeus; and the prophecy at *PV* 1026-9, that Prometheus's sufferings cannot end until a god is found willing to descend to Tartarus, was probably fulfilled by the **Centaur** Chiron, who had accidentally received an incurable wound from Heracles and longed for death. Presumably in return for his release Prometheus revealed to Zeus the secret concerning Thetis (though the sequence of events and their motivation are controversial here).

The existence of two plays about Prometheus, evidently belonging together, is generally thought to imply a connected **tetralogy**; but if so it is impossible to reconstruct the contents of the two remaining plays. Aeschylus did write a **satyr** play about Prometheus's gift of fire to men, but unfortunately this was performed with *Persians* and other plays in 472, not with the other Prometheus plays. There *may* also have been a *tragedy* called *Prometheus the Fire-Bearer*, and this *may* have been either the first play in the Prometheus tetralogy (if it concerned the gift of fire) or the third (if it concerned the foundation of his cult at Athens);

but its very existence is quite uncertain.

As far as we know (and that is not far), no scholar in antiquity questioned the ascription of *PV* to Aeschylus. In many respects, however, some of them obvious, the play is unlike the rest of his surviving work. The Chorus is relatively unimportant and its songs are brief and uncomplicated. The depiction of Zeus as a vicious and vindictive tyrant (see *tyrannos*) is extraordinary by any standard; this remains true even when it has been pointed out that he was eventually reconciled with Prometheus (and might therefore have become a reformed character) and that even in the undoubtedly Aeschylean plays he is something very different from the Christian God. The construction of the play is odd at several points, the Oceanus scene being especially badly integrated with its context. The text seems to call for elaborate stage machinery — the flying chariots of the Chorus, the 'four-legged bird' of Oceanus (see *deus ex machina*), the earthquake at the end — which is used more for spectacular effect than for any good dramatic purpose. These anomalies would not by themselves show that the play was not by Aeschylus, but careful investigation of its language and metrical practice has recently shown that here too it constantly differs from the six undoubtedly Aeschylean plays more than these six differ from one another, and that it resembles them no more than a play of Sophocles does. Since *PV* has sometimes (mainly in the nineteenth century) been regarded as Aeschylus's greatest play, the conclusion that it is probably not by him at all may seem embarrassing; but this is the conclusion that must be drawn from the evidence now available.

If this is correct, then presumably the *Prometheus Unbound* was not by Aeschylus either. The two plays can perhaps be dated to the 430s.

prophecy   See **dreams, omens, oracles, seers.**

protagonist   See **actors.**

Proteus [prō'tūs]   According to **Homer** (*Odyssey* 4. 354-575) Proteus was a sea-god whom **Menelaus**, on his way home from **Troy**, encountered on the island of Pharos off the coast of **Egypt**. The *Proteus* of Aeschylus, the **satyr** play belonging to the *Oresteia*, was evidently based on this episode. **Stesichorus** and **Herodotus** (2. 112-20), however, made Proteus a king of Egypt with whom **Helen** stayed when the Greeks thought that she was in **Troy**; Eur. *El.* 1280-1 alludes to this, and Eur. *Hel.* 5 attempts to reconcile the two accounts.

purification   See **catharsis, pollution**.

Pylades [pī′ladēz]   Son of **Strophius** of **Phocis**; companion of **Orestes** on his return from exile. He is a speaking character in Eur. *IT* and *Or.*, a silent one in Soph. *El.* and Eur. *El.*; for his role in Aesch. *Cho.* see **extras**. In the end, according to Euripides, he married **Electra**.

Pylos [pī′los]   The city of **Nestor**; an important Bronze-Age site in the western **Peloponnese**.

Pytho [pī′thō]   Another name for **Delphi**, supposedly derived from that of the Python, a monster which **Apollo** killed there. Hence Pythian [pī′thian] is a title of Apollo; the games held at Delphi were the Pythian Games; and the inspired priestess of Apollo (see **oracles**) was the Pythia [pī′thia] (sometimes wrongly called the Pythoness in English). At Soph. *OC* 1047-8 the 'Pythian shores' are not those close to Delphi but those close to a certain temple of Pythian Apollo, i.e. the eastern shores of the Bay of **Eleusis** (the 'lamp-lit shores' being those at Eleusis itself).

The Pythian Games were modelled on those of **Olympia**; they were similarly held every four years, and one of the main events was chariot-racing (at **Crisa**). They did not acquire this form until 582 BC (before that date there was only a musical festival), so the references to chariot-racing in Soph. *El.* (49-50, 681-763) allude to a relatively modern institution.

R

recognition   See *anagnōrisis*.

religion   See the Classified List of Entries, pp. 20-1.

Rhea [rē′a]   Daughter of **Uranus** and **Earth**; sister of **Cronus**, and mother by him of **Zeus** and other gods (the son mentioned at Soph. *OC* 1073 is **Poseidon**). She is sometimes identified with **Cybele** and for that reason associated with orgiastic cults; see also **Earth, tympanum**. For the Gulf of Rhea see **Io's wanderings**.

Rhesus [rē′sus]   A king of **Thrace**; son of one of the **Muses**. In the tenth year of the Trojan War he came to the aid of **Troy** with some miraculous horses, but he was killed, and the horses were stolen, in a night raid by **Odysseus** and **Diomedes**, as is told in **Homer**, *Iliad* 10 and Eur. *Rhes*.

Some ancient scholars doubted whether this play was a genuine work of Euripides. Modern scholars are generally agreed that it is not, and that it was written in the fourth century.

rhetoric   In any society in which there are no newspapers or political pamphlets, and in which men have some freedom of action, it is natural that there should be a strong interest in means of influencing them through persuasive speech (see **persuasion**). Thus it is not surprising that even in **Homer** there are many speeches of a distinctly rhetorical kind. In the **democracy** of fifth-century **Athens**, however, anyone who hoped to get on in life at all had to be able to win over the Assembly and the mass juries of the law-courts; and one of the ways in which the rich could still use their wealth in pursuit of political influence was by paying for lessons in public speaking. In these circumstances it was natural that supply should meet demand and that there should arise a craft of rhetoric with professors to teach it.

These professors were the **Sophists**, and the skill which they taught immediately captured the imagination of the Athenians and influenced all forms of literature. The study of rhetorical theory at Athens is sometimes said to date from the first visit of the Sicilian sophist Gorgias in 427; but there had been rhetoric, and indeed sophists, in Athens before that, and the year 427 does not mark any noticeable change in the practice of the tragedians. What is noticeable is that, although much of the dialogue of all three tragedians is in a sense rhetorical, there is a marked increase from Aeschylus to Sophocles, and again from Sophocles to Euripides, in the priority that is given to placing persuasive arguments in the characters' mouths, and in the self-conscious deployment of rhetorical techniques. Thus in Euripides, and to a lesser extent in Sophocles, we find a frequent use of set-piece speeches, often placed side by side to form an *agōn*; of carefully marshalled arguments, often proceeding *a priori* from generalisations about what is natural or probable; and of stock legalistic formulae, often alluding to the art of speaking itself (e.g. Eur. *Med*. 522-5, *Hipp*. 983-93, *El*. 907-13, 1060, *Tro*. 914-17, *Bacch*. 266-71).

It should not be assumed that rhetoric is necessarily inimical to the proper concerns of a dramatist. Conflict between characters, verbally expressed, is of the essence of drama, and the more persuasively the characters argue, the more sharply the issues of the play are brought out. Thus the scenes between **Clytemnestra** and **Electra** at Soph. *El.* 516-633 and Eur. *El.* 1011-123 effectively depict the relationship and moral issue between the two, although each of these scenes can certainly be classed as a rhetorical *agōn*. The attractiveness of **Medea**'s case against **Jason** (Eur. *Med.* 230-66, 465-519, etc.) contributes greatly to the interest of the character and to the depth of the play, which might otherwise seem little more than a melodrama; but this attractiveness cannot be divorced from Euripides' desire, as a rhetorician, to place the best possible arguments in the mouth of a potentially unsympathetic figure (he was certainly not moved by any feminist principles; see **women**). More problematic, for the modern reader, are passages in which the public and argumentative language of Greek rhetoric is employed to analyse a decision which we might expect to be entirely private and irrational, such as the decision of Medea to kill her children (*Med.* 1021-80, 1236-50) or that of **Oedipus** to blind himself (Soph. *OT* 1369-90); but the tragedians had no other language in which decisions could be explored, and we should at least recognise the bold and interesting use to which the rhetoric is put. It must be admitted, however, that there are places in Euripides where the rhetoric is less easy to defend; the inevitably one-sided *agōn* between Electra and the severed head of **Aegisthus** (Eur. *El.* 907-56) is perhaps not a passage over which many readers linger in admiration.

The element which **Aristotle** (*Poetics* 6, 19) calls *dianoia*, 'thought, mind, intellect', and which he considers essential to tragedy, seems almost identical with rhetoric. And Aristotle's *Rhetoric* makes frequent use of examples from tragedy.

Rhipae [rī'pē] or Rhipaean [-ē'an] Mountains   Fabulous mountains in the far North.

ritual   Those writing on the origins of **tragedy** can point to early representations of various kinds of masked dancers from various parts of the Greek world (see **masks**). These dancers are presumably engaged in some religious activity, and the early development of tragedy can hardly be entirely unconnected with such rituals. Attempts to connect early tragedy with any known ceremony, however, seem to have been quite unsuccessful.

In any case, it is now generally agreed that tragedy as we know it from the fifth century cannot usefully be described as a ritual. Certainly it was performed at the **Great Dionysia** in honour of **Dionysus**, but then all festivities and entertainments tended to be given a religious justification. The celebrations at the Great Dionysia pleased the genial god and won his favour, and no doubt the dramatic performances were vaguely thought to contribute to this process, but this explains nothing about their form or content. The awarding of prizes and the importance attached to competition shows how much value was placed on the individual tragedian's recreation and interpretation of a **myth**; and, while it is true that poetic **originality** was not considered incompatible with ritual purpose (as the songs of **Pindar** and others demonstrate), it is hardly likely that any performance had a ritual purpose which it did not openly express. Tragedies did occasionally portray Dionysus, as Eur. *Bacch.* does, but they were more directly concerned with men than with gods; there is no good evidence that tragedy ever had any more to do with Dionysus than the poems of **Homer**, which were recited at the Great Panathenaea, had to do with **Athena**.

There are, however, a large number of rituals performed *within* tragedies – **supplication** and **lamentation**, the singing of **paeans** and **hymns**, and occasionally other activities such as the pouring of **libations** or the raising of a ghost. No doubt the audience was drawn into the spirit of these rituals; the 173 lines of the Great *Kommos* in Aesch. *Cho.*, for instance (306-478), would have fallen very flat if it was not (see **chorus**). Their religious purpose lay within the fictional framework of the drama, but there were rituals outside drama that rested on similar fictions (in particular certain heroes, such as Adonis and **Hippolytus**, were regularly mourned as though they had died recently), and the effect on the audience in the dramatic and the non-dramatic context cannot have been very different. But whatever emotional effect may be produced by a ritual performed within a tragedy, it is certainly produced for the sake of its contribution to the effect of the tragedy as a whole.

S

sacrifice   The Greeks offered various kinds of food and drink to their gods; Aesch. *Ag.* 69-70 distinguishes between burnt and unburnt offerings, the latter covering **libations** and gifts of grain or fruit. The word 'sacrifice', however, normally refers to the slaughter of an animal followed by a burnt offering, and this was a rite that stood at the centre of Greek religion. A sacrifice could be held in prayer or in thanksgiving (Eur. *El.* 626), to sanctify an oath (Aesch. *Sept.* 42-8) or in fulfilment of a vow (*Sept.* 275-6), for purposes of divination (see **omens**), or simply as part of a regular religious festival. The social and psychological reasons for the rite are controversial; a fifth-century Greek would probably have said that its purpose was to obtain the gods' favour by providing them with food in a manner which they approved, but some modern scholars believe that the religious trappings of a sacrifice served to sanctify and excuse a slaughter which itself had an entirely practical purpose.

In the Heroic Age sacrifice might be performed by any king or head of a household, though in the fifth century the sacrificer would normally hold a priesthood (see **priests**). Sacrifices to gods of the **Underworld** were performed at pits in the ground, those to the gods above at altars. These altars normally stood in the open air, often in front of **temples**. Occasionally the victim would be burnt whole, but more often the feast would be shared between the god and his worshippers. Different gods on different occasions required different types of victims, and there were many variations of ceremonial procedure, but the procedure described at Eur. *El.* 777-839 can be taken as typical.

Here **Aegisthus** is sacrificing a calf to the local **nymphs** in a meadow, apparently beside a building (787-90, 802). Those attending the sacrifice are garlanded with myrtle (777-8), and must purify themselves by washing in water from a bowl (791-2; here it seems that **Orestes** and **Pylades**, as strangers, are asked to give themselves a preliminary wash before the main one, but avoid this so as not to be full participants in the ceremony). Equipment is brought from the building, and a fire is lit by the altar (798-802). Aegisthus throws barley-meal at the altar as he prays to the nymphs (803-7). He takes a knife from a basket (where it would previously have been hidden beneath the barley-meal) and cuts off a lock of the victim's hair (810-12); the first cut is harmless in itself, but the victim is now dedicated to death. The victim is lifted up, so that its blood can run into a bowl on the altar (compare the way in which **Iphigenia** is lifted at Aesch. *Ag.* 232), and Aegisthus cuts its throat with the knife (813-14). It is flayed and cut up so that Aegisthus may read the omens contained in its innards (819-29); and, if the ritual had not been interrupted at this point, the victim's thigh-bones, wrapped in fat, would have been burnt on the fire (Aesch. *PV* 496), and the meat would have been roasted and eaten by the worshippers (835-6; for an example of an uninterrupted sacrifice see **Homer**, *Odyssey* 3. 430-63). One detail not mentioned in Eur. *El.*, but relevant to the perversion of sacrificial procedure at Aesch. *Ag.* 228-47, Eur. *IA* 1467-569, is that the victim was expected to walk willingly to the altar, without uttering any sound of protest, which would be a bad omen.

At the **Great Dionysia** the dramatic performances were preceded by the sacrifice of a sucking-pig at an altar in the theatre. A recently discovered **fragment** suggests that Aeschylus may actually have staged a sacrifice in the course of a play, though this was certainly unusual. For the possible connection between the word 'tragedy' and a goat-sacrifice see **tragedy**.

The custom of animal sacrifice must imply the theoretical possibility, in extreme cases, of *human* sacrifice. This does not seem to have been regularly practised in any part of Greece in historical times, though it may have occurred in emergencies; it was felt to be characteristic of barbarian peoples, like those of Eur. *IT*. **Myth**, however, typically deals in theoretical possibilities and extreme cases; hence the legends of Iphigenia and **Polyxena**, and indeed that of Abraham and Isaac. The ordinary, unsanctified homicides of Greek tragedy are very often figuratively referred to by a perversion of sacrificial language; this is especially true in the *Oresteia*, where such language recalls the literal sacrifice of Iphigenia.

Salamis [sa′lamis]   An island off the coast of **Attica**; the kingdom of **Telamon** and **Ajax (i)**. At Eur. *Tro.* 801 the 'sacred hill' opposite Salamis is the Athenian **Acropolis**, visible from the island. For the Battle of Salamis see **Persia**.

Salmydessus [salmide′sus]   A town in **Thrace** on the shore of the Black Sea; or the stretch of coast near the town. See **Ares, Cleopatra, Io's wanderings**.

Sardis [sar′dis]   The capital of **Lydia**, on the River **Pactolus**, north of Mount **Tmolus** (at Eur. *Bacch.* 463 the mountain is inaccurately said to surround the city); site of a cult of **Cybele**. Electrum, a natural alloy of gold and silver, was mined in the neighbourhood.

Saronic [saro′nik] **Gulf** or Strait or Sea   The bay between **Attica**, the **Isthmus** of **Corinth** and the north-east **Peloponnese**; or the inner part of that bay, west of **Aegina**. See **Beacon Speech**.

satyrs [sa′terz]   Drunken, lecherous creatures who lived in wild places and attended **Dionysus**. In fifth-century **Athens** they were pictured as uncouth men with horses' tails (Plate IIIa).

A satyr play was a play with a chorus of satyrs, written by a tragedian on a mythical subject but treating it in a spirit of humorous burlesque.

At the **Great Dionysia** it was usual to perform a satyr play in fourth place after three tragedies by the same tragedian. The only example to survive complete is Eur. *Cycl.* (see **Cyclops**), but we also have a good deal of Sophocles' *Ichneutae* (*Trackers*), based on the Homeric Hymn to **Hermes** (see **Homer**), and some scraps of satyr plays by Aeschylus, who was regarded by ancient critics as the greatest exponent of the genre (see **fragments**). The tragedy Eur. *Alc.* was performed in fourth place as though it were a satyr play, and this may account for its shortness and its undignified portrayal of a drunken **Heracles**.

Aristotle claims in *Poetics* 4 that **tragedy** itself developed from a satyric form. There has been much argument as to what this statement means and how, if at all, it is to be reconciled with the claim made slightly earlier that tragedy arose 'from those who led off the **dithyramb**', or with the tradition that satyr plays were introduced by Pratinas, a contemporary of Aeschylus.

Scamander [skama′nder]   A river flowing close to **Troy**, famous from **Homer** (compare **Simois**). The statement at Aesch. *Eum.* 397-402, that the Greek chiefs after the Trojan War dedicated land by the Scamander to **Athena**, as a gift for the sons of **Theseus**, is probably intended to back the claim of fifth-century **Athens** to a settlement at **Sigeum**.

scholia [skō′lia]   Explanatory notes written in the margins of a text (singular 'scholium' or 'scholion'; a writer of them is a scholiast). Many medieval manuscripts of Greek tragedy (see **text**) contain scholia; some of these are wrong, and most tell us nothing that we could not have worked out for ourselves, but a few preserve valuable scraps of ancient scholarship.

Sciron [ski′ron]   A brigand who lived by the Scironian [skirō′nian] Rocks on the coast west of Megara, and whom **Theseus** killed on his first journey from **Trozen** to **Athens**.

Scylla [si′la]   (i) A proverbially grim monster (described by **Homer** at *Odyssey* 12. 85-97) living in the sea opposite **Charybdis**. Scylla and Charybdis were often located in the Strait of Messina between **Italy** and **Sicily**, and that is why Scylla is 'Tyrrhenian', loosely used to mean Italian, at Eur. *Med.* 1342-3, 1359.

(ii) Daughter of **Nisus**, a king of Megara who could not be killed as long as a certain lock of his hair remained uncut. He was besieged by

Minos of **Crete**, who bribed Scylla with a gold necklace, so that she cut the magic lock and caused her father's death.

Scyros [ski'ros]   An island east of **Euboea**; kingdom of **Lycomedes**; foster-home of **Neoptolemus**.

Scythia [si'thia]   A land to the north of the Black Sea, home of a nomadic people who were said to travel about in wagons; see **Herodotus** 4. 1-82 and **Io's wanderings**. They were famous for their archery (the 'Scythian weapons' at Aesch. *Cho*. 161-2 are a bow and arrows) and for their ferocity; they were believed to scalp their enemies, so hair cut short can be figuratively said to have received Scythian treatment (Eur. *El*. 241). Occasionally, however, they were thought of as 'noble savages' with good laws, and that seems to be the point at Aesch. *Eum*. 703. They can also be identified with the **Chalybes**, and hence regarded as inventors of iron. In a wider sense Scythia was sometimes felt to include the uninhabited regions of the furthest North, as at Aesch. *PV* 2.

seers   Since the **omens** sent by the gods are obscure, it is natural that there should be a class of men, like **Tiresias** (the seer mentioned at Aesch. *Sept*. 24), **Calchas**, **Amphiaraus** and **Helenus**, claiming special skill in interpreting them. In the fifth century we hear of professional seers travelling with armies to advise their commanders, just as Calchas and Amphiaraus do. One might logically expect the ability to understand omens to be separate from direct prophetic inspiration, but in tragedy, as no doubt in actual belief, the two tend to be combined; the seer begins by witnessing an omen, but then is divinely inspired in his interpretation of it. Although prophecies in tragedy, for good dramatic reasons, are always fulfilled, the Greeks were well aware that seers could in practice be venal and fraudulent, so the charges made against Tiresias at Soph. *Ant*. 1033-63, *OT* 387-9, Eur. *Bacch*. 255-7, are not in themselves implausible or impious.

The 'second sight' of **Cassandra**, which has nothing to do with omens that anyone else can see, is rather different. Here the real-life models must have been cases of actual insanity, which would be regarded with awe and attributed to possession by a god; so Cassandra's madness is fully compatible with true prophetic inspiration. The word *mantis*, which can be used of any kind of seer or prophet, is probably connected with a word for madness, as Eur. *Bacch*. 299 implies.

In token of their sacred calling seers might wear strips of wool as garlands (Aesch. *Ag.* 1265, Eur. *Tro.* 451) or hang them in places of divination (Eur. *Bacch.* 350). Besides predicting the future, they might claim an inspired knowledge of the past, and use this as proof of their supernatural powers, as at Aesch. *Ag.* 1195-7, *PV* 824-6, 842-3; in each place the dramatist uses this as a way of motivating an account of past events.

For the Pythia at **Delphi** see **oracles**. **Apollo** himself, as god of prophecy, is sometimes called a seer also.

Semele [se'melē]   Daughter of **Cadmus**; bride of **Zeus** (the 'Cadmean bride' of Soph. *Ant.* 1115); mother of **Dionysus** (Fig. 3). When she was pregnant with Dionysus, the jealous **Hera** tricked her into asking Zeus, who had promised to grant any request that she might make, to visit her in the same form in which he visited Hera. He came in the form of a lightning bolt, and she was consumed by its fire, though he was able to rescue the unborn Dionysus from the flames.

Like all places struck by lightning, the remains of the building in **Thebes** where she was supposed to have died were regarded as sacred, and men were forbidden to walk there. At Eur. *Bacch.* 8 this precinct is said to be still miraculously smoking, and at *Bacch.* 596-9 it bursts into flame; it is doubtful whether these effects were made visible in the theatre.

Semele was herself sometimes worshipped as a goddess together with Dionysus. Aeschylus, among others, wrote a *Semele*.

Semnai Theai [se'mni the'ï]   The words simply mean 'August Goddesses', the adjective *semnos* — 'august, awesome, holy' — being commonly applied to various divinities. Specifically, however, 'Semnai Theai' was the name of certain goddesses worshipped at **Athens**, who resembled the **Eumenides** and are identified with them at Soph. *OC* 89-90. At the end of Aesch. *Eum.* they are implicitly identified with the newly benevolent **Erinyes**, who are in fact called *semnai* at *Eum.* 1041.

Seneca [se'neka] (died AD 65)   Stoic philosopher; tutor of the Emperor Nero; author of the only Roman tragedies that survive (apart from one or two later works written in imitation of his style). These plays are largely exercises in rhetorical exaggeration, evidently not intended for the stage and not much admired today, but of great historical importance as a link between Greek tragedy and that of the Renaissance.

Seven against Thebes   When **Polynices**, banished from **Thebes**, had
married the daughter of **Adrastus** of **Argos**, he gathered an army with
which to attack his brother **Eteocles**. This army was led by seven
champions from Argos and elsewhere. According to Aesch. *Sept.*, Eur.
Supp. and Soph. *OC* 1313-25 the Seven were **Tydeus, Capaneus,
Eteoclus, Hippomedon, Parthenopaeus, Amphiaraus** and Polynices
himself. Eur. *Phoen.*, however, includes Adrastus among the Seven in
place of Eteoclus.

In the ensuing battle each of the Seven faced one of the gates of
Thebes, and all were killed in one way or another (except Adrastus, if
he is counted). Aesch. *Sept.* and Eur. *Phoen.* both deal with this battle,
which is also foreshadowed in Soph. *OC*. In Aeschylus each of the
Seven, except Amphiaraus, bears a shield with a boastful device, but
Eteocles is able to ensure the deaths of most of them by showing that
these devices reveal arrogance in the face of the gods (see *hybris*) and
by interpreting them as **omens** favourable to the Theban side. Eur.
Supp., in which the characters of the Seven are very differently presented, deals with their burial, won for them by Adrastus with the aid
of **Theseus** and in defiance of Thebes. The battle for Thebes also lies
in the background of Soph. *Ant.*

Aesch. *Sept.* was the third play in a connected **tetralogy** of which
the other plays were *Laius*, *Oedipus* and the **satyr** play *Sphinx*. About
the lost plays we know very little more than can be gathered from
Sept. 720-91; and that is not much, for we cannot be sure how many
of the incidents narrated here occurred within the action of *Laius* or
Oedipus, nor even how consistent Aeschylus was over the wording of
Apollo's oracle or **Oedipus**'s curse (see **Chalybes**). For the problem of
the ending of Aesch. *Sept.* see **Antigone**.

Sicily   Most of the island was settled by Greek colonists between the
late eighth and early sixth centuries BC, and by the fifth it was an
important part of the Greek world. Naturally, however, it was not
normally regarded as such in myth, epic and tragedy; and this makes it
difficult to understand the praise of the island at Eur. *Tro.* 220-3. The
passage has often been connected with the fact that, when the play was
produced in 415, **Athens** was preparing a huge (and disastrous) expedition against Sicily, whose strongest city, Syracuse, was an ally of **Sparta**
in the **Peloponnesian War**. If the conquest of Sicily should succeed,
there was talk of proceeding to southern **Italy** (mentioned at *Tro.*
224-9) and even Carthage (mentioned at *Tro.* 221). It is far from easy,
however, to see *how* the terms in which Sicily is praised here can relate

to the Sicilian Expedition, or what can be the purpose of such an allusion in the dramatic context.

The Sicilian Sea is that between Sicily and Greece.

Sidon [sī'don]   A city in **Phoenicia**; so 'Sidonian' [sīdō'nian] can be used to mean Phoenician.

Sigeum [sijē'um]   A coastal town close to **Troy**. At Soph. *Phil.* 355 it is 'bitter' or 'cruel' to **Neoptolemus** because his father **Achilles** is buried there. See also **Scamander**.

Simois [simō'is]   A small river flowing past **Troy** and into the **Scamander**.

Sinis [si'nis]   A brigand who lived at the **Isthmus** of **Corinth**, and whom **Theseus** killed on his first journey from **Trozen** to **Athens**.

Sipylus [si'pilus]   A mountain in **Lydia**; see **Niobe**.

Sirius [si'rius]   The Dog Star. It was associated with heat because the start of the hottest part of the year was marked by the time, in the latter part of July, when its rising first became visible before dawn (so that it was obviously overhead during the day).

Sisyphus [si'sifus]   A king of **Corinth** and a notorious trickster. He managed to cheat death by telling his wife not to bury his body when he died; he was permitted to return to earth in order to haunt her, and stayed there. He was punished for this by eternal torment in the **Underworld**. Euripides' **satyr** play *Sisyphus* was the fourth play of the **tetralogy** that included Eur. *Tro*.

Although **Odysseus** is always called the son of **Laertes** in **Homer**, a later story claimed that, when Laertes bought Odysseus's mother Anticleia as his concubine, she was already pregnant by Sisyphus. **Philoctetes** and others in tragedy therefore call Odysseus the bastard son of Sisyphus when they wish to discredit him. There is probably some similar scorn in the suggestion at Eur. *Med.* 405 that the family of the Corinthian **Creon (ii)** is descended from Sisyphus.

skēnē   The scene-building, a wooden structure facing the audience from the far side of the *orchēstrā* (Plate I). Actors changed their costumes inside it, and made some of their entrances and exits through a doorway in its façade (others were made by the *parodoi* (ii)). In most plays it represents a palace or other building in front of which the action takes place. It seems to be ignored, however, in Aesch. *Pers.*, *Sept.*, *Supp.* and *PV*, and perhaps also in Soph. *OC* and the second half of Soph. *Aj.*; and it is doubtful whether it had yet been built at the time when the first three of these plays were performed. It may, then, have been a novelty at the time of the *Oresteia* (458 BC), in which attention is constantly drawn to it (see **house**). It is unlikely that the façade was painted or modified in any way for particular plays (if it were, it would have to be modified *during* Soph. *Aj.*); a sentence in **Aristotle** (*Poetics* 4), which most scholars attempt to believe, states that Sophocles introduced 'scene-painting', but it seems very doubtful whether the sentence is either authentic or true. The roof of the *skēnē* could be used for the appearance of gods to mortal characters (see *deus ex machina*), and occasionally for other purposes, as at the beginning of Aesch. *Ag.* and the end of Eur. *Or.*

Solon [sǒ'lon]   The great Athenian law-giver of the early sixth century, often regarded as the founder of the Athenian constitution. We possess a number of **fragments** of his poetry, in which he explained his political aims and also gave expression to traditional Greek wisdom in terms which are often echoed by the tragedians.

sophists   The word *sophistēs* essentially means simply a skilled, clever or wise man. When applied to **Prometheus** at Aesch. *PV* 62 and 944, however, it seems to have already acquired a contemptuous tone; and by the late fifth century it had come to be used, often pejoratively, of a specific class of professional teachers and thinkers who were offering a novel kind of higher education at **Athens** and elsewhere.

The sophists claimed to provide any young man who could afford their fees with the skills that he needed to achieve success and political influence in his city. This meant, above all, skill in **rhetoric**, and the sophists were the first to develop conscious rhetorical techniques; they were accused by their enemies of cynically enabling their pupils to argue on either side of the same question. As thinkers they tended to be highly sceptical, questioning accepted moral, social and religious values, and some went so far as to claim that **justice** was a matter of mere convention, which a strong man should ignore. They were bitterly attacked as immoral and impious by such writers as **Aristophanes** and **Plato**, and much of our knowledge of them derives from these attacks; but they strongly influenced the literature of their day, including tragedy.

This influence is particularly noticeable in the work of Euripides, who is closely associated with the sophists by Aristophanes. It can be seen in the self-conscious rhetoric of his debates (see *agōn*); in his fondness for abstract language and *a priori* generalisation; and in the sceptical, unconventional and rationalistic opinions expressed by many of his characters (for *Med*. 230-51 see **women**; for *Tro*. 884-8 see **Zeus**; for *El*. 367-90 see **politics**; for *Bacch*. 272-318 see **Dionysus, Tiresias**). Certainly Euripides' plays are not propaganda for such opinions, for conventional opinions are expressed at least as often, and it is not necessarily the sophistical characters who are vindicated; but Euripides does, under sophistic influence, expand the range of ideas that are available for a dramatist to use. Such influence can also, however, be seen in the work of the supposedly conventional Sophocles, though here it is more unobtrusively woven into the fabric of the plays.

The two most famous sophists were Gorgias, whose rhetorical exercise in defence of **Helen** is extant and appears to have influenced Eur. *Tro*. 914-65; and Protagoras, whose account of the development of civilisation (see Plato, *Protagoras* 320C-322D) is thought to have influenced Aesch. *PV* 442-506, Soph. *Ant*. 332-75, Eur. *Supp*. 201-13.

Sparta [spar'ta]　The major city of **Laconia** in the southern **Peloponnese**; the home of **Tyndareus** and his children, and, according to **Homer**, Sophocles and Euripides, the home of **Menelaus** (for Aeschylus's version see **Argos**). In fifth-century prose Sparta is usually called by the later name Lacedaemon, which is also found at Eur. *Tro*. 250, the 'Lacedaemonian bride' being **Clytemnestra**.

Fifth-century Sparta was famous for its highly restrictive systems of government and education, dedicated to military efficiency and to holding down a large population of serfs (the Helots). It was hostile to **Athens** for most of the century, and led the alliance which fought and defeated Athens in the **Peloponnesian War**. The attacks on Sparta at Eur. *Andr*. 445-63, 595-601, evidently reflect fifth-century Athenian attitudes.

Spartoi [spar'toi]　See **Cadmus**.

Spercheus [sperkē'us]　The main river of **Malis**.

Sphinx [sfingks]　A monster, usually portrayed with the head of a woman, the body of a lioness and the wings of an eagle. For her story see **Oedipus**. Surviving tragedies do not tell us what her riddle was, and the version that is well known today ('What creature has four legs in the morning, two at midday and three in the evening, and is weakest when it has most? Answer: Man') may not be older than the fourth century BC, unless Aesch. *Ag.* 79-82 alludes to it. The *Sphinx* of Aeschylus was the **satyr** play of the **tetralogy** to which Aesch. *Sept.* belongs. The plural Sphinxes of Eur. *El.* 471 do not occur in Greek myth, but would be a quite normal motif in art.

stage directions   Almost all stage directions in translations of Greek drama (not counting marginal notes to indicate which character is speaking) have been inserted by the translators. The only genuine exceptions in tragedy are the moans and groans of the Chorus at Aesch. *Eum.* 117-29, which are given as stage directions in the manuscripts (see **text**); but even these probably do not go back to the dramatist. Sometimes a translator may render an inarticulate cry in the Greek text by a stage direction (e.g. at Soph. *Phil.* 745-6 *papai, apappapai, papappapappapappapai* might become '*A prolonged cry of agony*'), but all other stage directions refer to actions or sounds which have been inferred, rightly or wrongly, from what the characters say. It is natural that these should often be matters of controversy, though it is not likely that Greek tragedies contained actions of any significance that were *not* marked and explained in spoken words.

Notes to indicate the identity of speakers do generally go back to medieval manuscripts, but not to the dramatists themselves, who probably only put a mark at the point at which one speech ended and another began. In places, therefore, there is controversy as to who delivers a certain line or passage (e.g. **Clytemnestra** or the Chorus at Aesch. *Ag.* 489-500, **Antigone** or **Ismene** at Soph. *Ant.* 572), though the formal patterning of tragic dialogue makes serious doubt less common than might be expected.

stasimon (plural *stasima*)   The word is generally used to mean any choral song, other than the *parodos* **(i)**, which serves to separate two distinct sections of a play (see **chorus**, **episode**). By this definition all choral songs, except for a few brief ones within 'acts', are either *parodoi* or *stasima*. This does not quite correspond to the definition given in **Aristotle**, *Poetics* 12, but that definition is problematic.

Stesichorus [stēsi'korus]   A poet of the late seventh century BC, who wrote long lyric poems, resembling epics, on mythical subjects. They are known to us only from **fragments**, but several seem to have provided material for tragedies, notably the *Palinode on Helen* (see **Helen, Proteus**), the *Oresteia*, the *Sack of Troy*, and a poem about **Eteocles** and **Polynices**.

stichomythia [stikomi'thia]   Dialogue in which each utterance by each participant consists of a single line of verse. In tragedy most passages of rapid dialogue between two characters, or between a character and a chorus-leader, consist of stichomythia, unless they are very brief. Such passages can be prolonged – some in Euripides last for over 100 lines – and the dramatists sometimes resort to filling out a line with 'padding' so that the pattern can be sustained.

Under this general heading come also the less common forms in which each utterance consists of half a line (hemistichomythia; see *antilabē*) or of two lines (distichomythia).

Strength   Like other abstractions, strength or might (*kratos*) can on occasion be personified as a god (e.g. Aesch. *Cho*. 244), and force or violence (*biā*) as a goddess (the Greek word being feminine). **Hesiod** at *Theogony* 385-403 says allegorically that Strength and Force dwell always with **Zeus** and aided him in his war against the **Titans**; hence the author of Aesch. *PV* brings them on stage as Zeus's brutal ministers (see also **extras**).

strophe [stro'fē]   See **verse**.

Strophius [stro'fius]   The King of **Phocis** by whom **Orestes** was brought up; father of **Pylades**.

Strymon [stri'mon]   A large river in **Thrace**.

Styx [stiks] (adjective Stygian [sti'jian])   A river of the **Underworld**. The name is connected with the Greek for 'hate'.

Sun   See **Helios**.

supplication   A person in trouble might find himself unable either to protect his own interests or to demand protection from others. This could happen if, for instance, he had been exiled, perhaps for some **pollution**, and had come to a city where he had no rights; or if he lacked power within his own city; or if his city had been defeated in war and he was at the mercy of its conquerors. In such a case his only resource was to *beg* for protection. If he could place himself in the position of a suppliant before a man with the power to help or to spare him, there was some hope that that man might be shamed into doing so, since suppliants were considered to be under the protection of **Zeus** himself, and there was a strong religious feeling against rejecting them.

There existed, therefore, well-defined **rituals** of supplication, intended to mark the suppliant's special status and to show that he was abandoning any claim to power of his own and throwing himself on the mercy of others. In an emergency the suppliant might touch the beard or chin of the prospective helper (Eur. *Med*. 709) or, more often, kneel before him and touch his knees (e.g. *Med*. 324, 710). More formally, he would sit at an altar (Soph. *OT* 15-16, *OC* 1156-9) or in some other sacred place (Aesch. *Eum*. 40-1, Soph. *OT* 19-21), perhaps grasping the image of a god (Aesch. *Eum*. 80, Eur. *El*. 1254-5) and perhaps holding an olive branch wound round with strips of wool (Aesch. *Cho*. 1035, *Eum*. 43-4, Soph. *OT* 3, 19) as a token of supplication. A ritual of this kind would bring pressure on men as well as on a god, since the god would punish anyone who ignored the pleas of a suppliant at his altar or shrine, and still more anyone who dragged the suppliant away or killed him (Eur. *Tro*. 69-75).

Three surviving tragedies — Aesch. *Supp*. (see **Danaids (i)**), Eur. *Supp*. (see **Seven against Thebes**) and *Heracl*. (see **Heracles**) — are built entirely round a successful act of supplication by a group of exiles, and its consequences for them and for the city that befriends them. Aesch. *Eum*. and Soph. *OC*, while not conforming quite so strictly to the pattern of the 'suppliant plays', are very much influenced by it.

swan   This bird was believed by the Greeks to be a model of filial piety, and to acquire the power of singing just before its death.

Symplegades [simple'gadēz]   See **Clashing Rocks**.

Syria   Known to the Greeks as a source of incense.

T

Talaus [ta'lā-us]   Father of **Hippomedon**.

Talthybius [talthi′bius]   Herald of the Greek army at **Troy**; a character in Eur. *Hec.* and *Tro.*

Tanaus [ta′nā-us]   A river flowing between the territory of **Argos** and
that of **Sparta**.

Tantalus [ta′ntalus]   Son of **Zeus**; King of part of **Lydia**; father of
Pelops and **Niobe** (Fig. 2). He was eternally punished in the **Underworld**
for having abused the friendship of the gods in one way or another.

Tartarus [tar′tarus]   A place of punishment deep below the earth; see
Underworld.

Teiresias   See **Tiresias**.

Telamon [te′lamon]   King of **Salamis**; father of **Ajax (i)** and **Teucer**.
He accompanied **Heracles** on his expedition against **Troy**; see **Laomedon**.

temples   A Greek temple was a building sacred to a god or goddess,
generally designed to house his image and objects dedicated to him.
Oracles might be delivered there, but **sacrifices** and other religious
rituals were usually held in the open air. The temples of any city were a
major focus of patriotic sentiment, as well as religious sentiment,
among its citizens.

Tethys [tē′this]   A Titaness; consort of **Oceanus**; mother by him of
various gods and **nymphs** of the sea and rivers.

tetralogy   Each tragic poet competing in the **Great Dionysia** did so
with four plays, normally comprising three tragedies and one **satyr** play.
These plays might either be completely separate from one another or
more or less closely linked in subject matter. The word *tetralogiā* is
used by ancient critics to mean a set of four *linked* plays, but some
modern ones use 'tetralogy' to mean any set, whether linked or not. To
avoid confusion, therefore, this book, like some others, uses the term
'connected tetralogy' to mean a *tetralogiā* in the ancient sense. The set
of three tragedies from a tetralogy, in either sense of the word, is called
a trilogy.

Connected tetralogies are particularly associated with Aeschylus. We
know of at least four by him (not counting the doubtful **Prometheus**
tetralogy), and he probably wrote several others, though he also wrote

unconnected plays, such as the set produced in 472 − *Phineus*, the surviving *Persians*, *Glaucus Potnieus* and the satyric *Prometheus*. The only complete trilogy to survive is the *Oresteia* of 458 − *Agamemnon*, *Choephori* and *Eumenides* − and its satyr play, *Proteus*, is lost. Aesch. *Sept.* (see **Seven against Thebes**) and *Supp.* (almost certainly; see **Danaids (i)**) belonged to connected tetralogies also. We can see in the *Oresteia*, and glimpse in the *Septem*, how the tetralogic form enabled Aeschylus to depict the history of a family and to explore long chains of cause and effect, prophecy and fulfilment, crime and punishment, curse and destruction − or salvation. The connection between the plays of the Danaid tetralogy was presumably closer still; *Supp.*, unlike *Ag.*, reads more like a first act than a complete drama. The other Aeschylean tetralogy that we know of for certain was the *Lycurgeia*, but we cannot be sure of the relation between its plays; they may not all have concerned **Lycurgus**.

Other tragedians produced connected tetralogies on occasion, and the form survived until at least the fourth century. It is doubtful, however, whether Sophocles ever produced one; and from Euripides we know of only one or two examples, notably that produced in 415 − *Alexander* (see **Paris**), *Palamedes* (see **Odysseus**), the surviving *Trojan Women* and the satyric *Sisyphus*. Here the connections will have been less close than in the *Oresteia*, but connections of crime and punishment, prophecy and fulfilment can certainly be discerned.

Teucer [tū'ser]   Son of **Telamon**; half-brother of **Ajax (i)**. He was the most prominent archer in the Greek army at **Troy**, and is a character in Soph. *Aj.* and Eur. *Hel.*

Teucrian [tū'krian] **Land**   A name of **Troy**, from an early king Teucer (distinct from the **Teucer** above).

text   The oldest surviving manuscript containing complete plays by Aeschylus and Sophocles dates from the tenth century AD, and the oldest containing complete plays by Euripides dates from the twelfth. For many centuries, therefore, the plays that we have were preserved by being repeatedly copied from manuscript to manuscript in various parts of the Greek, Roman and Byzantine world. At some places and times − notably at Alexandria in the third and second centuries BC − manuscripts were carefully collated to produce scholarly editions; at others little interest was taken in the plays and their preservation was much more hazardous. It is for this reason that the vast majority of the

Greek tragedies that were produced, like most other Greek literature, have been lost, and what we do possess has survived largely by chance. In the past hundred years our knowledge has been increased a little by the discovery of Greek papyri in **Egypt**; see **fragments**.

In the course of repeated copying the texts have naturally become corrupted. Surviving manuscripts often disagree in their readings, and there are many places where none of them can be giving us what the poet wrote. Hence the need for textual criticism. A scholar wishing to produce an edition must for some plays collate a large number of manuscripts, for others a few or only one. Where readings differ, he must choose between them, using his knowledge of Greek language and metre, of the author's style, of the descent of the manuscripts and of the habits of scribes; and where no manuscript gives a plausible reading he must either attempt to heal the fault by conjectural emendation or warn the reader that the corruption is incurable.

Of simple errors made in the course of copying the majority are trivial and easily remedied, but all too often there are real issues; it is unlikely, for instance, that agreement will ever be reached on whether Sophocles really wrote 'the bloody dust of the gods below mows it down' at *Ant*. 601-2, or '*hybris* breeds a *tyrannos*' at *OT* 873. Some lyric passages are in such poor condition that for long stretches we can form only an approximate idea of the general sense; Aesch. *Cho*. 783-837 is a particularly bad example, and some of the lyrics in Aesch. *Supp*. are worse still.

Gaps in the text, called lacunae, are naturally incurable, and often difficult to detect. We know, however, that the beginning of Aesch. *Cho*. – perhaps some 30 lines – is missing from our one manuscript, which begins with what we call line 10 (the lines numbered 1-9 in our texts are ones which are quoted by **Aristophanes** and others and which partly fill the gap). There is a long lacuna after Eur. *Bacch*. 1329, and very probably one after *Bacch*. 1300 also; here again quotations by later writers supply some of what is missing (see **Agave**).

The question of interpolations – material inserted by someone other than the dramatist – causes much controversy. Insertions of a line or two are probably quite common, especially in Euripides. More seriously, the end of Aesch. *Sept*. has almost certainly suffered rewriting (see **Antigone**), as have the last few lines of Soph. *OT* (*OT* 1524-30 have probably replaced a different ending by Sophocles). The authenticity of Soph. *Ant*. 904-20 has been endlessly debated, and that of two inter-related passages at Aesch. *Cho*. 205-10 (with 228) and Eur. *El*. 518-44 (see **Electra**) is also uncertain. Eur. *IA*, which Euripides probably left unfinished, has been extensively tampered with at more than one period (see **Iphigenia, prologue**), and similar tampering, on a rather smaller scale, is suspected in Eur. *Phoen.*

Lines can also become misplaced. Thus the description of the robe at Aesch. *Cho.* 997-1004 can hardly belong where it stands in the manuscript, and the most likely place for it is before line 983.

The layman can hardly be expected to make his own judgements on textual issues, or indeed to be greatly interested in them, but he should perhaps be prepared to listen to what the experts tell him. Not all of those experts are fools, and, where they are agreed in rejecting the testimony of the manuscripts, they are more likely to be right than wrong.

Thebes [thēbz] or Thebe [thē′bē]   The dominant city of **Boeotia**, about 30 miles north-west of **Athens**; very important in both myth and history. For its foundation, and the story of the dragon's teeth and the Spartoi, see **Cadmus** (Thebes itself is pictured as a dragon or snake at Soph. *Ant.* 127, and the 'seed of the dragon' refers to it at *Ant.* 1125). Different myths tell of different families of Theban royalty, which poets and mythographers relate to one another by more or less artificial means (e.g. Soph. *OT* 267-8, Eur. *HF* 1-34). Thus we can distinguish (a) Cadmus, his daughters, and **Pentheus** (Fig. 3); (b) **Labdacus** and his various descendants, together with **Creon (i)** (Fig. 3); (c) **Amphion**, Zethus and **Niobe**; (d) Amphitryon, **Alcmene** and **Heracles**, together with the usurper Lycus. In legend the city had seven gates, each of which was attacked by one of the **Seven against Thebes**; according to Aesch. *Sept.* (the list varies slightly in other authors) these gates were the Proetid (see **Proetus**), the **Electran**, the **Neïstan**, the gate of **Athena Onca**, the **Borrhaean**, the **Homoloean**, and one merely called the seventh. In this play, for some reason, the name 'Thebes' does not actually occur, being always replaced with 'Cadmea', 'city of Cadmus' or the like.

Historically Thebes was often hostile to Athens, notably during the **Peloponnesian War**, a fact which is relevant to Soph. *OC* (see especially the prophecy at *OC* 606-23, but note also the complimentary reference at 919-31) and to Eur. *Supp.*

Themis [the′mis]   The word *themis*, meaning 'right' or 'righteousness', is sometimes personified as a deity observing human conduct and punishing crime. In myth she is more specifically a Titaness, mother of **Prometheus**, and her prophetic power is the source of his knowledge of

Figure 3: The Royal House of Thebes

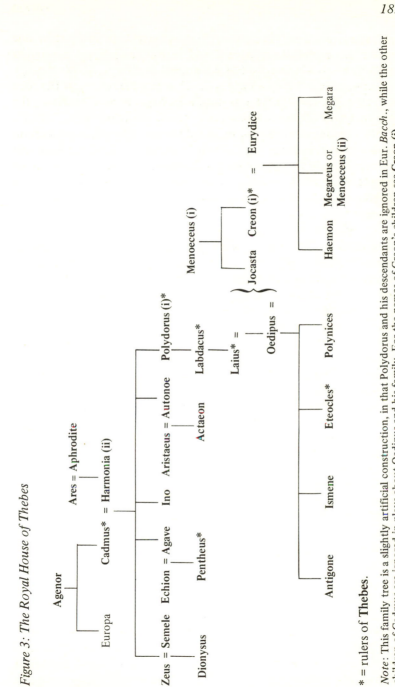

* = rulers of **Thebes**.

Note: This family tree is a slightly artificial construction, in that Polydorus and his descendants are ignored in Eur. *Bacch.*, while the other children of Cadmus are ignored in plays about Oedipus and his family. For the names of Creon's children see Creon (i).

the future. At Aesch. *PV* 209-10 she is identified with **Earth**, but at
Aesch. *Eum*. 2-4 and Eur. *IT* 1259-83 she is Earth's daughter; for the
oracle of hers which is mentioned in these last two passages see **Delphi**.

Themiscyra [themiski'ra]   See **Io's wanderings**.

theōris   A sacred ship; especially one that sailed from **Athens** to
Delos and back every spring to commemorate the voyage of **Theseus** to
Crete (see **Plato**, *Phaedo* 58A-B). At Aesch. *Sept*. 857-60 the Chorus
reverses the normally auspicious associations of the word, describing
the ship of the dead as a black-sailed *theōris* sailing to a land very
different from Delos.

Thermodon [thermō'don]   See **Io's wanderings**.

Thersites [thersi'tēz]   A character in **Homer**, *Iliad* 2. 210-77, 'the
worst man who came to **Troy**'. Homer tells how he impudently abused
Agamemnon and was beaten for this by **Odysseus**, to the approval of
the other chiefs.

Figure 4: The Family of Theseus

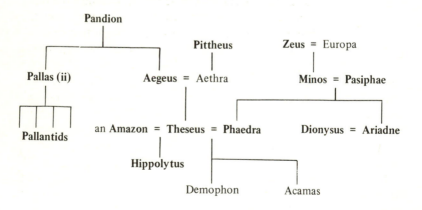

Theseus [thē′sūs]   King of **Athens**; son of **Aegeus** (Fig. 4) by most accounts, but sometimes said to be the son of **Poseidon** (in Eur. *Hipp*. he has been granted the fulfilment of three wishes, or curses, by his father Poseidon, but he is inconsistently called the son of Aegeus at lines 1283 and 1431). His mother was Aethra, daughter of **Pittheus**. Although the Athenians regarded him as their greatest hero, the people of **Trozen** also claimed him as a native and hero of *their* city, and several features of his myth as it is found in tragedy are evidently attempts to reconcile Athenian and Trozenian legends.

He was born and brought up, then, at Trozen, while Aegeus reigned at Athens (for the explanation see **Aegeus**). When he grew old enough, he claimed certain tokens which his father had left for him and travelled to Athens along the coast, defeating on the way such brigands as **Sinis**, **Sciron** and Procrustes. On his arrival he had, by some accounts, to evade the wiles of his stepmother **Medea** before being recognised as Aegeus's son.

Athens was at this time subject to **Minos** of **Crete**, who demanded an annual tribute of seven youths and seven virgins, to be fed to the Minotaur, a monster born to **Pasiphae** and kept by Minos in his Labyrinth. Theseus offered to be one of the tributary youths. When he reached Crete, Minos's daughter **Ariadne** fell in love with him; she helped him to escape from the Labyrinth, after he had killed the Minotaur, and then eloped with him, but was killed (or abandoned by him) on Naxos. As he approached Athens he forgot to change the black sails of his ship to white in token of his success, and Aegeus, seeing the black sails and assuming that his son had been killed, leapt to his death.

Theseus now became King of Athens; and, when his grandfather Pittheus grew too old to rule, he became King of Trozen also. At some stage he had to fight off a challenge from his cousins the **Pallantids**, whom he killed. He also defeated an invasion by the **Amazons**, and took their leader, Antiope or Hippolyta, as his wife or concubine; she bore him a son, **Hippolytus**. He later married Ariadne's sister **Phaedra**, but the events dramatised in Eur. *Hipp*. led to her death and that of Hippolytus.

Theseus also visited the **Underworld** in the company of his friend **Pirithous**. The usual version of the myth says that the two heroes were attempting to abduct **Persephone** and were imprisoned for a time, if not permanently, by **Hades**, but the tragedians say little about these discreditable details.

Patriotic Athenian legends present Theseus as a strong, wise and pious king, who ruled with the consent of his people (he can even be treated as a hero of Athenian **democracy**), and who befriended heroes from other cities. It is in this last capacity that he appears in Soph. *OC* and in Eur. *HF* and *Supp*.

Besides Hippolytus he had two sons (by Phaedra, according to most writers), called Demophon (the King of Athens in Eur. *Heracl*.) and Acamas. They survived Theseus and fought in the Trojan War; for the land assigned to them at Aesch. *Eum*. 397-402 see **Scamander**.

Thespis [the'spis]   The earliest tragedian whose name was known to ancient scholars. He was active at **Athens** in the second half of the sixth century BC. Most of the traditions concerning him are quite unreliable, but he is said to have invented the first **actor** (the poet himself), the use of **masks**, and other features familiar to us from fifth-century drama. It is impossible to assess, however, how much tragedy owes to his inspired invention, and how far he was working within an existing dramatic or semi-dramatic tradition (see **tragedy**). It is unlikely that his plays, if written down at all, survived much beyond his life-time.

Thesprotia [thesprō'shia]   See **Io's wanderings**.

Thessaly [the'sali]   A large region of northern Greece, normally considered to include **Phthia** (Thessaly and Phthia may be distinguished at Eur. *Tro*. 241-2, but the **text** is doubtful). It was noted for its horses and horsemen, and for its javelins. A Thessalian hat was one with a wide brim, worn by travellers (seen in Plate V).

The praise of Thessaly at *Tro*. 214-19 is less incongruous than that of **Sicily** at 220-3 (since Thessalians did take part in the Trojan War), but still not easy to explain. When the play was produced (in 415) an old alliance between **Athens** and the Thessalian cities may still have been nominally in force, but there is no evidence that those cities had done anything at all to honour it since the first year of the **Peloponnesian War** (431).

Thestius [the'stius]   Father of **Althaea**.

Thetis [the'tis]   A sea-**nymph**. For the prophecy alluded to at Aesch. *PV* 764 see **Prometheus**. Since **Zeus** was warned of this prophecy in time to avoid mating with her, she married **Peleus**, and became the mother of **Achilles**. She is a character in Eur. *Andr*.

Thorician [thori'shian] **Stone**   Thoricus [tho'rikus] was a village near the southern tip of **Attica**. Why a stone at **Colonus**, mentioned only at Soph. *OC* 1595, should have been called Thorician is unknown.

Thrace [thrās]   A barbarian land north of the **Aegean** and east of the Black Sea. Since cold north winds blew from there to Greece, the Greeks thought of Thrace itself as a cold place and as the home of **Boreas**. The 'Thracian [thrā'shan] wave' at Soph. *OT* 197 refers to the Black Sea.

Thyestes [thī-e'stēz]   Son of **Pelops**; brother of **Atreus**; father of **Aegisthus** (Fig. 2). The gods gave Atreus a golden lamb, delivered to him by **Pan**, as a symbol of sovereignty. Thyestes, however, seduced his brother's wife, Aerope (this is the 'original crime' which is seen as the source of the family's troubles at Aesch. *Ag.* 1191-3), and she secretly gave the lamb to him. When Atreus was about to be proclaimed king, Thyestes produced the lamb amid the celebrations and claimed the kingship for himself. **Zeus**, to show his displeasure at this crime, altered the course of the sun (the details of the alteration, as given at Eur. *El.* 727-36, are obscure); thus the deception was exposed, and Thyestes was banished.

Later he returned as a suppliant, and Atreus, feigning friendship, invited him to a banquet, at which he was served with the flesh of his own children, whom Atreus had murdered (this is alluded to at Aesch. *Ag.* 1095-7, 1106, 1502-4, 1511-12, *Cho.* 1068-9, as well as being described at *Ag.* 1590-7). Thyestes, on realising what he was eating, cursed Atreus and his descendants, but was again banished, together with the infant Aegisthus, the only child who had survived the slaughter.

He was the subject of plays by Sophocles, Euripides and others.

Thyiads [thwī'adz]   Female attendants of **Dionysus**. The word is usually synonymous with **Maenads** and **Bacchae**, though the Thyiads of Soph. *Ant.* 1151 may be **nymphs** rather than human worshippers.

thyrsus [ther'sus]   A staff made from a fennel stalk with a bunch of ivy leaves tied to one end. It was carried by worshippers of **Dionysus**, who waved it in their dances (Plate III), and the god might magically transform it into an effective weapon.

Tiresias [tīrē'sias]   The blind **seer** of **Thebes**. Various accounts are given of the origin of his blindness and his prophetic powers, but both qualities are taken for granted in the plays in which he appears (Soph. *Ant.* and *OT*, Eur. *Phoen.* and *Bacch.*; he is also the unnamed seer of Aesch. *Sept.* 24). He was said to have lived through seven (or nine) generations of men, and this is how it is possible for him to appear as a contemporary of anyone from **Cadmus** to **Antigone**. In Eur. *Bacch.* his prophetic powers are unimpressive and his pointless rationalisations of **myth** make him sound surprisingly like a fifth-century **sophist**; there seems to be an element of satire here, but Euripides' intentions are far from obvious.

Titans [ti'tanz] and Titanesses   A race of divine beings, children of **Uranus** and **Earth** (though the Titan **Prometheus** belongs to the next generation), who were believed by the Greeks of historical times to have existed earlier than most of the gods whom they themselves worshipped. They include **Cronus**, **Rhea**, **Oceanus**, **Atlas**, **Phoebe**, **Themis** and Prometheus. Some Titans, such as Rhea and Prometheus, received some worship in historical times; others may preserve a memory of gods worshipped at some earlier period, but this is quite uncertain. The later generation of gods, led by **Zeus**, established their power by defeating most of the Titans, led by Cronus, in a great battle. Zeus then consigned these Titans to **Tartarus**, though by some accounts he later released them.

Tithonus [titho'nus]   See **Eos**.

Tmolus [tmo'lus]   A mountain ridge south of **Sardis**, where the **Maenads** of **Lydia** were said to perform their rites.

Trachis [tra'kis]   A city in **Malis**. The 'Trachinian ridge' at Soph. *Phil.* 491 is one that dominates the city. For Sophocles' *Trachiniae* [traki'ni-e] or *Women of Trachis* (set at Trachis and called after the role of its chorus) see **Heracles**.

tragedy   The immediate source of the Greek word *tragōidiā*, 'tragedy', is *tragōidos*, which seems to have been used to mean a tragic performer, but which looks as if it should mean 'goat-singer'. Numerous attempts have been made by ancient and modern scholars to explain what, if anything, a goat could ever have had to do with tragedy (it is possible that at one time a goat was awarded as a prize in the tragic competitions, and sacrificed), but the answer, even if we knew it, would be unlikely to tell us much about any tragedies that we possess. In general few topics can have been discussed more endlessly and fruitlessly by classicists than that of the origin of tragedy (see **chorus, Dionysus, dithyramb, masks, ritual, satyrs, Thespis**); certainly **Aristotle**'s account at *Poetics* 3-4 is more bewildering than enlightening.

To a fifth-century Athenian, in any case, a *tragōidiā* would have meant a drama in verse, performed by a small number of **actors** and a chorus, treating a theme from **myth** (or exceptionally from recent history, but never from contemporary Athenian life) in a serious and dignified style. Elements of form, content and style seem equally essential to the definition (for Aristotle's more abstract and theoretical definition at *Poetics* 6 see *mimēsis*, **catharsis**). The seriousness and dignity can be seen in a negative way as the absence of features specifically associated with comedy (see **Aristophanes**): obscenity, outright humour (Greek tragedy may raise a smile on occasion, but hardly a laugh), reference to the trivial concerns of daily life, and breaches of 'dramatic illusion' (such as mention of the audience in the theatre or of contemporary Athenians). We may suspect that tragedy and comedy grew up in reaction to one another, and that Greek tragedy as we know it could not have existed without the presence of comedy as its antitype.

It was by no means essential for a Greek tragedy to have an unhappy ending; the majority of surviving examples do, but several do not, and these include not only the relatively light-hearted plays, such as Eur. *Hel.* and *IT*, but some that are entirely serious, such as Aesch. *Eum.*, Soph. *Phil.* and Eur. *Supp.* (others, such as Aesch. *Sept.* and *Cho.* and Soph. *OC*, have endings that are too emotionally ambiguous to be placed in simple 'happy' or 'unhappy' categories). Aristotle's *Poetics* seems flagrantly inconsistent as to which type of ending is preferable, Chapter 13 being immediately contradicted by Chapter 14. The fact that a Greek tragedy *can* end unhappily, however, is a remarkable feature of the genre, distinguishing it not only from comedy and satyr play but from most dramatic traditions that have arisen independently in other cultures. It is thus quite natural that later ages came to regard an unhappy ending as the one essential feature of a tragedy, applying the word to any play that had such an ending even if it lacked other features, such as a chorus, that were essential to a Greek *tragōidiā*.

Some modern critics, however, have given the word 'tragedy' an almost mystical significance, claiming that all 'genuine' tragedies, of whatever period, have certain qualities in common beyond those entailed by a common-sense definition of the word.

Triton [tri͞ton]   A river in **Libya**, more often called Tritonis. An obscure title of **Athena**, Tritogeneia, was explained by saying that she had been born beside this river, and at Aesch. *Eum*. 292-4 she is imagined as haunting her birthplace, rather as **Apollo** and **Artemis** haunt **Delos**.

Troy [troi] (adjective Trojan [trō͞jan])   A city of **Phrygia** in northwest Asia Minor; often called Ilium (its usual name in **Homer**), sometimes also **Pergamum**, Pergama or the **Teucrian Land**. Its walls were built by **Apollo** and **Poseidon** in the time of King **Laomedon**. It was twice captured by Greeks, first by **Heracles** and **Telamon** in the time of Laomedon, and second by a great expedition under the command of **Agamemnon** in the time of **Priam**. The Trojan War described in Homer's *Iliad* was the war that preceded this second capture; it may have a historical foundation in a war fought in the thirteenth century BC, when a destruction of Troy is attested archaeologically, but this is far less certain than has sometimes been claimed.

For the cause of the war see **Paris**; for events during it see **Achilles**, **Ajax (i)**, **Chryseis**, **Hector**, **Odysseus**, **Philoctetes**, **Rhesus**. It was brought to an end, after a ten-year siege, by the strategem of the Trojan or Wooden Horse, as is told in Homer, *Odyssey* 8. 492-520, Eur. *Tro*. 511-67. The bulk of the Greek army pretended to sail away, leaving a few warriors concealed in an image of a horse, constructed by **Epeus** on the advice of **Athena**. The Trojans, believing that the Horse was an offering to Athena, dragged it into the city. That night the Greek army secretly returned, and were let into Troy by the warriors who had emerged from the Horse. For the sack which followed see **Ajax (ii)**, **Neoptolemus**.

Eur. *Tro*. deals with various events that befall **Hecabe**, **Cassandra** and **Andromache** after the sack. It was the third play in a loosely connected **tetralogy**, the others being *Alexander* (see **Paris**), *Palamedes* (see **Odysseus**) and the **satyr** play *Sisyphus*. See also **Peloponnesian War**.

In tragedy, as in Homer, Trojans speak Greek (though at Aesch. *Ag*. 1050-61 **Clytemnestra** thinks that Cassandra may not). In general it is only the more unattractive of Greek characters who look down on the Trojans as **barbarians**.

Trozen [trō͞zen] (less correctly Troezen or Troizen)   A city in the eastern **Peloponnese**, on the **Saronic Gulf**; the kingdom of **Pittheus**. **Theseus** and **Hippolytus** were honoured there as Trozenian heroes, and some account is taken of this even in Athenian versions of their myths.

Eur. *Hipp.* is set at Trozen, though other accounts of the same events locate them at **Athens**. It may be of some relevance that Trozen was an Athenian possession for a period in the middle of the fifth century, some twenty years before the production of Eur. *Hipp.*

Hipp. 148-50, 228 and 1133 refer to a shallow lagoon close to the city, separated from the open sea by a sandbar.

tyche Greek for 'luck' or 'chance'. The word can be used superstitiously, luck being treated as an active force or even a goddess; or it can be used to counter superstition, 'mere chance' being opposed to **fate** or to divine intervention.

Tydeus [tĭ'dŭs] Son of **Oeneus**; father of **Diomedes**; one of the **Seven against Thebes**. He fled from his native Calydon to **Argos** after murdering a kinsman (Aesch. *Sept.* 572 probably alludes to this), married a daughter of **Adrastus**, and was active (with **Polynices** and in opposition to **Amphiaraus**) in fomenting war between Argos and **Thebes**. In the battle for Thebes Aesch. *Sept.* implies merely that he was killed by **Melanippus**, but the portrayal of his character in this play may reflect a more elaborate story, according to which Tydeus killed Melanippus but was himself wounded, and then succumbed to the temptation of gnawing the skull of his dead enemy, with the result that **Athena** killed him in disgust.

tympanum [tĭ'mpanum] A small drum resembling a tambourine, held in one hand and beaten with the other (Plate IIIb), supposedly used (with the *aulos*) in the ecstatic rites of **Dionysus** and **Cybele**. According to Eur. *Bacch.* 120-34 it was invented in **Crete** by the **Curetes** (equated here with the **Corybantes**) as a means of drowning the cries of the infant **Zeus**; they then passed it on to Zeus's mother **Rhea** (implicitly identified with Cybele); and it was in turn obtained from her by the **satyrs**, who used it in the worship of Dionysus (Euripides may have in mind a story that Rhea/Cybele cured Dionysus of a madness sent by **Hera**). The language used here fuses together elements of different cults throughout.

Tyndareus [tĭ'ndarŭs] King of **Sparta**; husband of **Leda**; father of **Clytemnestra** and perhaps **Castor** (Fig. 2). **Helen** and Polydeuces, Leda's children by **Zeus**, can also be referred to loosely as Tyndarids (children of Tyndareus); it is Helen who is meant at Eur. *El.* 480, *Tro.* 766. He is a character in Eur. *Or.*

Typho [tĭ'fō] or Typhon   A hundred-headed fire-breathing monster;
son of **Earth**; associated with **Cilicia**; see **Hesiod**, *Theogony* 820-68,
Aesch. *PV* 351-72. After the fall of the **Titans** Typho challenged the
rule of **Zeus**, who blasted him with a thunderbolt and hurled him to
Tartarus (according to Hesiod) or buried him under Mount **Etna**
(according to *PV*, following **Pindar**), whose volcanic activity is caused
by his restlessness.

tyrannos   The word generally means an unconstitutional monarch of
the type that forcibly seized power in many Greek cities, including
Athens, in the seventh or sixth century BC. These 'tyrants' were not
necessarily cruel, nor unpopular in their day; but in the fifth century,
when there were no longer any 'tyrants' in mainland Greece (they
persisted later in **Sicily**), the word *tyrannos* acquired a derogatory over-
tone. Thus in Aesch. *PV*, where the cruel upstart **Zeus** is repeatedly
called a *tyrannos* (see **Prometheus**), the word evidently means much the
same as 'tyrant' in English (note especially *PV* 221-5).

   In other tragedies, however, for some unexplained reason, the word
shows an opposite development, being used to mean simply 'king' (for
which other words existed) and to refer even to such clearly admirable
and legitimate monarchs as **Theseus**. The word is frequently applied in
this sense to **Oedipus** in Soph. *OT*; so the title *Oedipus Tyrannus* is a
reasonable one, and is correctly translated *Oedipus Rex* or *King
Oedipus*. At *OT* 873, on the other hand, if Sophocles really wrote
'*hybris* breeds a *tyrannos*', the word must bear the same bad sense as in
Aesch. *PV* (some scholars change the text to read 'tyranny (i.e. kingship) breeds *hybris*', removing the problem contained in the word
tyrannos, though not the problem of the line's relevance to the play).

Tyrrhenians [tĭrē'nianz]   A Greek name for the Etruscans, who were
the dominant race in fifth-century **Italy**; so 'Tyrrhenian' is used to
mean Italian at Eur. *Med.* 1342, 1359. They were believed to have
invented the trumpet.

U

Underworld   The Greeks usually, though by no means consistently
(see **death and burial**), believed that the dead inhabited a shadowy
realm ruled over by **Hades** and **Persephone** and generally located
beneath the earth. Though their lot was far from enviable, most of

them were not positively punished, and a man who had been a great king in his life might remain one among the dead (Aesch. *Cho.* 354-62, Soph. *El.* 839-41). Certain notorious criminals, however, such as **Ixion**, **Sisyphus** and **Tantalus**, are being eternally tormented in the Underworld, or more specifically in **Tartarus**, which was said to be far below the realm of Hades; and the **Erinyes** can continue their punishment of a polluted man after his death (Aesch. *Eum.* 267-75, 339-40).

These Erinyes have their home in the Underworld, like other dark and sinister powers (see **gods**). The rites paid to such 'gods below the earth' differ from those paid to the gods of **Olympus** (see **libations**), who are sometimes thought of as shunning them (e.g. Aesch. *Eum.* 179-97, 364-6). Nevertheless, the 'gods below the earth' are fully entitled to expect worship, and a person who honours them is in general displaying piety and not wickedness (though **Clytemnestra** at *Eum.* 106-9 has clearly honoured them in a very different spirit from e.g. **Oedipus** and **Ismene** at Soph. *OC* 466-506).

The Underworld also contains rivers with expressive names, such as **Acheron**, **Cocytus** and **Styx**, across which the dead may have to row or sail in order to reach their final home. Several heroes visited the Underworld, for one reason or another, during their lives, notably **Heracles**, **Odysseus** (see **Homer**, *Odyssey* 11), **Orpheus** and **Theseus**.

unities   The three 'tragic unities' — those of time, place and action — are a notion foisted on **Aristotle** by seventeenth-century critics.

Unity of Time derives from *Poetics* 5, where Aristotle remarks that tragedy 'tries as far as possible to limit itself to a single revolution of the sun, or a little more'. In fact the action of most Greek tragedies is notionally continuous, and so limited to the time taken to perform the play, though several plays include offstage journeys that might take hours or days in practice.

Unity of Place is nowhere mentioned by Aristotle, but the tragedians usually observe it. It is explicitly broken after Aesch. *Eum.* 234 and Soph. *Aj.* 814, where a change of scene is signalled by the departure of the Chorus (in *Eum.* there is also a considerable lapse of time). Aeschylean plays can also contain less explicit 'refocusings' of scene while the Chorus remains visible; thus in *Cho.* the scene changes at some undefined point from the tomb of **Agamemnon** to the exterior of the palace, and in *Eum.* it similarly changes from the Athenian **Acropolis** to the **Areopagus**.

Unity of Action derives from the requirement, on which Aristotle does insist (*Poetics* 7-8, etc.), that a work of art should be an organic whole. Critics argue about how far certain plays conform to it. In Soph. *Ant.* and Eur. *Hipp.*, for instance, difficulties seem to arise more from the modern requirement that each play should be about a single 'hero' than from Aristotle's requirement of necessary or probable connection between incidents; but Eur. *Tro.* makes no attempt to meet either requirement (being unified in theme and mood rather than action), and there are other Euripidean plays which show a more or less episodic construction.

Uranus [ū'ranus]   Sky or heaven personified as a god; consort of **Earth**; father of most of the **Titans**. For his castration and overthrow at the hands of his son **Cronus**, vaguely alluded to at Aesch. *Ag.* 168-70, see **Hesiod**, *Theogony* 147-210.

V

Veneti [ve'neti] or Enetoi   A tribe — 'Venetians' — at the north end of the Adriatic, famous for their horses.

verse   All Greek tragedy is written in verse. All ancient Greek verse is unrhymed but rhythmical, the rhythm being created, not by a pattern of stressed and unstressed syllables as in English, but by a pattern of long and short syllables (some prefer to call them 'heavy' and 'light'), which allows greater metrical complexity. The various metres used in tragedy can be divided into three classes.
   1. *Spoken dialogue* This carries most of the action of the plays. It is used mainly by **actors**, but sometimes also by the **Chorus**-Leader; and it is used both for **stichomythia** and for longer speeches. Most spoken dialogue (almost all in Sophocles and the earlier plays of Euripides) consists of lines called iambic trimeters, resembling the Alexandrines of classical French drama. The basic pattern is

$$x - u - \mid x - u - \mid x - u -$$

where — means a position occupied by a long syllable, u a position occupied by a short syllable, and x a position that can be occupied by either. Sometimes a 'long' position is occupied instead by two short syllables. This metre must restrict the poet's choice of words rather more than English blank verse, but less than heroic couplets.
   A few spoken passages (e.g. Aesch. *Pers.* 155-75, 215-48, 697-9,

703-58, *Ag.* 1649-73, Soph. *OT* 1515-30, Eur. *Tro.* 444-61, *Bacch.*
604-41) employ a longer line, the trochaic tetrameter, which, according
to **Aristotle** (*Poetics* 4), was the normal metre of dialogue in the earliest
tragedies. Here the basic pattern is

$$- u - x \mid - u - x \mid - u - x \mid - u -$$

2. *Sung lyrics* Choruses sing *parodoi* (**i**), *stasima* and sometimes
shorter songs within scenes; actors sometimes sing **monodies**; and
choruses and actors join in *amoibaia*. The metres used are very complex
and varied, and may change repeatedly within a few lines, so that the
modern reader has difficulty in perceiving any rhythmical effect at all.
The great majority of songs, however, have an overall antistrophic
structure; that is to say, they consist of pairs of stanzas, and the metres
of the first stanza in each pair (the strophe) are recapitulated exactly in
the second (the antistrophe). A song may consist of anything from one
such strophic pair to eleven (in the case of Aesch. *Cho.* 315-475), and
the last strophic pair may be followed by an epode, i.e. a single stanza
of which the metres are not repeated. Astrophic lyrics, i.e. ones which
lack any metrical recapitulation, occasionally occur at the beginnings of
songs and elsewhere; there are some long astrophic passages in late
Euripides.

All songs were accompanied on the *aulos*. Little is known about the
music, but it appears that each syllable was normally sung to a single
note, and that there was no harmony or counterpoint.

3. *Intermediate types* There is some dispute as to precisely which
passages were delivered in a style between speech and song, but for
practical purposes the only important 'intermediate' metre is one that is
best called 'non-lyric anapaests' (but often inaccurately 'marching
anapaests' or 'recitative anapaests'). The exact manner of delivery is
also uncertain. In Aeschylus passages in this metre often act as preludes
to choral songs (*Ag.* 40-103 is an unusually long example); in all the
tragedians the metre is used for brief choral comments of various kinds
(e.g. Aesch. *Ag.* 1331-42, Soph. *Ant.* 526-30, and the 'tail-pieces',
often of doubtful authenticity, with which most Euripidean plays end),
sometimes also for dialogue of an emotional sort (e.g. Eur. *Hipp.* 176-
266), and sometimes alternating with lyrics in *amoibaia* (e.g. Aesch. *Ag.*
1448-576). The basic pattern is

$$u u - u u - \mid u u - u u - \mid \ldots$$

(with frequent substitution of — for u u and vice versa), continued *ad lib.* until after a few lines a cadence is reached with u u — —; after which the pattern may resume.

Victory   See **Nike**.

W

women   Women in fifth-century **Athens** led very restricted lives. Legally they could not own property, take any direct part in politics or lawsuits, or make their own decisions on marriage or divorce. A woman remained in the tutelage of her father, or another male relative, until her marriage, and then passed, on payment of a dowry (Eur. *Med.* 232-3, *Hipp.* 628-9), into that of her husband (though the father retained the right to sue the husband for divorce and return of the dowry). Socially the women of a household had their own quarters (Aesch. *Cho.* 878) where they could avoid meeting the master's male visitors, and, unless the household was so poor that the women had to work out of doors, they might barely leave the house except to attend certain religious festivals (they probably did attend dramatic performances, though the dramatists certainly wrote with male spectators principally in mind).

Much of this may at first sight surprise a reader of the tragedies, in which female characters often have very active and important roles. The discrepancy can, however, be explained. The Athenians learned from myth and epic (whether factually or not) of earlier societies in which women had led freer lives. The tragedians dealt with events in the mythical past, and this was an area in which they often found it convenient not to impose the conventions of the fifth century. The stories that they were dramatising commonly involved relations between men and women (see **myth**), while the action of the plays had to be performed, and set, in the open air, and to be witnessed by a public within the drama (the **chorus**) as well as by the audience outside it. It was thus impossible to take full account of the conventions of Athenian life if female characters on a public stage were to be given the same importance which women must always have had within the family and in men's emotions. Sometimes, however, the tragedians do make a point of giving a woman a particular reason for leaving the house (e.g. Soph. *Ant.* 18-19, Eur. *Med.* 214-15, *Hipp.* 181; note also Soph. *El.* 516-18, Eur. *El.* 343-4). For Aesch. *Ag.* 242-7 see **Iphigenia**.

And in matters of more substance the plays do reflect fifth-century male attitudes, if not always in a straightforward and unthinking way. The attacks on womankind at Aesch. *Sept*. 181-202, Eur. *Med*. 569-75, *Hipp*. 616-68, while they doubtless seemed extreme and one-sided, cannot have seemed absurd; and **Eros** is often regarded with fear and mistrust. The argument at Aesch. *Eum*. 657-66, seeking to show that a mother is no true parent, can be paralleled from Greek philosophers (notably Anaxagoras, writing at Athens around the middle of the fifth century) and must be intended quite seriously (though this is not to say that Aeschylus is committed to its truth). The two most memorably dominant women in tragedy are doubtless Aeschylus's **Clytemnestra** and Euripides' **Medea**; and both are criminals, whose dominance is a masculine characteristic upsetting the natural order. Although the dramatists take good care that the crimes of both women should be well motivated, and indeed put some highly attractive arguments into their mouths (Aesch. *Ag*. 1412-18, Eur. *Med*. 230-66, 465-519, etc.), the murders that they commit still reflect the danger which a masterful and unrestrained woman would present to the mind of a male Athenian (note the parallels cited by the Chorus at Aesch. *Cho*. 585-638, Eur. *Med*. 1282-92). The other acts of revenge committed or attempted by Euripidean women (Hermione in *Andr*., **Hecabe** in *Hec*., **Electra** in *El*. and *Or*., Creusa in *Ion*) are similarly alarming.

Conversely, the virtues on which **Andromache** prides herself at Eur. *Tro*. 645-56 are those of an ideal fifth-century wife; another example of such a wife is Deianira in Soph. *Trach*., who lives only for her husband and indulges in much soul-searching (*Trach*. 531-97) before her one modest (and fatal) act of daring. And as for the heroic women in Euripides, whom we are clearly invited to admire (**Alcestis** in *Alc*., Macaria in *Heracl*., **Polyxena** in *Hec*., Iphigenia in *IA*), their heroism always resides in an act of self-sacrifice, which can be seen as carrying the passive virtue expected of women to its logical conclusion.

To this pattern of aggressive criminality contrasted with conformity or passive heroism there are, indeed, exceptions. These include such resourceful Euripidean ladies as Iphigenia in *IT* and Theonoe in *Hel*.; ingenuity, in a good cause as well as a bad, can be regarded as a feminine quality. More interesting, however, are **Antigone** and Electra in Sophocles. Both are *actively* heroic, and we must admire them for it, but neither case is simple; neither woman's character is straightforwardly sympathetic, neither woman commits or plans an action which in itself is obviously right, and both would seem much less admirable if they were not willing to sacrifice themselves for their convictions. As so often, Sophocles is being disturbingly paradoxical, and the paradoxes cannot be fully appreciated until normal fifth-century expectations have been taken into account.

Wooden Horse   See **Troy**.

Z

Zephyr [ze'fer] or Zephyrus   The west wind personified; surprisingly called a **Giant** at Aesch. *Ag.* 692, probably because it can carry ships across the sea.

Zeus [zūs]   The supreme god; son of **Cronus** and **Rhea**; brother of **Poseidon**, **Hades**, **Hera**, **Demeter** and **Hestia**; husband of Hera, and lover of various goddesses and mortal women; father of **Apollo**, **Artemis**, **Athena**, **Dionysus**, **Heracles** and many other mythical figures. (The 'child of Zeus' at Aesch. *Sept.* 161 is probably Athena; that at Soph. *OT* 470 is Apollo; in Eur. *Tro.* 'daughter of Zeus' means Athena at 526, Artemis at 554, **Helen** at 1109.)

He was born in a cave on **Crete** (or hidden in it by Rhea after his birth), and there his cries were drowned by the loud music of the **Curetes** so that Cronus, who knew that he was fated to be overthrown by his own child, might not find and swallow him. When he grew to maturity Zeus did overthrow Cronus and the other **Titans**, with the help of **Prometheus**, and established himself as the ruler of the world (**Uranus** and Cronus are the two predecessors mentioned in vague terms at Aesch. *Ag.* 168-72, *PV* 957).

His ancient function as a god of the sky and weather is sometimes mentioned in tragedy. His weapon is the thunderbolt (the bow of Aesch. *Ag.* 364 is metaphorical), and he is the god of lightning referred to at Soph. *Phil.* 1198. In a remarkable image at Aesch. *Ag.* 1388-92 **Clytemnestra** compares the joy that she felt when sprinkled with her husband's blood to the joy that Zeus's rain gives to the corn, the swelling of the grain being in turn metaphorically described as birth-pangs.

More emphasis, however, is placed by the tragedians, and especially by Aeschylus, on his supremacy over gods, men and the world in general (with the famous 'Hymn to Zeus', so-called, at Aesch. *Ag.* 160-83 compare especially Aesch. *Supp.* 86-103, 524-99). There was a tendency (to which the Cretan legend about his birth is an exception) to imagine him rather less anthropomorphically than the other gods, and the tragedians usually — perhaps always — avoided presenting him on stage. No one can defeat or overrule Zeus (he is the 'all-subduing god' of Soph. *Phil.* 1467-8), and he is thought of in a general way as controlling all that happens, so that a character can say of any past event, without fear of contradiction, that it was Zeus's will. This can be true even of the most unpleasant events, as at Soph. *Trach.* 1275-8; and indeed Zeus can be explicitly described as omnipotent, as at Aesch. *Ag.* 1485-8 (but the passage at Eur. *Tro.* 884-8, where 'Zeus' is treated as the name of some abstract principle, is quite untypical of tragedy and clearly influenced by the speculations of philosophers and **sophists**). None of this, however, was felt to be inconsistent with the belief that other gods had wills and powers of their own, or with the belief that human beings were responsible for their actions and, in a common-sense way, free to make their own decisions (see **fate**). Zeus did not make the world, and as a rule his 'omnipotence' was assumed to be subject to its laws.

Men tended to project onto Zeus their need for **justice**. He was, at least, often thought of as enforcing justice on earth by ensuring the punishment of crimes, especially the more unnatural and disturbing crimes such as those against kindred or gods (the person punished at Aesch. *Ag.* 1022-4 is **Asclepius**; that at Soph. *Phil.* 676-80 is **Ixion**). His conduct in myths, however (seducing mortal women, for instance, and imprisoning his father Cronus), did not suggest that he felt bound to observe the rules of justice himself. Not everyone in the fifth century was content simply to accept this paradox (no doubt the invention of **democracy** at **Athens** made it less easy to tolerate an arbitrary and unconstitutional ruler for the world), and the myths about Zeus were beginning to cause some embarrassment, as can be seen from e.g. Aesch. *Eum.* 640-51, Eur. *HF* 339-47, 1340-6. The presentation of him in Aesch. *PV*, on the other hand, where he is concerned with his own power to the complete exclusion of justice, is altogether exceptional; see **Prometheus**.

Zeus presided over oaths, and punished those who broke them; and certain groups who had no human protector and who could all too easily be wronged in the absence of a strong religious sanction against doing so — suppliants (see **supplication**), beggars, strangers and guests — were under his special protection. On the other hand he also protected kings, whose authority could be seen as a 'divine right' conferred by him.

The greatest centre of Zeus's worship was at **Olympia**, but he gave

oracles at **Dodona** (see **Io's wanderings**), and Mount Athos was also sacred to him (see **Beacon Speech**). His bird and emblem was the **eagle**. His numerous titles, some more official than others, include the King, the Highest, the Saviour (see **libations**), the Averter (of evil), the Router (of enemies), the Accomplisher, the Loud-Thunderer; the God of Suppliants (*Hikesios*), of Guests or Strangers (*Xenios*), of Fathers or Ancestors (*Patrōios*), of Possessions (*Ktēsios*, worshipped at a humble shrine in storerooms), of the Market Place or Assembly (*Agoraios*, associated with persuasive speech), of Oaths (*Horkios*), of Curses (*Araios*), of Kindred (*Synaimos*), of the Courtyard (*Herkeios*, worshipped by a whole household at an altar in the courtyard of the house), of the Sacred **Olive** Trees (*Morios, moriai* being olive trees in **Attica** that were public property and so placed under Zeus's protection). For 'the Zeus below the earth' see **Hades**.

BIBLIOGRAPHY

Note: The Bibliography is confined to works in English. Parts A 1-4 are intended to cover all translations of Greek tragedies that seem at all readily available (even if at present out of print). All other parts are much more selective, and only include works that are in some degree recommended.

A Translations

1. Collected or Selected Tragedies

An Anthology of Greek Drama, ed. C.A. Robinson, Jr., various translators, 2 vols. (Holt, Rinehart & Winston, New York, 1949). *An odd assortment of translations in diverse styles.*

The Chicago series: The Complete Greek Tragedies, ed. D. Grene and R. Lattimore, various translators (University of Chicago Press). Aeschylus, 2 vols. (1953, 1956). Sophocles, 2 vols. (1954, 1957). Euripides, 5 vols. (1955-9). Also a selection, *Greek Tragedies*, 3 vols. (1960). *An overall 'best buy'; though the quality varies from play to play, most of the translators provide accurate, unpretentious and readable versions.*

The Frogs and other Greek Plays, trans. K. McLeish (Heritage of Literature Series, Longman, London, 1970). *Includes Aesch. PV and Eur. Med., much simplified and adapted for young readers.*

Kelly's Keys to the Classics, various translators, 1 play per vol. (James Brodie, Bath, dates unspecified). *Schoolboy cribs, avowedly literal but impossibly archaic.*

The Loeb Classical Library (Heinemann, London, and Harvard University Press). Aeschylus, ed. and trans. H.W. Smyth, 2 vols. (1922, 1926; vol. 2 with an Appendix by H. Lloyd-Jones, 1957). Sophocles, ed. and trans. F. Storr, 2 vols. (1912, 1913). Euripides, ed. and trans. A.S. Way, 4 vols. (1912). *Loeb editions, giving text and translation, can be most useful for anyone who knows a little of the original language, but those of the tragedians are in urgent need of replacement. Smyth's Aeschylus is still usable (and invaluable for the*

199

fragments); Storr's Sophocles and Way's Euripides are barely so. A good volume in the same series is the following, which includes important fragments of tragedy:
Select Papyri, vol. 3 (Literary Papyri, Poetry), ed. and trans. D.L. Page (1941).
Gilbert Murray's translations, 1 play per vol., also various collections (Allen & Unwin, London, various dates). *Often available second-hand, and still sometimes reprinted. Greek tragedy ingeniously and incongruously romanticised.*
The OUP series: The Greek Tragedy in New Translations, ed. W. Arrowsmith, various translators, 1 play per vol. (Oxford University Press, New York, from 1973 (series not yet complete)). *Pretentious and expensive translations, of very uneven quality; but Eur. IT, trans. R. Lattimore, in this series (1974) should be used in preference to W. Bynner's version in the Chicago series.*
Penguin Classics (Harmondsworth). Aeschylus, trans. P. Vellacott, 2 vols. (1956, 1961). Sophocles, trans. E.F. Watling, 2 vols. (1947, 1953). Euripides, trans. P. Vellacott, 4 vols. covering 16 of the plays (1963-74). *Usable, but sometimes inaccurate and often inelegant. For R. Fagles's Oresteia see Part 2 below.*
The Prentice-Hall Greek Drama Series, ed. E.A. Havelock and M. Mack, various translators, 1 play per vol. (Prentice-Hall, Englewood Cliffs, NJ, from 1970). *Literal prose translations with extensive notes. A useful though uneven series, never completed and now out of print. But 4 vols. have been reprinted by other publishers; see Lloyd-Jones's Oresteia in Part 2, Kirk's Bacchae in Part 4.*
The Tenth Muse: Classical Drama in Translation, ed. C. Doria, various translators (Ohio University Press, 1980). *Includes Aesch. Supp., PV, Soph. Phil., Eur. Cycl., Bacch. Not recommended.*

2. Aeschylus

Oresteia, trans. R. Fagles (Penguin, Harmondsworth, 1977). *Well reviewed and certainly usable, but Fagles does not always resist the temptation to try to improve on Aeschylus.*
Oresteia, trans. T. Harrison (Rex Collings, London, 1981). *The National Theatre version; an interesting and worthwhile poetic experiment.*
Oresteia, trans. H. Lloyd-Jones, 3 vols. (Duckworth, London, 1979). *Literal prose translations with extensive commentary; useful work by a distinguished scholar, but the notes can be careless. A one-volume edition is about to be published (1982).*
Oresteia, 'trans.' R. Lowell (Faber, London, 1979). *An adaptation, not*

made from the Greek text.

Oresteia, trans. D. Young (University of Oklahoma Press, 1974). *Not recommended.*

The Orestes Plays (i.e. the *Oresteia*), trans. P. Roche (Mentor Classics, New York, 1963). *Not recommended.*

The Serpent Son (i.e. the *Oresteia*), trans. F. Raphael and K. McLeish (Cambridge University Press, 1979). *Less bad than the BBC television production might suggest.*

Agamemnon, ed. E. Fraenkel, 3 vols. (Oxford University Press, 1950). *A vast scholarly edition, including a literal translation.*

Agamemnon, trans. L. MacNeice (Faber, London, 1936). *Faithful and readable.*

Prometheus Bound, adapted by R. Lowell (Faber, London, 1970). *Not a translation of the Greek text.*

3. Sophocles

Plays, trans. T.H. Banks, 2 vols. (Oxford University Press, New York, 1956, 1966). *Straightforward and useful.*

The Plays and Fragments, ed. R.C. Jebb, 1 play per vol. (Cambridge University Press, latest edns 1892-1900). *Scholarly editions of the plays (not the fragments), including literal translations.*

Electra, Antigone, Philoctetes, trans. K. McLeish (Translations from Greek and Roman Authors, Cambridge University Press, 1979). *Somewhat simplified and adapted for use in schools.*

Four Greek Plays, trans. K. McLeish (Heritage of Literature Series, Longman, 1964). *Includes OT and Ant., much adapted and simplified.*

The Oedipus Plays (Ant., OT, OC), trans. P. Roche (Mentor Classics, New York, 1958). *Not recommended.*

The Theban Plays (Ant., OT, OC), trans. R. Fagles (Allen Lane, London, 1982). *This was published too late for me to study it, but looks good. A Penguin edition will doubtless appear in due course.*

Three Tragedies (Ant., OT, El.), trans. H.D.F. Kitto (Oxford University Press, 1962). *Straightforward and useful.*

Electra, trans. R.C. Jebb (The Library of Liberal Arts, Bobbs-Merrill, Indianapolis, 1950). *A reprint of a scholarly but dated version; see above.*

Oedipus the King, trans. R. Bagg (University of Massachusetts Press, 1982). *Not recommended.*

Oedipus Tyrannus, trans. L. Berkowitz and T.F. Brunner (W.W. Norton, New York, 1970). *A sensible translation, usefully coupled with some comparative material and a collection of critical studies.*

Oedipus Tyrannus, trans. J. Ferguson in J. Ferguson and P. Berthoud, *Two Oedipus Plays* (Open University Press, Milton Keynes, 1976). *A competent translation with intensely irritating notes. A translation of OC is not included.*

Women of Trachis, trans. E. Pound (Faber, London, 1969). *A travesty.*

4. Euripides

Three Great Plays (Med., Hipp., Hel.), trans. R. Warner (Mentor Classics, New York, 1958). *Straightforward and useful.*

The Trojan Women, Helen, the Bacchae, trans. N. Curry (Translations from Greek and Roman Authors, Cambridge University Press, 1981). *Somewhat simplified and adapted for use in schools.*

Bacchae, trans. G.S. Kirk (Cambridge University Press, 1979). *Literal prose translation with extensive and extremely useful notes.*

Bacchae, trans. W. Soyinka (Eyre Methuen, London, 1973). *A free adaptation.*

Bakkhai, trans. R. Bagg (University of Massachusetts Press, 1978). *Not recommended.*

Hippolytus, trans. G. and S. Lawall in G. and S. Lawall and G. Kunkel (eds.), *The Phaedra of Seneca* (Bolchazy-Carducci, Chicago, 1982). *Competent.*

5. Aristotle's 'Poetics'

Ed. and trans. S.H. Butcher, *Aristotle's Theory of Poetry and Fine Art*, 4th edn (Dover Publications, New York, 1951). *Text, translation and interpretative essays; reprinted from a 1911 edn, but still of use.*

Trans. T.S. Dorsch in *Classical Literary Criticism* (Penguin, Harmondsworth, 1965). *A good translation, but with very scanty notes.*

Trans. G.F. Else (University of Michigan Press, 1970). *Scholarly and painstaking, but not all of Else's views are widely accepted.*

Trans. L. Golden, with commentary by O.B. Hardison, Jr. (Prentice-Hall, Englewood Cliffs, NJ, 1968). *Extensive and thoughtful commentary, not always convincing.*

Trans. M.E. Hubbard in *Ancient Literary Criticism*, ed. D.A. Russell and M. Winterbottom (Oxford University Press, 1972). *Probably the best version for most purposes. The same volume contains much other material relevant to tragedy.*

6. Other Greek Authors

Aristophanes, trans. A. Sommerstein and (for one vol.) D. Barrett, 3 vols. (Penguin, Harmondsworth, 1970-8)

Greek Lyric, ed. and trans. D.A. Campbell (Loeb Classical Library, Heinemann, London, and Harvard University Press, vol. 1 1982, others forthcoming)

Herodotus, trans. A. de Sélincourt, revised by A.R. Burn (Penguin, Harmondsworth, 1972)

Hesiod, the Homeric Hymns and Homerica, ed. and trans. H.G. Evelyn-White, 2nd edn (Loeb Classical Library, Heinemann, London, and Harvard University Press, 1936)

Homer, *The Iliad*, trans. R. Lattimore (University of Chicago Press, 1951)

—— *The Odyssey*, trans. W. Shewring (Oxford University Press, 1980)

Pindar, trans. Sir M. Bowra (Penguin, Harmondsworth, 1960)

Plato, *The Republic*, trans. Sir D. Lee, 2nd edn (Penguin, Harmondsworth, 1974)

B Books on Greek Tragedy

1. Origins

Else, G.F. *The Origin and Early Form of Greek Tragedy* (Harvard University Press, 1965). *Provocative but largely convincing.*

Pickard-Cambridge, A.W. *Dithyramb Tragedy and Comedy*, 2nd edn revised by T.B.L. Webster (Oxford University Press, 1962). *A standard, and excellent, work of scholarship.*

2. Staging

Arnott, P.D. *Introduction to the Greek Theatre* (Macmillan, London, 1959). *A straightforward account.*

Baldry, H.C. *The Greek Tragic Theatre* (Chatto & Windus, London, 1971). *Another useful introduction.*

Pickard-Cambridge, A.W. *The Dramatic Festivals of Athens*, 2nd edn revised by J. Gould and D.M. Lewis (Oxford University Press, 1968)

—— *The Theatre of Dionysus in Athens* (Oxford University Press, 1946). *Both standard scholarly treatments.*

Simon, E. *The Ancient Theatre*, trans. C.E. Vafopoulou-Richardson (Methuen, London, 1982). *Scholarly but very brief.*

Walcot, P. *Greek Drama in its Theatrical and Social Context* (University of Wales Press, 1976). *A helpful account of the relation between the*

plays and their audience.
Note: Some of the most reliable and helpful information on staging can be found in Taplin's two books; see Parts 3 and 4 below.

3. The Plays in General

Gould, T.F. and C.J. Herington (eds.), *Greek Tragedy* (Yale Classical Studies, vol. 25, Cambridge University Press, 1977). *An uneven collection of articles, including some valuable studies, notably of Aesch. Sept. and Eur. Med.*

Jones, J. *On Aristotle and Greek Tragedy* (Chatto & Windus, London, 1962). *Difficult and one-sided, but highly stimulating.*

Kitto, H.D.F. *Form and Meaning in Drama* (Methuen, London, 1956). *Discusses the Oresteia and Soph. Phil., Ant., Aj., in more detail than the following book.*

— *Greek Tragedy*, 3rd edn (Methuen, London, 1961). *A lively and justly popular introduction, becoming dated.*

— *Poiesis* (University of California Press, 1966). *Includes discussion of problems in Aeschylus and Sophocles.*

Lattimore, R. *The Poetry of Greek Tragedy* (Johns Hopkins Press, Baltimore, 1958)

— *Story Patterns in Greek Tragedy* (Athlone Press, London, 1964). *Both helpful little books.*

Lesky, A. *Greek Tragedy*, trans. H.A. Frankfort (Ernest Benn, London, 1965). *A sober and factual introduction.*

Taplin, O. *Greek Tragedy in Action* (Methuen, London, 1978). *Bitty but otherwise excellent; the last chapter is essential reading for anyone thinking of producing a Greek tragedy.*

Vernant, J.-P. and P. Vidal-Naquet, *Tragedy and Myth in Ancient Greece*, trans. J. Lloyd (Harvester Press, Brighton, 1981). *Leaden prose, but some valuable insights.*

Vickers, B. *Towards Greek Tragedy* (Longman, London, 1973). *Long-winded and bad-tempered, but useful in parts.*

4. Aeschylus

Conacher, D.J. *Aeschylus' Prometheus Bound: A Literary Commentary* (University of Toronto Press, 1980). *Not really a commentary, but a good introduction to the play.*

Gagarin, M. *Aeschylean Drama* (University of California Press, 1976). *Mainly on ethical and social values; excellent within its range.*

Rosenmeyer, T.G. *The Art of Aeschylus* (University of California Press, 1982). *The only usable introductory book, but to be used with caution.*

Taplin, O. *The Stagecraft of Aeschylus* (Oxford University Press, 1977). *An admirable work of scholarship, with wide implications for all of Greek tragedy.*

5. Sophocles

Berkowitz, L. and T.F. Brunner (eds.), *Oedipus Tyrannus* (see Part A3 above)

Gellie, G.H. *Sophocles: A Reading* (Melbourne University Press, 1972). *An extremely clear and level-headed introduction.*

Kirkwood, G.M. *A Study of Sophoclean Drama* (Cornell University Press, 1958). *Another good introduction.*

Knox, B.M.W. *The Heroic Temper* (University of California Press, 1964). *A stimulating study of the Sophoclean hero (mainly on Ant., Phil. and OC).*

—— *Oedipus at Thebes* (Yale University Press, 1957). *A subtle (sometimes over-subtle) study of OT.*

O'Brien, M.J. (ed.) *Twentieth Century Interpretations of Oedipus Rex* (Prentice-Hall, Englewood Cliffs, NJ, 1968). *A useful collection.*

Reinhardt, K. *Sophocles*, trans. H. and D. Harvey (Blackwell, Oxford, 1979). *A translation of a classic (but difficult) pre-war German account.*

Seale, D. *Vision and Stagecraft in Sophocles* (Croom Helm, London, 1982). *Perceptive and helpful.*

Winnington-Ingram, R.P. *Sophocles: An Interpretation* (Cambridge University Press, 1980). *An exceptionally sensitive and penetrating book.*

6. Euripides

Barlow, S.A. *The Imagery of Euripides* (Methuen, London, 1971). *Useful, though sometimes careless.*

Burnett, A.P. *Catastrophe Survived* (Oxford University Press, 1971). *A good study of Alc., IT, Hel., Ion, Andr., HF, Or.*

Collard, C. *Euripides* (Greece & Rome New Surveys in the Classics No. 14, Oxford University Press, 1981). *A very useful bibliographical survey.*

Conacher, D.J. *Euripidean Drama* (University of Toronto Press, 1967). *A good introduction, covering all the plays.*

Grube, G.M.A. *The Drama of Euripides* (Methuen, London, 1941). *Another introductory book, still useful.*

Winnington-Ingram, R.P. *Euripides and Dionysus* (Hakkert, Amsterdam, 1969 (originally Cambridge, 1948)). *A subtle account of Bacch.*

C Other Relevant Books

1. The Greeks in General

Adkins, A.W.H. *Merit and Responsibility: A Study in Greek Values* (Oxford University Press, 1960). *A difficult but important book.*

Andrewes, A. *Greek Society* (Penguin, Harmondsworth, 1971). *A sane and reliable introduction.*

Bowder, D. (ed.) *Who Was Who in the Greek World* (Phaidon, Oxford, 1982). *Brief biographies, including some of tragedians by the present author.*

Bury, J.B. and R. Meiggs *A History of Greece*, 4th edn (Macmillan, London, 1975). *Probably the better of the two standard histories.*

Dodds, E.R. *The Greeks and the Irrational* (University of California Press, 1951). *A classic of classical scholarship, brilliant and enduring.*

—— *The Ancient Concept of Progress and other Essays* (Oxford University Press, 1973). *Essays on Greek literature (mainly tragedy) and belief, all excellent, some intended for the general reader.*

Finley, M.I. *The Ancient Greeks* (Penguin, Harmondsworth, 1971). *A good introduction.*

Hammond, N.G.L. and H.H. Scullard (eds.) *The Oxford Classical Dictionary*, 2nd edn (Oxford University Press, 1970). *A standard reference book.*

2. Greek Myths and Religion

Guthrie, W.K.C. *The Greeks and their Gods* (Methuen, London, 1950). *Sane and reliable.*

Kirk, G.S. *The Nature of Greek Myths* (Penguin, Harmondsworth, 1974). *An excellent account.*

Rose, H.J. *A Handbook of Greek Mythology*, 6th edn (Methuen, London, 1958). *Not inspiring, but the best available handbook.*

3. Greek Literature

Dover, K.J. (ed.) *Ancient Greek Literature* (Oxford University Press, 1980). *A good brief introduction, including an excellent essay by Dover on tragedy.*

Easterling, P.E. and B.M.W. Knox (eds.), *The Cambridge History of Classical Literature*, vol. 1 (Cambridge University Press, forthcoming).

Will perhaps largely supersede the following book.

Lesky, A. *A History of Greek Literature*, trans. J. Willis and C. de Heer (Methuen, London, 1966). *A standard history*.

D Treatments of Particular Topics

Note: This is a brief and quite unsystematic list of recommended books and articles relating to some of the topics covered by entries in this book. Many of these books and articles have strongly influenced those entries. More specialised discussions have been admitted into this list than into other sections of the Bibliography, and some, though not all, of the items here will prove heavy going for many readers.

Areopagus

Dodds, E.R. 'Morals and Politics in the *Oresteia*', *Proceedings of the Cambridge Philological Society* 186 (1960), pp. 19-31, reprinted in *The Ancient Concept of Progress* (see Part C1 above), pp. 45-63

ātē

Dawe, R.D. 'Some Reflections on Ate and Hamartia', *Harvard Studies in Classical Philology* 72 (1967), pp. 89-123

catharsis

Lucas, D.W. in Aristotle, *Poetics*, ed. Lucas (Oxford University Press, 1968), pp. 273-90

character

Easterling, P.E. 'Presentation of Character in Aeschylus', *Greece & Rome* 2nd ser. 20 (1973), pp. 3-19

—— 'Character in Sophocles', *Greece & Rome* 2nd ser. 24 (1977), pp. 121-9

Gould, J. 'Dramatic character and "human intelligibility" in Greek tragedy', *Proceedings of the Cambridge Philological Society* 204 (1978), pp. 43-67

chorus

Dale, A.M. 'The Chorus in the Action of Greek Tragedy', in Dale, *Collected Papers* (Cambridge University Press, 1969), pp. 210-20

death and burial

Vermeule, E.T. *Aspects of Death in Early Greek Art and Poetry* (University of California Press, 1979)

democracy

Davies, J.K. *Democracy and Classical Greece* (Harvester Press/Fontana/ Collins, Brighton etc., 1978)

Dionysus

Dodds, E.R. in Euripides, *Bacchae*, ed. Dodds, 2nd edn (Oxford University Press, 1960), pp. xi-xxv

episode and other structural terms

Taplin, O. *The Stagecraft of Aeschylus* (see Part B4 above), pp. 49-60, 470-9

Erinys

Brown, A.L. 'The Erinyes in the *Oresteia*', forthcoming in *Journal of Hellenic Studies* 103 (1983)

fate

Lesky, A. 'Decision and Responsibility in the Tragedy of Aeschylus', *Journal of Hellenic Studies* 86 (1966), pp. 78-85

Freud

Vernant, J.-P. 'Oedipus without the complex', in Vernant and Vidal-Naquet, *Tragedy and Myth* (see Part B3 above), pp. 63-86

hamartiā

Stinton, T.C.W. '*Hamartia* in Aristotle and Greek Tragedy', *Classical Quarterly* n.s. 25 (1975), pp. 221-54

hybris

Fisher, N.R.E. '*Hybris* and Dishonour', *Greece & Rome* 2nd ser. 23 (1976), pp. 177-93; *ibid*. 26 (1979), pp. 32-47

imagery

Lebeck, A. *The Oresteia* (Center for Hellenic Studies, Washington, 1971)

See also Barlow in Part B6 above.

Io's wanderings

Bolton, J.D.P. *Aristeas of Proconnessus* (Oxford University Press, 1962)

justice

See Adkins in Part C1, Gagarin in Part B4, above.

lamentation

Alexiou, M. *The Ritual Lament in Greek Tradition* (Cambridge University Press, 1974)

Nietzsche

Silk, M.S. and J.P. Stern, *Nietzsche on Tragedy* (Cambridge University Press, 1981)

oracles

Fontenrose, J. *The Delphic Oracle* (University of California Press, 1978)

Paris

Stinton, T.C.W. *Euripides and the Judgement of Paris* (Society for the Promotion of Hellenic Studies, London, 1965)

Prometheus
Griffith, M. *The Authenticity of 'Prometheus Bound'* (Cambridge University Press, 1977)
sacrifice
Burkert, W. 'Greek tragedy and sacrificial ritual', *Greek, Roman & Byzantine Studies* 7 (1966), pp. 87-121
sophists
Guthrie, W.K.C. *The Sophists* (Cambridge University Press, 1971)
stage directions
Taplin, O. 'Did Greek dramatists write stage instructions?', *Proceedings of the Cambridge Philological Society* 203 (1977), pp. 121-32
supplication
Gould, J. 'Hiketeia', *Journal of Hellenic Studies* 93 (1973), pp. 74-103
text
Reynolds, L.D. and N.G. Wilson, *Scribes and Scholars*, 2nd edn (Oxford University Press, 1974)
tyrannos
Andrewes, A. *The Greek Tyrants* (Hutchinson, London, 1956)
verse
Maas, P. *Greek Metre*, trans. H. Lloyd-Jones (Oxford University Press, 1962)
women
Gould, J.P. 'Law, custom and myth: aspects of the social position of women in classical Athens', *Journal of Hellenic Studies* 100 (1980), pp. 38-59
Zeus
Lloyd-Jones, H. 'Zeus in Aeschylus', *Journal of Hellenic Studies* 76 (1956), pp. 55-67
—— *The Justice of Zeus* (University of California Press, 1971)